EinFach Englisch

Echoes of the Empire – The Mixed Voices of a Colonial Past

20th Century English Short Stories

Die Textausgabe folgt der Zusammenstellung für das Schwerpunkt-thema Englisch ab Abiturprüfung 2007 in Baden-Württemberg

by Dr. Karola Schallhorn
Alexandra Peschel

Editor: Dr. Karola Schallhorn

Series Editor:
Hans Kröger

Zu dieser Textausgabe ist eine Audio-CD erhältlich (Best.-Nr. 062405).

Sprachliche Betreuung: Simone Duxbury-Ziemer

westermann GRUPPE

Druck A[13] / Jahr 2020
Alle Drucke der Serie A sind im Unterricht parallel verwendbar.

Umschlagabbildung (vorne und hinten): alamy images, Abingdon/Oxfordshire (Joerg Boethling)
Umschlaggestaltung: Jennifer Kirchhof
Druck und Bindung: Westermann Druck GmbH, Braunschweig

ISBN 978-3-14-041224-7

Contents

Getting started

This collage depicts scenes, symbols and characters from some of the short stories you are going to read.

1. What will they be about? Guess first without browsing the book.
2. Associate your ideas with the name of the collection "One language – Many Voices" and the individual titles of the stories.

Colonial Encounters

Joseph Conrad

An Outpost of Progress

1

There were two white men in charge of the trading station. Kayerts, the chief; was short and fat; Carlier, the assistant, was tall, with a large head and a very broad trunk perched upon a long pair of thin legs. The third man on the staff was a Sierra Leone nigger, who maintained that his name ⁵ was Henry Price. However, for some reason or other, the natives down the river had given him the name of Makola, and it stuck to him through all his wanderings about the country. He spoke English and French with a warbling accent, wrote a beautiful hand, understood book-keeping, and ¹⁰ cherished in his innermost heart the worship of evil spirits. His wife was a Negress from Loanda, very large and very noisy. Three children rolled about in sunshine before the door of his low, shed-like dwelling. Makola, taciturn and impenetrable, despised the two white men. He had charge ¹⁵ of a small clay storehouse with a dried-grass roof, and pretended to keep a correct account of beads, cotton cloth, red kerchiefs, brass wire, and other trade goods it contained. Besides the storehouse and Makola's hut, there was only one large building in the cleared ground of the station. It ²⁰ was built neatly of reeds, with a verandah on all the four sides. There were three rooms in it. The one in the middle was the living-room, and had two rough tables and a few stools in it. The other two were the bedrooms for the white men. Each had a bedstead and a mosquito net for all furni- ²⁵ ture. The plank floor was littered with the belongings of the white men; open half-empty boxes, town wearing apparel, old boots; all the things dirty, and all the things broken, that accumulate mysteriously round untidy men. There was also another dwelling-place some distance away from the build- ³⁰ ings. In it, under a tall cross much out of the perpendicular, slept the man who had seen the beginning of all this; who had planned and had watched the construction of this outpost of progress. He had been, at home, an unsuccessful painter who, weary of pursuing fame on an empty stomach, ³⁵ had gone out there through high protections. He had been

trunk torso

taciturn unpleasantly quiet
impenetrable here: impossible to understand
to despise to dislike and have no respect for sb/sth

apparel clothes

perpendicular *Lot*

weary [ˈwɪərɪ] very tired

the first chief of that station. Makola had watched the energetic artist die of fever in the just finished house with his usual kind of 'I told you so' indifference. Then, for a time, he dwelt alone with his family, his account books, and the
5 Evil Spirit that rules the lands under the equator. He got on very well with his god. Perhaps he had propitiated him by a promise of more white men to play with, by and by. At any rate the director of the Great Trading Company, coming up in a steamer that resembled an enormous sardine
10 box with a flat-roofed shed erected on it, found the station in good order, and Makola as usual quietly diligent. The director had the cross put up over the first agent's grave, and appointed Kayerts to the post. Carlier was told off as second in charge. The director was a man ruthless and ef-
15 ficient, who at times, but very imperceptibly, indulged in grim humour. He made a speech to Kayerts and Carlier, pointing out to them the promising aspect of their station. The nearest trading-post was about three hundred miles away. It was an exceptional opportunity for them to distin-
20 guish themselves and to earn percentages on the trade. This appointment was a favour done to beginners. Kayerts was moved almost to tears by his director's kindness. He would, he said, by doing his best, try to justify the flattering confidence, etc., etc. Kayerts had been in the Administration of
25 the Telegraphs, and knew how to express himself correctly. Carlier, an ex-non-commissioned officer of cavalry in an army guaranteed from harm by several European Powers, was less impressed. If there were commissions to get, so much the better; and, trailing a sulky glance over the river,
30 the forests, the impenetrable bush that seemed to cut off the station from the rest of the world, he muttered between his teeth, 'We shall see, very soon.'
Next day, some bales of cotton goods and a few cases of provisions having been thrown on shore, the sardine-box
35 steamer went off, not to return for another six months. On the deck the director touched his cap to the two agents, who stood on the bank waving their hats, and turning to an old servant of the Company on his passage to headquarters, said, 'Look at those two imbeciles. They must be mad at
40 home to send me such specimens. I told those fellows to plant a vegetable garden, build new storehouses and fences, and construct a landing-stage. I bet nothing will be done! They won't know how to begin. I always thought the station on this river useless, and they just fit the station!'
45 'They will form themselves there,' said the old stager with a quiet smile.
'At any rate, I am rid of them for six months,' retorted the director.

---

to propitiate to stop sb from being angry by trying to please them

shed *Schuppen*

diligent showing care and effort in your work or duties

ruthless [ruːθləs] determined to get what you want, not caring if you hurt other people

imperceptible hardly to be seen or felt

to indulge in sth *in etwas schwelgen*

to distinguish yourself to do sth so well that people notice and admire you

non-commissioned officer a soldier in the army, etc who has a rank such as sergeant or corporal but not a higher rank

sulky silent or bad-tempered

impenetrable here: that cannot be entered

imbecile idiot

specimen [ˈspesɪmən] an example of sth

to retort to reply quickly in an angry, offended or humorous way

slope *Hang*

dull not interested in sth because it is boring, not exciting

to render to cause to become
vigorous very active, full of life, strong and healthy

audacity brave but rude or shocking behaviour
composure *Fassung, Beherrschung*

unmitigated complete (in a bad sense)
savagery behaviour that is very cruel and violent

repulsive causing a feeling of strong dislike
to discompose to disturb

intrusion into/on/upon sb/sth the act of entering a place which is private or where you may not be wanted
to intrude into/on/upon sb/sth
intrusive

to assent to agree
voluble [ˈvɒljʊbl; AmE ˈvɒljʊbl] talking a lot, expressed in many words
indignation *Entrüstung, Empörung*

jocular humorous

The two men watched the steamer round the bend, then, ascending arm in arm the slope of the bank, returned to the station. They had been in this vast and dark country only a very short time, and as yet always in the midst of other white men, under the eye and guidance of their superiors. And now, dull as they were to the subtle influences of surroundings, they felt themselves very much alone, when suddenly left unassisted to face the wilderness; a wilderness rendered more strange, more incomprehensible by the mysterious glimpses of the vigorous life it contained. They were two perfectly insignificant and incapable individuals, whose existence is only rendered possible through the high organization of civilized crowds. Few men realize that their life, the very essence of their character, their capabilities and their audacities, are only the expression of their belief in the safety of their surroundings. The courage, the composure, the confidence; the emotions and principles; every great and every insignificant thought belongs not to the individual but to the crowd: to the crowd that believes blindly in the irresistible force of its institutions and of its morals, in the power of its police and of its opinion. But the contact with pure unmitigated savagery, with primitive nature and primitive man, brings sudden and profound trouble into the heart. To the sentiment of being alone of one's kind, to the clear perception of the loneliness of one's thoughts, of one's sensations – to the negation of the habitual, which is safe, there is added the affirmation of the unusual, which is dangerous; a suggestion of things vague, uncontrollable, and repulsive, whose discomposing intrusion excites the imagination and tries the civilized nerves of the foolish and the wise alike.

Kayerts and Carlier walked arm in arm, drawing close to one another as children do in the dark; and they had the same, not altogether unpleasant, sense of danger which one half suspects to be imaginary. They chatted persistently in familiar tones. 'Our station is prettily situated,' said one. The other assented with enthusiasm, enlarging volubly on the beauties of the situation. Then they passed near the grave. 'Poor devil!' said Kayerts. 'He died of fever, didn't he?' muttered Carlier, stopping short. 'Why,' retorted Kayerts, with indignation, 'I've been told that the fellow exposed himself recklessly to the sun. The climate here, everybody says, is not at all worse than at home, as long as you keep out of the sun. Do you hear that, Carlier? I am chief here, and my orders are that you should not expose yourself to the sun!' He assumed his superiority jocularly, but his meaning was serious. The idea that he would, perhaps, have to bury Carlier and remain alone, gave him an

inward shiver. He felt suddenly that this Carlier was more precious to him here, in the centre of Africa, than a brother could be anywhere else. Carlier, entering into the spirit of the thing, made a military salute and answered in a brisk
5 tone, 'Your orders shall be attended to, chief!' Then he burst out laughing, slapped Kayerts on the back and shouted, 'We shall let life run easily here! Just sit still and gather in the ivory those savages will bring. This country has its good points, after all!' They both laughed loudly while
10 Carlier thought: That poor Kayerts; he is so fat and unhealthy. It would be awful if I had to bury him here. He is a man I respect. ... Before they reached the verandah of their house they called one another 'my dear fellow'.
The first day they were very active, pottering about with
15 hammers and nails and red calico, to put up curtains, make their house habitable and pretty; resolved to settle down comfortably to their new life. For them an impossible task. To grapple effectually with even purely material problems requires more serenity of mind and more lofty courage than
20 people generally imagine. No two beings could have been more unfitted for such a struggle. Society, not from any tenderness, but because of its strange needs, had taken care of those two men, forbidding them all independent thought, all initiative, all departure from routine; and forbidding it
25 under pain of death. They could only live on condition of being machines. And now, released from the fostering care of men with pens behind the ears, or of men with gold lace on the sleeves, they were like those lifelong prisoners who, liberated after many years, do not know what use to make
30 of their freedom. They did not know what use to make of their faculties, being both, through want of practice, incapable of independent thought.
At the end of two months Kayerts often would say, 'If it was not for my Melie, you wouldn't catch me here.' Melie
35 was his daughter. He had thrown up his post in the Administration of the Telegraphs, though he had been for seventeen years perfectly happy there, to earn a dowry for his girl. His wife was dead, and the child was being brought up by his sisters. He regretted the streets, the pavements, the
40 cafés, his friends of many years; all the things he used to see, day after day; all the thoughts suggested by familiar things – the thoughts effortless, monotonous, and soothing of a government clerk; he regretted all the gossip, the small enmities, the mild venom, and the little jokes of govern-
45 ment offices. 'If I had had a decent brother-in-law,' Carlier would remark, 'a fellow with a heart, I would not be here.' He had left the army and had made himself so obnoxious to his family by his laziness and impudence, that an exasper-

ivory objects like elephants' teeth and other tusks
savage a primitive person (offensive)

calico a heavy, rough cotton fabric

to grapple with *mit etw. ringen*
serenity calmness
lofty *hochmütig*

to foster to encourage sth to develop
lace *Spitzenborte, Band*

dowry money and/or property a bride or her family must pay to her husband when they get married

enmity feelings of hatred towards sb
enemy opposite of friend

venom poison; here: hate or anger
obnoxious *widerlich*
impudence rudeness

to procure to obtain

to compel to force sb to do sth

witticism a clever and amusing remark
grievance *Groll*

idleness laziness

void a large empty space

uncouth rude, coarse

startled surprised
to squat *hocken*
to bargain to discuss prices, conditions, etc

brute (derog) brutal, rude person

to swagger to move in an overconfident way because you think you are very important
haughty arrogant
indulgence approval

complacent *selbstgefällig*
shank (old) the part of the leg between the knee and the ankle

ated brother-in-law had made superhuman efforts to procure him an appointment in the Company as a second-class agent. Having not a penny in the world he was compelled to accept this means of livelihood as soon as it became quite clear to him that there was nothing more to squeeze 5 out of his relations. He, like Kayerts, regretted his old life. He regretted the clink of sabre and spurs on a fine afternoon, the barrack-room witticisms, the girls of garrison towns; but, besides, he had also a sense of grievance. He was evidently a much ill-used man. This made him moody, 10 at times. But the two men got on well together in the fellowship of their stupidity and laziness. Together they did nothing, absolutely nothing, and enjoyed the sense of idleness for which they were paid. And in time they came to feel something resembling affection for one another.   15
They lived like blind men in a large room, aware only of what came in contact with them (and of that only imperfectly), but unable to see the general aspect of things. The river, the forest, all the great land throbbing with life, were like a great emptiness. Even the brilliant sunshine disclosed 20 nothing intelligible. Things appeared and disappeared before their eyes in an unconnected and aimless kind of way. The river seemed to come from nowhere and flow nowhither. It flowed through a void. Out of that void, at times, came canoes, and men with spears in their hands would 25 suddenly crowd the yard of the station. They were naked, glossy black, ornamented with snowy shells and glistening brass wire, perfect of limb. They made an uncouth babbling noise when they spoke, moved in a stately manner, and sent quick, wild glances out of their startled, never-resting eyes. 30 Those warriors would squat in long rows, four or more deep, before the verandah, while their chiefs bargained for hours with Makola over an elephant tusk. Kayerts sat on his chair and looked down on the proceedings, understanding nothing. He stared at them with his round blue eyes, 35 called out to Carlier, 'Here, look! look at that fellow there – and that other one, to the left. Did you ever see such a face? Oh, the funny brute!'
Carlier, smoking native tobacco in a short wooden pipe, would swagger up twirling his moustaches, and surveying 40 the warriors with haughty indulgence, would say –
'Fine animals. Brought any bone? Yes? It's not any too soon. Look at the muscles of that fellow – third from the end. I wouldn't care to get a punch on the nose from him. Fine arms, but legs no good below the knee. Couldn't make 45 cavalry men of them.' And after glancing down complacently at his own shanks, he always concluded: 'Pah! Don't they stink! You, Makola! Take that herd over to the fetish'

(the store-house was in every station called the fetish, perhaps because of the spirit of civilization it contained) 'and
give them up some of the rubbish you keep there. I'd rather
see it full of bone than full of rags.'

5 Kayerts approved.

'Yes, yes! Go and finish that palaver over there, Mr. Makola. I will come round when you are ready, to weigh the
tusk. We must be careful.' Then turning to his companion:
'This is the tribe that lives down the river; they are rather
10 aromatic. I remember, they had been once before here.
D'ye hear that row? What a fellow has got to put up with in
this dog of a country! My head is split.'

Such profitable visits were rare. For days the two pioneers
of trade and progress would look on their empty courtyard
15 in the vibrating brilliance of vertical sunshine. Below the
high bank, the silent river flowed on glittering and steady.
On the sands in the middle of the stream, hippos and alliga-
tors sunned themselves side by side. And stretching away
in all directions, surrounding the insignificant cleared spot
20 of the trading post, immense forests, hiding fateful compli-
cations of fantastic life, lay in the eloquent silence of mute
greatness. The two men understood nothing, cared for
nothing but for the passage of days that separated them
from the steamer's return. Their predecessor had left some
25 torn books. They took up these wrecks of novels, and, as
they had never read anything of the kind before, they were
surprised and amused. Then during long days there were
interminable and silly discussions about plots and person-
ages. In the centre of Africa they made acquaintance of
30 Richelieu and of d'Artagnan, of Hawk's Eye and of Father
Goriot, and of many other people. All these imaginary per-
sonages became subjects for gossip as if they had been living friends. They discounted their virtues, suspected their
motives, decried their successes; were scandalized at their
35 duplicity or were doubtful about their courage. The accounts of crimes filled them with indignation, while tender
or pathetic passages moved them deeply. Carlier cleared
his throat and said in a soldierly voice, 'What nonsense!'
Kayerts, his round eyes suffused with tears, his fat cheeks
40 quivering, rubbed his bald head, and declared, 'This is a
splendid book. I had no idea there were such clever fellows
in the world.' They also found some old copies of a home
paper. That print discussed what it was pleased to call 'Our
Colonial Expansion' in high-flown language. It spoke
45 much of the rights and duties of civilization, of the sacred-
ness of the civilizing work, and extolled the merits of those
who went about bringing light, and faith and commerce to
the dark places of the earth. Carlier and Kayerts read, won-

rag a piece of old, often torn cloth

row [raʊ] quarrel, noise

predecessor the person who did the job before

gossip informal talk about other people's private lives that may be unkind or not true
to discount *herabsetzen*
to decry to condemn
duplicity *falsches Spiel*

bald having little or no hair

to extol to praise sb/sth very much

consolation comfort

to squint blinzeln

loins Lenden
mangy [meɪndʒi] shabby, dirty
staff a long, thick walking stick

occupation here: what one is doing at a particular moment

to inquire to ask for information

ammonia a colourless gas with a strong smell
attentive with close attention

dered, and began to think better of themselves. Carlier said one evening, waving his hand about, 'In a hundred years, there will be perhaps a town here. Quays, and warehouses, and barracks, and – and – billiard-rooms. Civilization, my boy, and virtue – and all. And then, chaps will read that two good fellows, Kayerts and Carlier, were the first civilized men to live in this very spot!' Kayerts nodded, 'Yes, it is a consolation to think of that.' They seemed to forget their dead predecessor; but, early one day, Carlier went out and replanted the cross firmly. 'It used to make me squint whenever I walked that way,' he explained to Kayerts over the morning coffee. 'It made me squint, leaning over so much. So I just planted it upright. And solid, I promise you! I suspended myself with both hands to the cross-piece. Not a move. Oh, I did that properly.'

At times Gobila came to see them. Gobila was the chief of the neighbouring villages. He was a gray-headed savage, thin and black, with a white cloth round his loins and a mangy panther skin hanging over his back. He came up with long strides of his skeleton legs, swinging a staff as tall as himself, and, entering the common room of the station, would squat on his heels to the left of the door. There he sat, watching Kayerts, and now and then making a speech which the other did not understand. Kayerts, without interrupting his occupation, would from time to time say in a friendly manner: 'How goes it, you old image?' and they would smile at one another. The two whites had a liking for that old and incomprehensible creature, and called him Father Gobila. Gobila's manner was paternal, and he seemed really to love all white men. They all appeared to him very young, indistinguishably alike (except for stature), and he knew that they were all brothers, and also immortal. The death of the artist, who was the first white man whom he knew intimately, did not disturb this belief, because he was firmly convinced that the white stranger had pretended to die and got himself buried for some mysterious purpose of his own, into which it was useless to inquire. Perhaps it was his way of going home to his own country? At any rate, these were his brothers, and he transferred his absurd affection to them. They returned it in a way. Carlier slapped him on the back, and recklessly struck off matches for his amusement. Kayerts was always ready to let him have a sniff at the ammonia bottle. In short, they behaved just like that other white creature that had hidden itself in a hole in the ground. Gobila considered them attentively. Perhaps they were the same being with the other – or one of them was. He couldn't decide – clear up that mystery; but he remained always very friendly. In consequence of that friend-

ship the women of Gobila's village walked in single file through the reedy grass, bringing every morning to the station, fowls, and sweet potatoes, and palm wine, and sometimes a goat. The Company never provisions the stations
5 fully, and the agents required those local supplies to live. They had them through the good-will of Gobila, and lived well. Now and then one of them had a bout of fever, and the other nursed him with gentle devotion. They did not think much of it. It left them weaker, and their appearance
10 changed for the worse. Carlier was hollow-eyed and irritable. Kayerts showed a drawn, flabby face above the rotundity of his stomach, which gave him a weird aspect. But being constantly together, they did not notice the change that took place gradually in their appearance, and also in
15 their dispositions.
Five months passed in that way.
Then, one morning, as Kayerts and Carlier, lounging in their chairs under the verandah, talked about the approaching visit of the steamer, a knot of armed men came out of
20 the forest and advanced towards the station. They were strangers to that part of the country. They were tall, slight, draped classically from neck to heel in blue fringed cloths, and carried percussion muskets over their bare right shoulders. Makola showed signs of excitement, and ran out of
25 the storehouse (where he spent all his days) to meet these visitors. They came into the courtyard and looked about them with steady, scornful glances. Their leader, a powerful and determined-looking Negro with bloodshot eyes, stood in front of the verandah and made a long speech. He
30 gesticulated much, and ceased very suddenly.
There was something in his intonation, in the sounds of the long sentences he used, that startled the two whites. It was like a reminiscence of something not exactly familiar, and yet resembling the speech of civilized men. It sounded like
35 one of those impossible languages which sometimes we bear in our dreams.
'What lingo is that?' said the amazed Carlier. 'In the first moment I fancied the fellow was going to speak French. Anyway, it is a different kind of gibberish to what we ever
40 heard.'
'Yes,' replied Kayerts. 'Hey, Makola, what does he say? Where do they come from? Who are they?'
But Makola, who seemed to be standing on hot bricks, answered hurriedly, 'I don't know. They come from very far.
45 Perhaps Mrs Price will understand. They are perhaps bad men.'
The leader, after waiting for a while, said something sharply to Makola, who shook his head. Then the man, after

---

to walk in single file *im Gänsemarsch gehen*

fowls (or fowl pl) birds like chicken

bout [baʊt] an attack or period of illness

irritable getting annoyed easily, showing one's anger
rotundity roundness
weird unusual, strange, frightening

fringed *gefranst*

to cease [siːs] to stop

reminiscence memory

lingo language
to fancy to think
gibberish (infml) nonsense

volubility *Redseligkeit*

an air of manner of, facial expression of

to congregate to come together in a group

sagacious wise

ravine a deep, very narrow valley with steep sides

appeal call

jet a stream of air, gas or fire that comes out very quickly of a narrow opening

looking round, noticed Makola's hut and walked over there. The next moment Mrs Makola was heard speaking with great volubility. The other strangers – they were six in all – strolled about with an air of ease, put their heads through the door of the storeroom, congregated round the grave, pointed understandingly at the cross, and generally made themselves at home.

'I don't like those chaps – and, I say, Kayerts, they must be from the coast; they've got firearms,' observed the sagacious Carlier.

Kayerts also did not like those chaps. They both, for the first time, became aware that they lived in conditions where the unusual may be dangerous, and that there was no power on earth outside of themselves to stand between them and the unusual. They became uneasy, went in and loaded their revolvers. Kayerts said, 'We must order Makola to tell them to go away before dark.'

The strangers left in the afternoon, after eating a meal prepared for them by Mrs Makola. The immense woman was excited, and talked much with the visitors. She rattled away shrilly, pointing here and there at the forests and at the river. Makola sat apart and watched. At times he got up and whispered to his wife. He accompanied the strangers across the ravine at the back of the station-ground, and returned slowly looking very thoughtful. When questioned by the white men he was very strange, seemed not to understand, seemed to have forgotten French – seemed to have forgotten how to speak altogether. Kayerts and Carlier agreed that the nigger had had too much palm wine.

There was some talk about keeping a watch in turn, but in the evening everything seemed so quiet and peaceful that they retired as usual. All night they were disturbed by a lot of drumming in the villages. A deep, rapid roll near by would be followed by another far off – then all ceased. Soon short appeals would rattle out here and there, then all mingle together, increase, become vigorous and sustained, would spread out over the forest, roll through the night, unbroken and ceaseless, near and far; as if the whole land had been one immense drum booming out steadily an appeal to heaven. And through the deep and tremendous noise sudden yells that resembled snatches of songs from a madhouse darted shrill and high in discordant jets of sound which seemed to rush far above the earth and drive all peace from under the stars.

Carlier and Kayerts slept badly. They both thought they had heard shots fired during the night – but they could not agree as to the direction. In the morning Makola was gone somewhere. He returned about noon with one of yesterday's

strangers, and eluded all Kayerts's attempts to close with him: had become deaf apparently. Kayerts wondered. Carlier, who had been fishing off the bank, came back and remarked while he showed his catch, 'The niggers seem to be
5 in a deuce of a stir; I wonder what's up. I saw about fifteen canoes cross the river during the two hours I was there fishing.' Kayerts, worried, said, 'Isn't this Makola very queer today?' Carlier advised, 'Keep all our men together in case of some trouble.'

to elude to escape or avoid
to close with here: to meet with and talk to

in a deuce of a stir
in Höllenaufruhr

queer strange

2

10 There were ten station men who had been left by the Director. Those fellows, having engaged themselves to the Company for six months (without having any idea of a month in particular and only a very faint notion of time in general), had been serving the cause of progress for up-
15 wards of two years. Belonging to a tribe from a very distant part of the land of darkness and sorrow, they did not run away, naturally supposing that as wandering strangers they would be killed by the inhabitants of the country; in which they were right. They lived in straw huts on the slope of a
20 ravine overgrown with reedy grass, just behind the station buildings. They were not happy, regretting the festive incantations, the sorceries, the human sacrifices of their own land; where they also had parents, brothers, sisters, admired chiefs, respected magicians, loved friends, and other ties
25 supposed generally to be human. Besides, the rice rations served out by the Company did not agree with them, being a food unknown to their land, and to which they could not get used. Consequently they were unhealthy and miserable. Had they been of any other tribe they would have made up
30 their minds to die – for nothing is easier to certain savages than suicide – and so have escaped from the puzzling difficulties of existence. But belonging, as they did, to a warlike tribe with filed teeth, they had more grit, and went on stupidly living through disease and sorrow. They did very lit-
35 tle work, and had lost their splendid physique. Carlier and Kayerts doctored them assiduously without being able to bring them back into condition again. They were mustered every morning and told off to different tasks – grass-cutting, fence-building, tree-felling, etc., etc., which no power
40 on earth could induce them to execute efficiently. The two whites had practically very little control over them.
In the afternoon Makola came over to the big house and found Kayerts watching three heavy columns of smoke rising above the forests. 'What is that?' asked Kayerts. 'Some
45 villages burn,' answered Makola, who seemed to have re-

faint vague
notion idea

to regret here: to miss
incantation special words that are spoken or sung to have a magic effect
sorcery magic that uses evil spirits

grit courage

assiduous [əˈsidjuəs; AmE -dʒuəs] working very hard and with great care, diligent

to induce to persuade or influence sb to do sth

gained his wits. Then he said abruptly: 'We have got very little ivory; bad six months' trading. Do you like get a little more ivory?'

'Yes,' said Kayerts, eagerly. He thought of percentages which were low.   5

'Those men who came yesterday are traders from Loanda who have got more ivory than they can carry home. Shall I buy? I know their camp.'

'Certainly,' said Kalyerts. 'What are those traders?'

'Bad fellows,' said Makola, indifferently. 'They fight with 10 people, and catch women and children. They are bad men, and got guns. There is a great disturbance in the country. Do you want ivory?'

'Yes,' said Kayerts. Makola said nothing for a while. Then:
to mutter to mumble 'Those workmen of ours are no good at all,' he muttered, 15 looking round. 'Station in very bad order, sir. Director will growl. Better get a fine lot of ivory, then he say nothing.'

'I can't help it; the men won't work,' said Kayerts. 'When will you get that ivory?'

'Very soon,' said Makola. 'Perhaps tonight. You leave it to 20 me, and keep indoors, sir. I think you had better give some palm wine to our men to make a dance this evening. Enjoy themselves. Work better tomorrow. There's plenty palm wine – gone a little sour.'

Kayerts said yes, and Makola, with his own hands, carried 25
calabash *Kürbisflasche* big calabashes to the door of his hut. They stood there till the evening, and Mrs Makola looked into every one. The men got them at sunset. When Kayerts and Carlier retired, a big bonfire was flaring before the men's huts. They could hear their shouts and drumming. Some men from Gobila's 30 village had joined the station hands, and the entertainment was a great success.

In the middle of the night, Cartier waking suddenly, heard a man shout loudly; then a shot was fired. Only one. Carlier ran out and met Kayerts on the verandah. They were 35 both startled. As they went across the yard to call Makola, they saw shadows moving in the night. One of them cried, 'Don't shoot! It's me, Price.' Then Makola appeared close to them. 'Go back, go back, please,' he urged, 'you spoil all.' 'There are strange men about,' said Carlier. 'Never 40 mind; I know,' said Makola. Then he whispered, 'All right. Bring ivory. Say nothing! I know my business.' The two white men reluctantly went back to the house, but did not sleep. They heard footsteps, whispers, some groans. It seemed as if a lot of men came in, dumped heavy things on 45
to squabble [skwɒbl, AmE the ground, squabbled a long time, then went away. They
skwɑːbl] to argue about sth lay on their hard beds and thought: 'This Makola is invalu-
invaluable extremely useful able.' In the morning Carlier came out, very sleepy, and

pulled at the cord of the big bell. The station hands mustered every morning to the sound of the bell. That morning nobody came. Kayerts turned out also, yawning. Across the yard they saw Makola come out of his hut, a tin basin of
5 soapy water in his hand. Makola, a civilized nigger, was very neat in his person. He threw the soapsuds skilfully over a wretched little yellow cur he had, then turning his face to the agent's house, he shouted from the distance, 'All the men gone last night!'
10 They heard him plainly, but in their surprise they both yelled out together: 'What!' Then they stared at one another. 'We are in a proper fix now,' growled Carlier. 'It's incredible!' muttered Kayerts. 'I will go to the huts and see,' said Carlier, striding off. Makola coming up found Kayerts
15 standing alone.
'I can hardly believe it,' said Kayerts, tearfully. 'We took care of them as if they had been our children.'
'They went with the coast people,' said Makola after a moment of hesitation.
20 'What do I care with whom they went – the ungrateful brutes!' exclaimed the other. Then with sudden suspicion, and looking hard at Makola, he added: 'What do you know about it?'
Makola moved his shoulders, looking down on the ground.
25 'What do I know? I think only. Will you come and look at the ivory I've got there? It is a fine lot. You never saw such.' He moved towards the store. Kayerts followed him mechanically, thinking about the incredible desertion of the men. On the ground before the door of the fetish lay six
30 splendid tusks.
'What did you give for it?' asked Kayerts, after surveying the lot with satisfaction.
'No regular trade,' said Makola. 'They brought the ivory and gave it to me. I told them to take what they most want-
35 ed in the station. It is a beautiful lot. No station can show such tusks. Those traders wanted carriers badly, and our men were no good here. No trade, no entry in books; all correct.'
Kayerts nearly burst with indignation. 'Why!' he shouted,
40 'I believe you have sold our men for these tusks!' Makola stood impassive and silent. 'I – I – will – I,' stuttered Kayerts. ''You fiend!' he yelled out.
'I did the best for you and the Company,' said Makola, imperturbably. 'Why you shout so much? Look at this
45 tusk.'
'I dismiss you! I will report you – I won't look at the tusk. I forbid you to touch them. I order you to throw them into the river. You – you!'

hand worker
to muster to gather in a military way
to yawn *gähnen*

wretched ill, unhappy, bad
cur aggressive dog, mongrel

to be in a fix to be in a mess, a difficult situation

hesitation indecision
to hesitate to be slow to speak or act because you feel uncertain or nervous

desertion act of deserting
to desert [diˈzɜːt] to run away from duty, to abandon

imperturbable
[ˌɪmpəˈtɜːbəbl, AmE -pəˈtɜːr-]
unerschütterlich, gelassen
to dismiss sb to send away, to sack sb

to contemplate to consider

menace threat
in the bosom [bʊzᵊm] **of one's family** *in den Schoß der Familie*

muffled low, soft

to stir [stɜːʳ] to move

to pounce upon to spring forward onto sth/sb

put-up job sth arranged in advance in order to cheat or deceive

conviction belief
to convince sb to make sb believe that sth is true
convincing (adj)

deference [ˈdefərəns] respect

'You very red, Mr Kayerts. If you are so irritable in the sun, you will get fever and die – like the first chief!' pronounced Makola impressively.

They stood still, contemplating one another with intense eyes, as if they had been looking with effort across im- 5 mense distances. Kayerts shivered. Makola had meant no more than he said, but his words seemed to Kayerts full of ominous menace! He turned sharply and went away to the house. Makola retired into the bosom of his family; and the tusks, left lying before the store, looked very large and val- 10 uable in the sunshine.

Carlier came back on the verandah. 'They're all gone, hey?' asked Kayerts from the far end of the common room in a muffled voice. 'You did not find anybody?'

'Oh, yes,' said Carlier, 'I found one of Gobila's people ly- 15 ing dead before the huts – shot through the body. We heard that shot last night.'

Kayerts came out quickly. He found his companion staring grimly over the yard at the tusks, away by the store. They both sat in silence for a while. Then Kayerts related his con- 20 versation with Makola. Carlier said nothing. At the midday meal they ate very little. They hardly exchanged a word that day. A great silence seemed to lie heavily over the station and press on their lips. Makola did not open the store; he spent the day playing with his children. He lay full-length 25 on a mat outside the door, and the youngsters sat on his chest and clambered all over him. It was a touching picture. Mrs Makola was busy cooking all day as usual. The white men made a somewhat better meal in the evening. After- wards, Carlier smoking his pipe strolled over to the store; 30 he stood for a long time over the tusks, touched one or two with his foot, even tried to lift the largest one by its small end. He came back to his chief, who had not stirred from the verandah, threw himself in the chair and said –

'I can see it! They were pounced upon while they slept 35 heavily after drinking all that palm wine you've allowed Makola to give them. A put-up job! See? The worst is, some of Gobila's people were there, and got carried off too, no doubt. The least drunk woke up, and got shot for his sobriety. This is a funny country. What will you do now?' 40

'We can't touch it, of course,' said Kayerts.

'Of course not,' assented Carlier.

'Slavery is an awful thing,' stammered out Kayerts in an unsteady voice.

'Frightful – the sufferings,' grunted Carlier with conviction. 45 They believed their words. Everybody shows a respectful deference to certain sounds that he and his fellows can make. But about feelings people really know nothing. We

talk with indignation or enthusiasm; we talk about oppression, cruelty, crime, devotion, self-sacrifice, virtue, and we know nothing real beyond the words. Nobody knows what suffering or sacrifice mean – except, perhaps the victims of
5 the mysterious purpose of these illusions.
Next morning they saw Makola very busy setting up in the yard the big scales used for weighing ivory. By and by Carlier said: 'What's that filthy scoundrel up to?' and lounged out into the yard. Kayerts followed. They stood watching.
10 Makola took no notice. When the balance was swung true, he tried to lift a tusk into the scale. It was too heavy. He looked up helplessly without a word, and for a minute they stood round that balance as mute and still as three statues. Suddenly Carlier said: 'Catch hold of the other end, Makola
15 – you beast!' and together they swung the tusk up. Kayerts trembled in every limb. He muttered, 'I say! O! I say!' and putting his hand in his pocket found there a dirty bit of paper and the stump of a pencil. He turned his back on the others, as if about to do something tricky, and noted stealth-
20 ily the weights which Carlier shouted out to him with unnecessary loudness. When all was over Makola whispered to himself: 'The sun's very strong here for the tusks.' Carlier said to Kayerts in a careless tone: 'I say, chief, I might just as well give him a lift with this lot into the store.'
25 As they were going back to the house Kayerts observed with a sigh: 'It had to be done.' And Carlier said: 'It's deplorable, but, the men being Company's men, the ivory is Company's ivory. We must look after it.' 'I will report to the Director, of course,' said Kayerts. 'Of course; let him
30 decide,' approved Carlier.
At midday they made a hearty meal. Kayerts sighed from time to time. Whenever they mentioned Makola's name they always added to it an opprobrious epithet. It eased their conscience. Makola gave himself a half-holiday, and bathed
35 his children in the river. No one from Gobila's villages came near the station that day. No one came the next day, and the next, nor for a whole week. Gobila's people might have been dead and buried for any sign of life they gave. But they were only mourning for those they had lost by the
40 witchcraft of white men, who had brought wicked people into their country. The wicked people were gone, but fear remained. Fear always remains. A man may destroy everything within himself, love and hate and belief, and even doubt; but as long as he clings to life he cannot destroy
45 fear; the fear, subtle, indestructible, and terrible, that pervades his being; that tinges his thoughts; that lurks in his heart; that watches on his lips the struggle of his last breath. In his fear, the mild old Gobila offered extra human sacri-

---

devotion love, affection

scales (pl) *Waage*
scale *Waagschale*

scoundrel *Schuft*

limb arm or leg

stealthy secret, furtive

deplorable *erbärmlich*

opprobrious disgraceful, bad
epithet nickname

to mourn [mɔːn] to feel and show sadness because sb has died; to grieve for
wicked morally bad, evil dangerous

to tinge [tɪndʒ] to add a small amount of colour to
to lurk *lauern*

to dissuade to convince sb not to do sth
woe grief, sorrow

solicitude feeling of worry
inarticulate not expressed clearly

as of yore as in the past

jaunty with a feeling of confidence
gloomy sad and without hope

game wild animals that people hunt like deer, ducks etc

carcase (also **carcass**) the dead body of an animal

to moon about to dream about

bleached tresses (literary) a woman's long hair made blonde or white by chemical treatment

fices to all the Evil Spirits that had taken possession of his white friends. His heart was heavy. Some warriors spoke about burning and killing, but the cautious old savage dissuaded them. Who could foresee the woe those mysterious creatures, if irritated, might bring? They should be left ₅ alone. Perhaps in time they would disappear into the earth as the first one had disappeared. His people must keep away from them, and hope for the best.

Kayerts and Carlier did not disappear, but remained above on this earth, that, somehow, they fancied had become big- ₁₀ ger and very empty. It was not the absolute and dumb solitude of the post that impressed them so much as an inarticulate feeling that something from within them was gone, something that worked for their safety, and had kept the wilderness from interfering with their hearts. The images ₁₅ of home; the memory of people like them, of men that thought and felt as they used to think and feel, receded into distances made indistinct by the glare of unclouded sunshine. And out of the great silence of the surrounding wilderness, its very hopelessness and savagery seemed to ap- ₂₀ proach them nearer, to draw them gently, to look upon them, to envelop them with a solicitude irresistible, familiar, and disgusting.

Days lengthened into weeks, then into months. Gobila's people drummed and yelled to every new moon, as of yore, ₂₅ but kept away from the station. Makola and Carlier tried once in a canoe to open communications, but were received with a shower of arrows, and had to fly back to the station for dear life. That attempt set the country up and down the river into an uproar that could be very distinctly heard for ₃₀ days. The steamer was late. At first they spoke of delay jauntily, then anxiously, then gloomily. The matter was becoming serious. Stores were running short. Carlier cast his lines off the bank, but the river was low, and the fish kept out in the stream.They dared not stroll far away from the ₃₅ station to shoot. Moreover, there was no game in the impenetrable forest. Once Carlier shot a hippo in the river. They had no boat to secure it, and it sank. When it floated up it drifted away, and Gobila's people secured the carcase. It was the occasion for a national holiday, but Carlier had a ₄₀ fit of rage over it and talked about the necessity of exterminating all the niggers before the country could be made habitable. Kayerts mooned about silently; spent hours looking at the portrait of his Melie. It represented a little girl with long bleached tresses and a rather sour face. His ₄₅ legs were much swollen, and he could hardly walk. Carlier, undermined by fever, could not swagger any more, but kept tottering about, still with a devil-may-care air, as became a

man who remembered his crack regiment. He had become
hoarse, sarcastic, and inclined to say unpleasant things. He
called it 'being frank with you'. They had long ago reckoned their percentages on trade, including in them that last
5 deal of 'this infamous Makola'. They had also concluded
not to say anything about it. Kayerts hesitated at first – was
afraid of the Director.
'He has seen worse things done on the quiet,' maintained
Carlier, with a hoarse laugh. 'Trust him! He won't thank
10 you if you blab. He is no better than you or me. Who will
talk if we hold our tongues? There is nobody here.'
That was the root of the trouble! There was nobody there;
and being left there alone with their weakness, they became
daily more like a pair of accomplices than like a couple of
15 devoted friends. They had heard nothing from home for
eight months. Every evening they said, 'Tomorrow we shall
see the steamer.' But one of the Company's steamers had
been wrecked, and the Director was busy with the other, relieving very distant and important stations on the main river.
20 He thought that the useless station, and the useless men,
could wait. Meantime Kayerts and Carlier lived on rice
boiled without salt, and cursed the Company, all Africa, and
the day they were born. One must have lived on such diet to
discover what ghastly trouble the necessity of swallowing
25 one's food may become. There was literally nothing else in
the station but rice and coffee; they drank the coffee without
sugar. The last fifteen lumps Kayerts had solemnly locked
away in his box, together with a half-bottle of Cognac, 'in
case of sickness,' he explained. Carlier approved. 'When one
30 is sick,' he said, 'any little extra like that is cheering.'
They waited. Rank grass began to sprout over the courtyard. The bell never rang now. Days passed, silent, exas-
perating, and slow. When the two men spoke, they snarled;
and their silences were bitter, as if tinged by the bitterness
35 of their thoughts.
One day after a lunch of boiled rice, Carlier put down his
cup untasted, and said: 'Hang it all! Let's have a decent cup
of coffee for once. Bring out that sugar, Kayerts!'
'For the sick,' muttered Kayerts, without looking up.
40 'For the sick,' mocked Carlier. 'Bosh! … Well! I am sick.'
'You are no more sick than I am, and I go without,' said
Kayerts in a peaceful tone.
'Come! out with that sugar, you stingy old slave-dealer.'
Kayerts looked up quickly. Carlier was smiling with
45 marked insolence. And suddenly it seemed to Kayerts that
he had never seen that man before. Who was he? He knew
nothing about him. What was he capable of? There was a
surprising flash of violent emotion within him, as if in the

---

crack regiment *Eliteregiment*

hoarse sounding harsh because
of a sore throat

to blab (infml) to tell sb
information that should be kept
secret

accomplice a person who helps
sb to commit a crime

to relieve to provide new staff
and supplies

to curse to say rude things
and swear

ghastly ['gɑːstli] extremely
unpleasant

lump piece
solemn *feierlich*

to snarl (of dogs, etc) to show
one's teeth and make a deep
angry noise in the throat

decent of a good enough
standard or quality

to mock to laugh at

stingy ['stɪndʒi] not giving
willingly
insolence *Unverschämtheit*

composure the state of being calm and in control of one's feelings

hypocrite ['hɪpəkrɪt] a person who pretends to have moral standards or opinions that they do not actually have

presence of something undreamt-of, dangerous, and final. But he managed to pronounce with composure –
'That joke is in very bad taste. Don't repeat it.'
'Joke!' said Carlier, hitching himself forward on his seat. 'I am hungry – I am sick – I don't joke! I hate hypocrites. ₅ You are a hypocrite. You are a slave-dealer. I am a slave-dealer. There's nothing but slave-dealers in this cursed country. I mean to have sugar in my coffee today, anyhow!'
'I forbid you to speak to me in that way,' said Kayerts with a fair show of resolution. ₁₀
'You! – What?' shouted Carlier, jumping up.
Kayerts stood up also. 'I am your chief,' he began, trying to master the shakiness of his voice.
'What?' yelled the other. 'Who's chief? There's no chief here. There's nothing here: there's nothing but you and I. ₁₅

pot-bellied having a fat, round stomach

Fetch the sugar – you pot-bellied ass.'
'Hold your tongue. Go out of this room,' screamed Kayerts. 'I dismiss you – you scoundrel!'

flabby fat

Carlier swung a stool. All at once he looked dangerously in earnest. 'You flabby, good-for-nothing civilian – take that!' ₂₀ he howled.
Kayerts dropped under the table, and the stool struck the grass inner wall of the room. Then, as Carlier was trying to upset the table, Kayerts in desperation made a blind rush, head low, like a cornered pig would do, and over-turning ₂₅ his friend, bolted along the verandah, and into his room. He locked the door, snatched his revolver, and stood panting.

to pant to breathe quickly with short breaths

In less than a minute Carlier was kicking at the door furiously, howling, 'If you don't bring out that sugar, I will shoot you at sight, like a dog. Now then – one – two – ₃₀ three. You won't? I will show you who's the master,'
Kayerts thought the door would fall in, and scrambled through the square hole that served for a window in his room. There was then the whole breadth of the house between them. But the other was apparently not strong ₃₅ enough to break in the door, and Kayerts heard him running round. Then he also began to run laboriously on his

laborious taking a long time and effort

swollen legs. He ran as quickly as he could, grasping the revolver, and unable yet to understand what was happening to him. He saw in succession Makola's house, the store, the ₄₀ river, the ravine, and the low bushes; and he saw all those things again as he ran for the second time round the house.

in succession in a series
to succeed to come next after sb/sth
successor a person or thing that comes after sb/sth else and takes their/its place

Then again they flashed past him. That morning he could not have walked a yard without a groan.
And now he ran. He ran fast enough to keep out of sight of ₄₅ the other man.
Then as, weak and desperate, he thought, 'Before I finish the next round I shall die,' he heard the other man stumble

heavily, then stop. He stopped also. He had the back and Carlier the front of the house; as before. He heard him drop into a chair cursing, and suddenly his own legs gave way, and he slid down into a sitting posture with his back to the
5 wall. His mouth was as dry as a cinder, and his face was wet with perspiration – and tears. What was it all about? He thought it must be a horrible illusion; he thought he was dreaming; he thought he was going mad! After a while he collected his senses. What did they quarrel about? That
10 sugar! How absurd! He would give it to him – didn't want it himself. And he began scrambling to his feet with a sudden feeling of security. But before he had fairly stood upright, a commonsense reflection occurred to him and drove him back into despair. He thought: If I give way now to
15 that brute of a soldier, he will begin this horror again tomorrow – and the day after – every day – raise other pretensions, trample on me, torture me, make me his slave – and I will be lost! Lost! The steamer may not come for days – may never come. He shook so that he had to sit
20 down on the floor again. He shivered forlornly. He felt he could not, would not move any more. He was completely distracted by the sudden perception that the position was without issue – that death and life had in a moment become equally difficult and terrible.
25 All at once he heard the other push his chair back; and he leaped to his feet with extreme facility. He listened and got confused. Must run again! Right or left? He heard footsteps. He darted to the left, grasping his revolver, and at the very same instant, as it seemed to him, they came into vio-
30 lent collision. Both shouted with surprise. A loud explosion took place between them; a roar of red fire, thick smoke; and Kayerts, deafened and blinded, rushed back thinking: I am hit – it's all over. He expected the other to come round – to gloat over his agony. He caught hold of an upright of
35 the roof – 'All over!' Then he heard a crashing fall on the other side of the house, as if somebody had tumbled headlong over a chair – then silence. Nothing more happened. He did not die. Only his shoulder felt as if it had been badly wrenched, and he had lost his revolver. He was disarmed
40 and helpless! He waited for his fate. The other man made no sound. It was a stratagem. He was stalking him now! Along what side? Perhaps he was taking aim this very minute!
After a few moments of an agony frightful and absurd, he
45 decided to go and meet his doom. He was prepared for every surrender. He turned the corner, steadying himself with one hand on the wall; made a few paces, and nearly swooned. He had seen on the floor, protruding past the other

---

cinder a small piece of ash or partly burnt coal, wood etc that is no longer burning but still hot
perspiration sweat

pretension claim

forlorn sad and without hope

to distract to take sb's attention away from what they are trying to do

to leap to jump

to gloat *sich hämisch freuen*
agony extreme physical or mental pain, fear of death

to wrench to twist

stratagem [ˈstrætədʒəm] a trick or plan that you use to gain an advantage over or to deceive an opponent
to stalk to hunt
doom unavoidable death or destruction
to swoon to faint
to protrude to stick out from a place

gratitude the feeling of being grateful and wanting to express thanks

corpse dead human body

expectant 1. awaiting
2. pregnant

exhausted [ɪgˈzɔːstɪd, eg-, AmE -zaːstɪd] very tired
serenity calmness
to plumb ausloten

contemptible not deserving any respect at all
to revel in seine wahre Freude haben an
lucidity clearness

noxious poisonous or harmful

corner, a pair of turned-up feet. A pair of white naked feet in red slippers. He felt deadly sick, and stood for a time in profound darkness. Then Makola appeared before him, saying quietly: 'Come along, Mr Kayerts. He is dead.' He burst into tears of gratitude; a loud, sobbing fit of crying. 5 After a time he found himself sitting in a chair and looking at Carlier, who lay stretched on his back. Makola was kneeling over the body.

'Is this your revolver?' asked Makola, getting up.

'Yes,' said Kayerts; then he added very quickly, 'He ran 10 after me to shoot me – you saw!'

'Yes, I saw,' said Makola. 'There is only one revolver; where's his?'

'Don't know,' whispered Kayerts in a voice that had become suddenly very faint. 15

'I will go and look for it,' said the other, gently. He made the round along the verandah; while Kayerts sat still and looked at the corpse. Makola came back empty-handed, stood in deep thought, then stepped quietly into the dead man's room, and came out directly with a revolver, which 20 he held up before Kayerts. Kayerts shut his eyes. Everything was going round. He found life more terrible and difficult than death. He had shot an unarmed man.

After meditating for a while, Makola said softly, pointing at the dead man who lay there with his right eye blown out – 25 'He died of fever.' Kayerts looked at him with a stony stare, 'Yes,' repeated Makola, thoughtfully, stepping over the corpse – 'I think he died of fever. Bury him tomorrow.'

And he went away slowly to his expectant wife, leaving the two white men alone on the verandah. 30

Night came, and Kayerts sat unmoving on his chair. He sat quiet as if he had taken a dose of opium. The violence of the emotions he had passed through produced a feeling of exhausted serenity. He had plumbed in one short afternoon the depths of horror and despair, and now found repose in 35 the conviction that life had no more secrets for him: neither had death! He sat by the corpse thinking; thinking very actively, thinking very new thoughts. He seemed to have broken loose from himself altogether. His old thoughts, convictions, likes and dislikes, things he respected and things 40 he abhorred, appeared in their true light at last! Appeared contemptible and childish, false and ridiculous. He revelled in his new wisdom while he sat by the man he had killed. He argued with himself about all things under heaven with that kind of wrong-headed lucidity which may be observed 45 in some lunatics. Incidentally he reflected that the fellow dead there had been a noxious beast anyway; that men died every day in thousands; perhaps in hundreds of thousands

– who could tell? – and that in the number, that one death could not possibly make any difference; couldn't have any importance, at least to a thinking creature. He, Kayerts, was a thinking creature. He had been all his life, till that
5 moment, a believer in a lot of nonsense like the rest of mankind – who are fools; but now he thought! He knew! He was at peace; he was familiar with the highest wisdom! Then he tried to imagine himself dead, and Carlier sitting in his chair watching him; and his attempt met with such
10 unexpected success, that in a very few moments he became not at all sure who was dead and who was alive. This extraordinary achievement of his fancy startled him, however, and by a clever and timely effort of mind he saved himself just in time from becoming Carlier. His heart thumped, and
15 he felt hot all over at the thought of that danger. Carlier! What a beastly thing! To compose his now disturbed nerves – and no wonder! – he tried to whistle a little. Then, suddenly, he fell asleep, or thought he had slept; but at any rate there was a fog, and somebody had whistled in the fog.
20 He stood up. The day had come, and a heavy mist had descended upon the land: the mist penetrating, enveloping, and silent; the morning mist of tropical lands; the mist that clings and kills; the mist white and deadly, immaculate and poisonous. He stood up, saw the body, and threw his arms
25 above his head with a cry like that of a man who, waking from a trance, finds himself immured forever in a tomb. *'Help! ... My God!'*
A shriek inhuman, vibrating and sudden, pierced like a sharp dart the white shroud of that land of sorrow. Three
30 short, impatient screeches followed, and then, for a time, the fog-wreaths rolled on, undisturbed, through a formidable silence. Then many more shrieks rapid and piercing, like the yells of some exasperated and ruthless creature, rent the air. Progress was calling to Kayerts from the river. Progress
35 and civilization and all the virtues. Society was calling to its accomplished child to come, to be taken care of, to be instructed, to be judged, to be condemned; it called him to return to that rubbish heap from which be had wandered away, so that justice could be done.
40 Kayerts heard and understood. He stumbled out of the verandah, leaving the other man quite alone for the first time since they had been thrown there together. He groped his way through the fog, calling in his ignorance upon the invisible heaven to undo its work. Makola flitted by in the
45 mist, shouting as he ran –
'Steamer! Steamer! They can't see. They whistle for the station. I go ring the bell. Go down to the landing, sir. I ring.'

fancy imagination

to compose to make calm

mist a light fog
to penetrate to go into or through
immaculate spotless, perfect

to immure to shut sb in a place so that they cannot get out
to pierce to make a hole through
shroud burial wrapping, covering
fog-wreath [fogriːθ] *Nebelkranz*

exasperated furious, annoyed
to rent to tear a hole in

to grope to try and reach a place by feeling with your hands because you cannot see clearly

smudge a dirty mark with no clear shape
stain a dirty mark that is difficult to remove
peal a loud sound or series of sounds

He disappeared. Kayerts stood still. He looked upwards; the fog rolled low over his head. He looked round like a man who has lost his way; and he saw a dark smudge, a cross-shaped stain, upon the shifting purity of the mist. As he began to stumble towards it, the station bell rang in a ₅ tumultuous peal its answer to the impatient clamour of the steamer.

incontinent uncontrollable
exceedingly extremely
dense *dicht*

to toil up to move with difficulty

The Managing Director of the Great Civilizing Company (since we know that civilization follows trade) landed first, and incontinently lost sight of the steamer. The fog down ₁₀ by the river was exceedingly dense; above, at the station, the bell rang unceasing and brazen.
The Director shouted loudly to the steamer:
'There is nobody down to meet us; there may be something wrong, though they are ringing. You had better come, too!' ₁₅
And he began to toil up the steep bank. The captain and the engine-driver of the boat followed behind. As they scrambled up the fog thinned, and they could see their Director a good way ahead. Suddenly they saw him start forward, calling to them over his shoulder: 'Run! Run to the house! ₂₀ I've found one of them. Run, look for the other!'

varied ['veərɪd] of many different types

rigid strict, stiff
irreverent disrespectful

He had found one of them! And even he, the man of varied and startling experience, was somewhat discomposed by the manner of this finding. He stood and fumbled in his pockets (for a knife) while he faced Kayerts, who was ₂₅ hanging by a leather strap from the cross. He had evidently climbed the grave, which was high and narrow, and after tying the end of the strap to the arm, had swung himself off. His toes were only a couple of inches above the ground; his arms hung stiffly down; he seemed to be standing rig- ₃₀ idly at attention, but with one purple cheek playfully posed on the shoulder. And, irreverently, he was putting out a swollen tongue at his Managing Director.

W. Somerset Maugham
(beginning) 🔊

The Force of Circumstance

blind *Jalousie, Rollo*

pallor pale colouring of the face, esp. because of illness or fear
dug-out canoe
wan pale and weak

She was sitting on the veranda waiting for her husband to come in for luncheon. The Malay boy had drawn the blinds ₃₅ when the morning lost its freshness, but she had partly raised one of them so that she could look at the river. Under the breathless sun of midday it had the white pallor of death. A native was paddling along in a dug-out so small that it hardly showed above the surface of the water. The ₄₀ colours of the day were ashy and wan. They were but the

various tones of the heat. (It was like an Eastern melody, in
the minor key, which exacerbates the nerves by its ambiguous monotony; and the ear awaits impatiently a resolution,
but waits in vain.) The cicadas sang their grating song with
5 a frenzied energy; it was as continual and monotonous as
the rustling of a brook over the stones; but on a sudden it
was drowned by loud singing of a bird, mellifluous and
rich; and for an instant, with a catch at her heart, she
thought of the English blackbird.
10 Then she heard her husband's step on the gravel path behind the bungalow, the path that led to the court-house in
which he had been working, and she rose from her chair to
greet him. He ran up the short flight of steps, for the bungalow was built on piles, and at the door the boy was waiting
15 to take his topee. He came into the room which served
them as a dining-room and parlour, and his eyes lit up with
pleasure as he saw her.
'Hulloa, Doris. Hungry?'
'Ravenous.'
20 'It'll only take me a minute to have a bath and then I'm
ready.'
'Be quick,' she smiled.
He disappeared into his dressing-room and she heard him
whistling cheerily while, with the carelessness with which
25 she was always remonstrating, he tore off his clothes and
flung them on the floor. He was twenty-nine, but he was
still a school-boy; he would never grow up. That was why
she had fallen in love with him, perhaps, for no amount of
affection could persuade her that he was good-looking. He
30 was a little round man, with a red face like the full moon,
and blue eyes. He was rather pimply. She had examined
him carefully and had been forced to confess to him that he
had not a single feature which she could praise. She had
told him often that he wasn't her type at all.
35 'I never said I was a beauty,' he laughed.
'I can't think what it is I see in you.'
But of course she knew perfectly well. He was a gay, jolly
little man, who took nothing very solemnly, and he was
constantly laughing. He made her laugh too. He found life
40 an amusing rather than a serious business, and he had a
charming smile. When she was with him she felt happy and
good-tempered. And the deep affection which she saw in
those merry blue eyes of his touched her. It was very satis-
factory to be loved like that. Once, sitting on his knees,
45 during their honeymoon she had taken his face in her hands
and said to him:
'You're an ugly, little fat man, Guy, but you've got charm. I
can't help loving you.'

key *Tonart*
exacerbate to make sth worse
ambiguous that can be understood in more than one way

brook a small stream
mellifluous sweet like honey

gravel small stones

pile large wooden, metal or stone post
topee *Tropenhelm*

ravenous extremely hungry

to remonstrate to protest or complain about sth/sb

pimply *pickelig*

gay (old fashioned) cheerful
jolly happy and cheerful
solemn serious

merry happy

to contort to become twisted

mentally deficient
geistig zurückgeblieben
to chuckle to laugh quietly

A wave of emotion swept over her and her eyes filled with tears. She saw his face contorted for a moment with the extremity of his feeling and his voice was a little shaky when he answered.

'It's a terrible thing for me to have married a woman who's 5 mentally deficient,' he said.

She chuckled. It was the characteristic answer which she would have liked him to make.

It was hard to realize that nine months ago she had never even heard of him. She had met him at a small place by the 10 seaside where she was spending a month's holiday with her mother. Doris was a secretary to a member of parliament. Guy was home on leave. They were staying at the same hotel, and he quickly told her all about himself. He was born in Sembulu, where his father had served for thirty years un- 15 der the second Sultan, and on leaving school he had entered the same service. He was devoted to the country.

'After all, England's a foreign land to me,' he told her. 'My home's Sembulu.'

And now it was her home too. He asked her to marry him 20 at the end of the month's holiday. She had known he was going to, and had decided to refuse him. She was her widowed mother's only child and she could not go so far away from her, but when the moment came she did not quite know what happened to her, she was carried off her feet by 25 an unexpected emotion, and she accepted him. They had been settled now for four months in the little outstation of which he was in charge. She was very happy.

She told him once that she had quite made up her mind to refuse him. 30

'Are you sorry you didn't?' he asked, with a merry smile in his twinkling blue eyes.

'I should have been a perfect fool if I had. What a bit of luck that fate or chance or whatever it was stepped in and took the matter entirely out of my hands!' Now she heard 35 Guy clatter down the steps to the bath-house. He was a noisy fellow and even with bare feet he could not be quiet. But he

to utter *äußern*

sibilant *zischend*
to waylay *abfangen*
to be vexed to be angry

uttered an exclamation. He said two or three words in the local dialect and she could not understand. Then she heard someone speaking to him, not aloud, but in a sibilant whis- 40 per. Really it was too bad of people to waylay him when he was going to have his bath. He spoke again and though his voice was low she could hear that he was vexed. The other voice was raised now; it was a woman's. Doris supposed it was someone who had a complaint to make. It was like a 45 Malay woman to come in that surreptitious way. But she was evidently getting very little from Guy, for she heard him say: Get out. That at all events she understood, and

surreptitious [ˌsʌrəpˈtɪʃəs] done secretly or quickly, in the hope that other people will not notice

then she heard him bolt the door. There was a sound of the
water he was throwing over himself (the bathing arrangements still amused her, the bath-houses were under the
bedrooms, on the ground; you had a large tub of water und
5 you sluiced yourself with a little tin pail) and in a couple of
minutes he was back again in the dining-room. His hair
was still wet. They sat down to luncheon.
'It's lucky I'm not a suspicious or a jealous person,' she
laughed. 'I don't know that I should altogether approve of
10 you having animated conversations with ladies while
you're having your bath.'
His face, usually so cheerful, had borne a sullen look when
he came in, but now it brightened.
'I wasn't exactly pleased to see her.'
15 'So I judged by the tone of your voice. In fact, I thought
you were rather short with the young person.'
'Damned cheek, waylaying me like that!'
'What did she want?'
'Oh, I don't know. It's a woman from the kampong. She's
20 had a row with her husband or something.'
'I wonder if it's the same one who was hanging about this
morning.'
He frowned a little.
'Was there someone hanging about?'
25 'Yes, I went into your dressing-room to see that everything
was nice and tidy, and then I went down to the bath-house.
I saw someone slink out of the door as I went down
the steps and when I looked out I saw a woman standing
there.'
30 'Did you speak to her?'
'I asked her what she wanted and she said something, but I
couldn't understand.'
'I'm not going to have all sorts of stray people prowling
about here,' he said. 'They've got no right to come.'
35 He smiled, but Doris, with the quick perception of a woman in love, noticed that he smiled only with his lips, not as
usual with his eyes also, and wondered what it was that
troubled him.
'What have you been doing this morning?' he asked.
40 'Oh, nothing much. I went for a little walk.'
'Through the kampong?'
'Yes. I saw a man send a chained monkey up a tree to pick
coconuts, which rather thrilled me.'
'It's rather a lark, isn't it?'
45 'Oh, Guy, there were two little boys watching him who
were much whiter than the others. I wondered if they were
half-castes. I spoke to them, but they didn't know a word of
English.'

---

to bolt to lock

to sluice to wash sth with
a stream of water
pail bucket

sullen silent and bad-tempered

cheek rudeness, lack of respect

kampong (Malay) a village
row [raʊ] quarrel

to frown die Stirn runzeln

to stray streunen
to prowl to move quietly and
carefully around an area, esp
with the intention of committing
a crime

lark joke

half-caste (offensive) a person
whose parents are from different
races

'There are two or three half-caste children in the kampong,'
he answered.
'Who do they belong to?'
'Their mother is one of the village girls.'
'Who is their father?'   5
'Oh, my dear, that's the sort of question we think it a little
dangerous to ask out here.' He paused. 'A lot of fellows
have native wives, and then when they go home or marry
they pension them off and send them back to their village.'
Doris was silent. The indifference with which he spoke   10
seemed a little callous to her. There was almost a frown on
her frank, open, pretty English face when she replied.
'But what about the children?'
'I have no doubt they're properly provided for. Within his
means, a man generally sees that there's enough money to   15
have them decently educated. They get jobs as clerks in a
government office, you know; they're all right.'
She gave him a slightly rueful smile.
'You can't expect me to think it's a very good system.'
'You mustn't be too hard,' he smiled back.   20
'I'm not hard. But I'm thankful you never had a Malay
wife. I should have hated it. Just think if those two little
brats were yours.'
The boy changed their plates. There was never much variety in their menu. They started luncheon with river fish,   25
dull and insipid, so that a good deal of tomato ketchup was
needed to make it palatable, and then went on to some kind
of stew. Guy poured Worcester Sauce over it.
'The old Sultan didn't think it was a white woman's country,' he said presently. 'He rather encouraged people to –   30
keep house with native girls. Of course things have changed
now. The country's perfectly quiet and I suppose we know
better how to cope with the climate.'
'But, Guy, the eldest of those boys wasn't more than seven
or eight and the other was about five.'   35
'It's awfully lonely on an outstation. Why, often one
doesn't see another white man for six months on end. A
fellow comes out here when he's only a boy.' He gave her
that charming smile of his which transfigured his round,
plain face. 'There are excuses, you know.'   40
She always found that smile irresistible. It was his best argument. Her eyes grew once more soft and tender.
'I'm sure there are.' She stretched her hand across the little
table and put it on his. 'I'm very lucky to have caught you
so young. Honestly, it would upset me dreadfully if I were   45
told that you had lived like that.'
He took her hand and pressed it.
'Are you happy here, darling?'

---

to pension sb off *jdn abfinden*

callous not caring about other people's feelings or suffering

means (pl) the money that a person has

rueful showing that sb is sorry

brat (infml) kid, child that behaves badly

insipid having almost no taste or flavour
palatable having a pleasant or acceptable taste

to transfigure to change the appearance of a person or thing so that they look more beautiful
plain simple, not attractive

'Desperately.'

She looked very cool and fresh in her linen frock. The heat did not distress her. She had no more than the prettiness of youth, though her brown eyes were fine; but she had a
5 pleasing frankness of expression, and her dark, short hair was neat and glossy. She gave you the impression of a girl of spirit and you felt sure that the member of parliament for whom she worked had in her a very competent secretary.

'I loved the country at once,' she said. 'Although I'm alone
10 so much I don't think I've ever once felt lonely.'

Of course she had read novels about the Malay Archipelago and she had formed an impression of a sombre land with great ominous rivers and a silent, impenetrable jungle. When a little coasting steamer set them down at the mouth
15 of the river, where a large boat, manned by a dozen Dyaks, was waiting to take them to the station, her breath was taken away by the beauty, friendly rather than awe-inspiring, of the scene. It had a gaiety, like the joyful singing of birds in the trees, which she had never expected. On each bank
20 of the river were mangroves and nipah palms, and behind them the dense green of the forest. In the distance stretched blue mountains, range upon range, as far as the eye could see. She had no sense of confinement nor of gloom, but rather of openness and widespaces where the exultant fan-
25 cy could wander with delight. The green glittered in the sunshine and the sky was blithe and cheerful. The gracious land seemed to offer her a smiling welcome.

They rowed on, hugging a bank, and high overhead flew a pair of doves. A flash of colour, like a living jewel, dashed
30 across their path. It was a kingfisher. Two monkeys, with their dangling tails, sat side by side on a branch. On the horizon, over there on the other side of the broad and turbid river, beyond the jungle, was a row of little white clouds, the only clouds in the sky, and they looked like a row of
35 ballet-girls, dressed in white, waiting at the back of the stage, alert and merry, for the curtain to go up. Her heart was filled with joy; and now, remembering it all, her eyes rested on her husband with a grateful, assured affection.

And what fun it had been to arrange their living-room! It
40 was very big. On the floor, when she arrived, was torn and dirty matting; on the walls of unpainted wood hung (much too high up) photogravures of Academy pictures, Dyak shields, and parangs. The tables were covered with Dyak cloth in sombre colours, and on them stood pieces of Bru-
45 nei brass-ware, much in need of cleaning, empty cigarette tins, and bits of Malay silver. There was a rough wooden shelf with cheap editions of novels and a number of old travel books in battered leather; and another shelf was

---

frock (old-fashioned) dress
to distress to bother

frankness an honest and direct way of behaving towards others

sombre dark, sad and serious
impenetrable that can not be entered, passed through or seen through

Dyak or **Dayak** [daɪæk] a member of a Malaysian tribe from the interior of Borneo: noted for their long houses

confinement imprisonment
gloom 1. feeling of being sad and without hope 2. almost total darkness
exultant triumphant
fancy imagination
blithe happy and carefree
to hug to keep close to sth for a distance

turbid full of mud, dirt

alert attentive, watchful

parang short and stout, straight-edged knife
Brunei a sultanate in NW Borneo
brass *Messing*

battered old and well-used

bachelor unmarried man

pathetic heart-rendering
dreary depressing

deft skilful

shrub bush
inordinate far more than is usual
poky (infml) too small

deliberate done on purpose,
intentional, careful
to display to show

banter friendly remarks and
jokes

tummy (infml) the stomach
and the area around the
stomach
to chaff to tease

racket *Tennisschläger*
press a device to keep wooden
rackets from warping

crowded with empty bottles. It was a bachelor's room, untidy but stiff; and though it amused her she found it intolerably pathetic. It was a dreary, comfortless life that Guy had led there, and she threw her arms round his neck and kissed him. 5

'You poor darling,' she laughed. She had deft hands and she soon made the room habitable. She arranged this and that, and what she could not do with she turned out. Her wedding-presents helped. Now the room was friendly and comfortable. In glass vases were lovely orchids and in great 10 bowls huge masses of flowering shrubs. She felt an inordinate pride because it was her house (she had never in her life lived in anything but a poky flat) and she had made it charming for him.

'Are you pleased with me?' she asked when she had finished. 15

'Quite,' he smiled.

The deliberate understatement was much to her mind. How jolly it was that they should understand each other so well! They were both of them shy of displaying emotion, and it 20 was only at rare moments that they used with one another anything but ironic banter.

They finished luncheon and he threw himself into a long chair to have a sleep. She went towards her room. She was a little surprised that he drew her to him as she passed and, 25 making her bend down, kissed her lips. They were not in the habit of exchanging embraces at odd hours of the day.

'A full tummy is making you sentimental, my poor lamb,' she chaffed him.

'Get out and don't let me see you again for at least two 30 hours.'

'Don't snore.'

She left him. They had risen at dawn and in five minutes were fast asleep.

Doris was awakened by the sound of her husband's splash- 35 ing in the bath-house. The walls of the bungalow were like a sounding board and not a thing that one of them did escaped the other. She felt too lazy to move, but she heard the boy bring the tea things in, so she jumped up and ran down into her own bath-house. The water, not cold but cool, was 40 deliciously refreshing. When she came into the sitting-room Guy was taking the rackets out of the press, for they played tennis in the short cool of the evening. The night fell at six. The tennis-court was two or three hundred yards from the bungalow and after tea, anxious not to lose time, they 45 strolled down to it.

'Oh, look,' said Doris, 'there's that girl that I saw this morning.'

Guy turned quickly. His eyes rested for a moment on a native woman, but he did not speak.

'What a pretty sarong she's got,' said Doris. 'I wonder where it comes from.'

5 They passed her. She was slight and small, with the large, dark, starry eyes of her race and a mass of raven hair. She did not stir as they went by, but stared at them strangely. Doris saw then that she was not quite so young as she had at first thought. Her features were a trifle heavy and her 10 skin was dark, but she was very pretty. She held a small child in her arms. Doris smiled a little as she saw it, but no answering smile moved the woman's lips. Her face remained impassive. She did not look at Guy, she looked only at Doris, and he walked on as though he did not see 15 her. Doris turned to him.

'Isn't that baby a duck?'

'I didn't notice.'

She was puzzled by the look of his face. It was deathly white, and the pimples which not a little distressed her 20 were more than commonly red.

'Did you notice her hands and feet? She might be a duchess.'

'All natives have good hands and feet,' he answered, but not jovially as was his wont; it was as though he forced himself to speak.

25 But Doris was intrigued.

'Who is she, d'you know?'

'She's one of the girls in the kampong.'

They had reached the court now. When Guy went up to the net to see that it was taut he looked back. The girl was still 30 standing where they had passed her. Their eyes met.

'Shall I serve?' said Doris.

'Yes, you've got the balls on your side.'

He played very badly. Generally he gave her fifteen and beat her, but today she won easily. And he played silently.

35 Generally he was a noisy player, shouting all the time, cursing his foolishness when he missed a ball and chaffing her when he placed one out of her reach.

'You're off your game, young man,' she cried.

'Not a bit,' he said.

40 He began to slam the balls, trying to beat her, and sent one after the other into the net. She had never seen him with this set face. Was it possible that he was a little out of temper because he was not playing well? The light fell, and they ceased to play. The woman whom they had passed stood in 45 exactly the same position as when they came and once more, with expressionless face, she watched them go.

The blinds on the veranda were raised now, and on the table between their two long chairs were bottles and soda-water.

---

sarong a long piece of fabric wrapped around the body from the waist or the chest worn by Malaysian and Indonesian men and women
to stir to move

features *Gesichtszüge*
a trifle a bit

duck dear, darling

wont habit, usual manner

to be intrigued to be very interested in sth/sb and wanting to know more about it/them

taut tight, properly stretched

to curse to swear

to be off one's game to play badly

to cease [si:s] to stop

under the weather sick, less
healthy than usual

This was the hour at which they had the first drink of the day and Guy mixed a couple of gin slings. The river stretched widely before them, and on the further bank the jungle was wrapped in the mystery of the approaching night. A native was silently rowing up-stream, standing at ₅ the bow of the boat, with two oars.

'I played like a fool,' said Guy, breaking a silence. 'I'm feeling a bit under the weather.'

'I'm sorry. You're not going to have fever, are you?'

'Oh, no. I shall be all right tomorrow.' ₁₀

Darkness closed in upon them. The frogs croaked loudly and now and then they heard a few short notes from some singing bird of the night. Fireflies flitted across the veranda and they made the trees that surrounded it look like Christmas trees lit with tiny candles. They sparkled softly. Doris ₁₅ thought she heard a little sigh. It vaguely disturbed her. Guy was always so full of gaiety.

'What is it, old man?' she said gently. 'Tell mother.'

breezy cheerful

'Nothing. Time for another drink,' he answered breezily.

Next day he was as cheerful as ever and the mail came. The ₂₀ coasting steamer passed the mouth of the river twice a month, once on its way to the coalfields and once on its way back. On the outward journey it brought mail, which Guy sent a boat down to fetch. Its arrival was the excitement of their uneventful lives. For the first day or two they ₂₅ skimmed rapidly all that had come, letters, English papers and papers from Singapore, magazines and books, leaving for the ensuing weeks a more exact perusal. They snatched the illustrated papers from one another. If Doris had not been so absorbed she might have noticed that there was a ₃₀ change in Guy. She would have found it hard to describe and harder still to explain. There was in his eyes a sort of watchfulness and in his mouth a slight droop of anxiety.

to skim to read sth quickly in
order to find a particular point or
the main points
perusal careful reading

droop hanging down

industrious busy
commotion sudden noisy
confusion or excitement
compound area, esp
surrounded by a fence
vituperative schmähend
scuffle short struggle

Then, perhaps a week later, one morning when she was sitting in the shaded room studying a Malay grammar (for she ₃₅ was industriously learning the language) she heard a commotion in the compound. She heard the house boy's voice, he was speaking angrily, the voice of another man, perhaps it was the water-carrier's, and then a woman's, shrill and vituperative. There was a scuffle. She went to the window ₄₀ and opened the shutters. The water-carrier had hold of a woman's arm and was dragging her along, while the house boy was pushing her from behind with both hands. Doris recognized her at once as the woman she had seen one

to loiter to hang around

morning loitering in the compound and later in the day out- ₄₅ side the tennis-court. She was holding a baby against her breast. All three were shouting angrily.

'Stop,' cried Doris. 'What are you doing?'

At the sound of her voice the water-carrier let go suddenly and the woman, still pushed from behind, fell to the ground. There was a sudden silence and the house boy looked sullenly into space. The water-carrier hesitated a
5 moment and then slunk away. The woman raised herself slowly to her feet, arranged the baby on her arm, and stood impassive, staring at Doris. The boy said something to her which Doris could not have heard even if she had understood: the woman by no change of face showed that his
10 words meant anything to her; but she slowly strolled away. The boy followed her to the gate of the compound. Doris called to him as he walked back, but he pretended not to hear. She was growing angry now and she called more sharply.
15 'Come here at once,' she cried.
Suddenly, avoiding her wrathful glance, he came towards the bungalow. He came in and stood at the door. He looked at her sulkily.
'What were you doing with that woman?' she asked abruptly.
20 'Tuan say she no come here.'
'You mustn't treat a woman like that. I won't have it. I shall tell the tuan exactly what I saw.'
The boy did not answer. He looked away, but she felt that he was watching her through his long eyelashes. She dis-
25 missed him.
'That'll do.'
Without a word he turned and went back to the servants' quarters. She was exasperated and she found it impossible to give her attention once more to the Malay exercises. In a
30 little while the boy came in to lay the cloth for luncheon. On a sudden he went to the door.
'What is it?' she asked.
'Tuan just coming.'
He went out to take Guy's hat from him. His quick ears had
35 caught the footsteps before they were audible to her. Guy did not as usual come up the steps immediately; he paused, and Doris at once surmised that the boy had gone down to meet him in order to tell him of the morning's incident. She shrugged her shoulders. The boy evidently wanted to get
40 his story in first. But she was astonished when Guy came in. His face was ashy.
'Guy, what on earth's the matter?'
He flushed a sudden hot red.
'Nothing. Why?'
45 She was so taken aback that she let him pass into his room without a word of what she had meant to speak of at once. It took him longer than usual to have his bath and change his clothes and luncheon was served when he came in.

sullen silent and bad-tempered
to hesitate to be slow to speak or act because you feel uncertain or nervous
slink, slunk, slunk to steal away

wrathful furious, scornful

sulky offended

tuan (in Malay speaking countries) sir, lord: a form of address used as a mark of respect

to dismiss to send away

exasperated extremely annoyed

to surmise [sə'maɪz] to guess

to be obliged to do sth
[əˈblaɪdʒd] to do sth because it is your duty

to pester sb (for/with sth) to annoy sb, esp by asking them sth many times

terse concise, short

irritable getting annoyed easily, showing anger

abstracted deep in thought

to exert oneself to make a big effort

sluggishness laziness

deliberation the quality of being slow and careful in considering, planning or discussing sth
relentlessness the quality of not stopping or getting weaker and being unwilling to compromise
fancy imagination
distress worry, unhappiness

'Guy,' she said, as they sat down, 'that woman we saw the other day was here again this morning.'
'So I've heard,' he answered.
'The boys were treating her brutally. I had to stop them. You must really speak to them about it.'   5
Though the Malay understood every word she said, he made no sign that he heard. He handed her the toast.
'She's been told not to come here. I gave instructions that if she showed herself again she was to be turned out.'
'Were they obliged to be so rough?'   10
'She refused to go. I don't think they were any rougher than they could help.'
'It was horrible to see a woman treated like that. She had a baby in her arms.'
'Hardly a baby. It's three years old.'   15
'How d'you know?'
'I know all about her. She hasn't the least right to come here pestering everybody.'
'What does she want?'
'She wants to do exactly what she did. She wants to make   20
a disturbance.'
For a little while Doris did not speak. She was surprised at her husband's tone. He spoke tersely. He spoke as though all this were no concern of hers. She thought him a little unkind. He was nervous and irritable.   25
'I doubt if we shall be able to play tennis this afternoon,' she said. 'It looks to me as though we were going to have a storm.'
The rain was falling when she awoke and it was impossible to go out. During tea Guy was silent and abstracted. She got her sewing and began to work. Guy sat down to read   30
such of the English papers as he had not yet gone through from cover to cover; but he was restless; he walked up and down the large room and then went out on the veranda. He looked at the steady rain. What was he thinking of? Doris was vaguely uneasy.   35
It was not till after dinner that he spoke. During the simple meal he had exerted himself to be his usual gay self, but the exertion was apparent. The rain had ceased and the night was starry. They sat on the veranda. In order not to attract insects they had put out the lamp in the sitting-room. At   40
their feet, with a mighty, formidable sluggishness, silent, mysterious, and fatal, flowed the river. It had the terrible deliberation and the relentlessness of destiny.
'Doris, I've got something to say to you,' he said suddenly. His voice was very strange. Was it her fancy that he had   45
difficulty in keeping it quite steady? She felt a little pang in her heart because he was in distress, and she put her hand gently into his. He drew it away.

'It's rather a long story. I'm afraid it's not a very nice one and I find it rather difficult to tell. I'm going to ask you not to interrupt me, or to say anything, till I've finished.'
In the darkness she could not see his face, but she felt that
5 it was haggard. She did not answer. He spoke in a voice so low that it hardly broke the silence of the night.

haggard tired, exhausted, worried

'I was only eighteen when I came out here. I came straight from school. I spent three months in Kuala Solor, and then I was sent to a station up the Sembulu river. Of course there
10 was a Resident there and his wife. I lived in the court-house, but I used to have my meals with them and spend the evening with them. I had an awfully good time. Then the fellow who was here fell ill and had to go home. We were short of men on account of the war and I was put in
15 charge of this place. Of course I was very young, but I spoke the language like a native, and they remembered my father. I was as pleased as punch to be on my own.'
He was silent while he knocked the ashes out of his pipe and refilled it. When he lit a match Doris, without looking
20 at him, noticed that his hand was unsteady.

to be pleased as punch (Punch) (idm) *sich wie ein Kind/ein Schneekönig freuen*

'I'd never been alone before. Of course at home there'd been father and mother and generally an assistant. And then at school naturally there were always fellows about. On the way out, on the boat, there were people all the time,
25 and at K.S., and the same at my first post. The people there were almost like my own people. I seemed always to live in a crowd. I like people. I'm a noisy blighter. I like to have a good time. All sorts of things make me laugh and you must have somebody to laugh with. But it was different here. Of
30 course it was all right in the day time; I had my work and I could talk to the Dyaks. Although they were headhunters in those days and now and then I had a bit of trouble with them, they were an awfully decent lot of fellows. I got on very well with them. Of course I should have liked a white
35 man to gas to, but they were better than nothing, and it was easier for me because they didn't look upon me quite as a stranger. I liked the work too. It was rather lonely in the evening to sit on the veranda and drink a gin and bitters by myself, but I could read. And the boys were about. My own
40 boy was called Abdul. He'd known my father. When I got tired of reading I could give him a shout and have a bit of a jaw with him.

blighter (old-fashioned, BrE, infml) *Lümmel, Mistkerl*

decent honest, fair, acceptable

to gas to sb (old-fashioned, infml) to chat with sb

to have a bit of a jaw with sb to chat with sb

'It was the nights that did for me. After dinner the boys shut up and went away to sleep in the kampong. I was all
45 alone. There wasn't a sound in the bungalow except now and then the croak of the chik-chak. It used to come out of the silence, suddenly, so that it made me jump. Over in the kampong I heard the sound of a gong or fire-crackers. They

chik-chak type of lizard

rotten terrible

to mend to repair

Straits dollars currency used in the Straits Settlements, formerly a British crown colony of SE Asia that included Singapore, Penang, Malacca, Labuan and some smaller islands

to blush to become red in the face
to snuggle up *sich ankuscheln*
to take to sb to start to like

were having a good time, they weren't so far away, but I had to stay where I was. I was tired of reading. I couldn't have been more of a prisoner if I'd been in jail. Night after night it was the same. I tried drinking three or four whiskies, but it's poor fun drinking alone, and it didn't cheer me ⁵ up; it only made me feel rather rotten next day. I tried going to bed immediately after dinner, but I couldn't sleep, I used to lie in bed, getting hotter and hotter, and more wide awake, till I didn't know what to do with myself. By George, those nights were long. D'you know, ¹⁰ I got so low, I was so sorry for myself that sometimes – it makes me laugh now when I think of it, but I was only nineteen and a half – sometimes I used to cry.

'Then, one evening, after dinner, Abdul had cleared away and was just going off, when he gave a little cough. He said, ¹⁵ wasn't I lonely in the house all night by myself? "Oh, no, that's all right," I said. I didn't want him to know what a damned fool I was, but I expect he knew all right. He stood there without speaking; and I knew he wanted to say something to me. "What is it?" I said. "Spit it out." Then he said ²⁰ that if I'd like to have a girl to come and live with me he knew one who was willing. She was a very good girl and he could recommend her. She'd be no trouble and it would be someone to have about the bungalow. She'd mend my things for me … I felt awfully low. It had been raining all ²⁵ day and I hadn't been able to get any exercise. I knew I shouldn't sleep for hours. It wouldn't cost me very much money, he said, her people were poor and they'd be quite satisfied with a small present. Two hundred Straits dollars. "You look," he said. "If you don't like her you send ³⁰ her away." I asked him where she was. "She's here," he said. "I call her." He went to the door. She'd been waiting on the steps with her mother. They came in and sat down on the floor. I gave them some sweets. She was shy, of course, but cool enough, and when I said something to her she gave ³⁵ me a smile. She was very young, hardly more than a child, they said she was fifteen. She was awfully pretty, and she had her best clothes on. We began to talk. She didn't say much, but she laughed a lot when I chaffed her. Abdul said I'd find she had plenty to say for herself when she ⁴⁰ got to know me. He told her to come and sit by me. She giggled and refused, but her mother told her to come, and I made room for her on the chair. She blushed and laughed, but she came, and then she snuggled up to me. The boy laughed too. "You see, she's taken to you already," he said. ⁴⁵ "Do you want her to stay?" he asked. "Do you want to?" I said to her. She hid her face, laughing, on my shoulder. She was very soft and small. "Very well," I said, "let her stay."'Guy leaned forward and helped himself to a whisky and soda.

'May I speak now?' asked Doris.

'Wait a minute, I haven't finished yet. I wasn't in love with
5 her, not even at the beginning. I only took her so as to have
somebody about the bungalow. I think I should have gone
mad if I hadn't or else taken to drink. I was at the end of
my tether. I was too young to be quite alone. I was never in
love with anyone but you.' He hesitated a moment. 'She
10 lived here till I went home last year on leave. It's the woman you've seen hanging about.'

'Yes, I guessed that. She had a baby in her arms. Is that
your child?'

'Yes. It's a little girl.'

15 'Is it the only one?'

'You saw the two small boys the other day in the kampong.
You mentioned them.'

'She has three children then?'

'Yes.'

20 'It's quite a family you've got.'

She felt the sudden gesture which her remark forced from
him, but she did not speak.

'Didn't she know that you were married till you suddenly
turned up here with a wife?' asked Doris.

25 'She knew I was going to be married.'

'When?'

'I sent her back to the village before I left here. I told her it
was all over. I gave her what I'd promised. She always
knew it was only a temporary arrangement. I was fed up
30 with it. I told her I was going to marry a white woman.'

'But you hadn't even seen me then.'

'No, I know. But I'd made up my mind to marry when I
was home.' He chuckled in his old manner. 'I don't mind
telling you that I was getting rather despondent about it
35 when I met you. I fell in love with you at first sight and
then I knew it was either you or nobody.'

'Why didn't you tell me? Don't you think it would have
been only fair to give me a chance of judging for myself? It
might have occurred to you that it would be rather a shock
40 to a girl to find out that her husband had lived for ten years
with another girl and had three children.'

'I couldn't expect you to understand. The circumstances
out here are peculiar. It's the regular thing. Five men out of
six do it. I thought perhaps it would shock you and I didn't
45 want to lose you. You see, I was most awfully in love with
you. I am now, darling. There was no reason that you
should ever know. I didn't expect to come back here. One
seldom goes back to the same station after home leave.

to be at the end of one's tether (BrE; idm) to feel that you cannot deal with a difficult situation any more because you are too tired, worried, unhappy, etc

to chuckle to laugh quietly

to be despondent about sad, without much hope

to occur [əˈkɜː(r)]
1. to take place, to happen
2. to exist
3. to come to mind
occurence [əˈkʌrəns; AmE əˈkɜːr-] something that happens or exists

to blackmail sb to force sb to give you money

to make a clean breast of sth to tell the whole truth about sth bad that one has done

jealous feeling angry or unhappy because sb you like or love is showing interest in sb else
I daresay ich meine/ich möchte sagen
perk (AmE) additional benefit, advantage

to provide for versorgen

touching cute, sweet

to reproach sb (for sth) to blame or criticize sb

slush (infml) silly stories

When we came here I offered her money if she'd go to some other village. First she said she would and then she changed her mind.'
'Why have you told me now?'
'She's been making the most awful scenes. I don't know how she found out that you knew nothing about it. As soon as she did she began to blackmail me. I've had to give her an awful lot of money. I gave orders that she wasn't to be allowed in the compound. This morning she made that scene just to attract your attention. She wanted to frighten me. It couldn't go on like that. I thought the only thing was to make a clean breast of it.'
There was a long silence as he finished. At last he put his hand on hers.
'You do understand, Doris, don't you? I know I've been to blame.'
She did not move her hand. He felt it cold beneath his.
'Is she jealous?'
'I daresay there were all sorts of perks when she was living here, and I don't suppose she much likes not getting them any longer. But she was never in love with me any more than I was in love with her. Native women never do really care for white men, you know.'
'And the children?'
'Oh, the children are all right. I've provided for them. As soon as the boys are old enough I shall send them to school at Singapore.'
'Do they mean nothing to you at all?'
He hesitated.
'I want to be quite frank with you. I should be sorry if anything happened to them. When the first one was expected I thought I'd be much fonder of it than I ever had been of its mother. I suppose I should have been if it had been white. Of course, when it was a baby it was rather funny and touching, but I had no particular feeling that it was mine. I think that's what it is; you see, I have no sense of their belonging to me. I've reproached myself sometimes, because it seemed rather unnatural, but the honest truth is that they're no more to me than if they were somebody else's children. Of course a lot of slush is talked about children by people who haven't got any.'
Now she had heard everything. He waited for her to speak, but she said nothing. She sat motionless.
'Is there anything more you want to ask me, Doris?' he said at last.
'No, I've got rather a headache. I think I shall go to bed.' Her voice was as steady as ever. 'I don't quite know what to say. Of course it's been all very unexpected. You must give me a little time to think.'

'Are you very angry with me?'

'No. Not at all. Only – only I must be left to myself for a while. Don't move. I'm going to bed.'

She rose from her long chair and put her hand on his shoul-
5 der.

'It's so very hot tonight. I wish you'd sleep in your dressing-room. Good night.'

She was gone. He heard her lock the door of her bedroom.
She was pale next day and he could see that she had not
10 slept.

There was no bitterness in her manner, she talked as usual,
but without ease; she spoke of this and that as though she
were making conversation with a stranger. They had never
had a quarrel, but it seemed to Guy that so would she talk
15 if they had had a disagreement and the subsequent reconciliation had left her still wounded. The look in her eyes
puzzled him; he seemed to read in them a strange fear. Immediately after dinner she said:

'I'm not feeling very well tonight. I think I shall go straight
20 to bed.'

'Oh, my poor darling, I'm so sorry,' he cried.

'It's nothing. I shall be all right in a day or two.'

'I shall come in and say good night to you later.'

'No, don't do that. I shall try and get straight off to sleep.'

25 'Well, then, kiss me before you go.'

He saw that she flushed. For an instant she seemed to hesitate, then, with averted eyes, she leaned towards him. He
took her in his arms and sought her lips, but she turned her
face away and he kissed her cheek. She left him quickly
30 and again he heard the key turn softly in the lock of her
door. He flung himself heavily on the chair. He tried to
read, but his ear was attentive to the smallest sound in his
wife's room. She had said she was going to bed, but he did
not hear her move. The silence in there made him unac-
35 countably nervous. Shading the lamp with his hand he saw
that there was a glimmer under her door; she had not put
out her light. What on earth was she doing? He put down
his book. It would not have surprised him if she had been
angry and had made him a scene, or if she had cried; he
40 could have coped with that; but her calmness frightened
him. And then what was that fear which he had seen so
plainly in her eyes? He thought once more over all he had
said to her on the previous night. He didn't know how else
he could have put it. After all, the chief point was that he'd
45 done the same as everybody else, and it was all over long
before he met her. Of course as things turned out he had
been a fool, but anyone could be wise after the event. He
put his hand to his heart. Funny how it hurt him there.

subsequent following
reconciliation an end to a
disagreement and the start of a
good relationship again

to flush to become red in the
face, to blush
to avert one's eyes to turn your
eyes away from what you do not
want to see
to seek, sought, sought to
search for

'I suppose that's the sort of thing people mean when they say they're heartbroken,' he said to himself. 'I wonder how long it's going on like this?'

Should he knock at the door and tell her he must speak to her? It was better to have it out. He *must* make her under- 5 stand. But the silence scared him. Not a sound! Perhaps it was better to leave her alone. Of course it had been a shock. He must give her as long as she wanted. After all, she knew how devotedly he loved her.

devoted having great love for sb/sth and being loyal to them

Patience, that was the only thing; perhaps she was fighting 10 it out with herself; he must give her time; he must have patience. Next morning he asked her if she had slept better.

'Yes, much,' she said.

'Are you very angry with me?' he asked piteously.

She looked at him with candid, open eyes. 15

'Not a bit.'

piteous deserving or causing pity
candid honest and sincere

'Oh, my dear, I'm so glad. I've been a brute and a beast. I know it's been hateful for you. But do forgive me. I've been so miserable.'

'I do forgive you. I don't even blame you.' 20

He gave her a little rueful smile, and there was in his eyes the look of a whipped dog.

'I haven't much liked sleeping by myself the last two nights.'

She glanced away. Her face grew a trifle paler. 25

'I've had the bed in my room taken away. It took up so much space. I've had a little camp bed put there instead.'

'My dear, what are you talking about?'

Now she looked at him steadily.

'I'm not going to live with you as your wife again.' 30

'Never?'

She shook her head. He looked at her in a puzzled way. He could hardly believe he had heard aright and his heart began to beat painfully.

'But that's awfully unfair to me, Doris.' 35

'Don't you think it was a little unfair to me to bring me out here in the circumstances?'

'But you just said you didn't blame me.'

'That's quite true. But the other's different. I can't do it.'

'But how are we going to live together like that?' 40

to ponder to think

She stared at the floor. She seemed to ponder deeply.

'When you wanted to kiss me on the lips last night I – it almost made me sick.'

'Doris.'

She looked at him suddenly and her eyes were cold and 45

hostile unfriendly or aggressive and ready to argue or fight

hostile.

'That bed I slept on, is that the bed in which she had her children?' She saw him flush deeply. 'Oh, it's horrible.

How could you?' She wrung her hands, and her twisting, tortured fingers looked like little writhing snakes. But she made a great effort and controlled herself. 'My mind is quite made up. I don't want to be unkind to you, but there
5 are some things that you can't ask me to do. I've thought it all over. I've been thinking of nothing else since you told me, night and day, till I'm exhausted. My first instinct was to get up and go. At once. The steamer will be here in two or three days.'
10 'Doesn't it mean anything to you that I love you?'
'Oh, I know you love me. I'm not going to do that. I want to give us both a chance. I have loved you so, Guy.' Her voice broke, but she did not cry. 'I don't want to be unreasonable. Heaven knows, I don't want to be unkind. Guy,
15 will you give me time?'
'I don't know quite what you mean.'
'I just want you to leave me alone. I'm frightened by the feelings that I have.'
He had been right then; she was afraid.
20 'What feelings?'
'Please don't ask me. I don't want to say anything to wound you. Perhaps I shall get over them. Heaven knows, I want to. I'll try, I promise you. I'll try. Give me six months. I'll do everything in the world for you, but just that one thing.'
25 She made a little gesture of appeal. 'There's no reason why we shouldn't be happy enough together. If you really love me you'll – you'll have patience.'
He sighed deeply.
'Very well,' he said. 'Naturally I don't want to force you to
30 do anything you don't like. It shall be as you say.'
He sat heavily for a little, as though, on a sudden grown old, it was an effort to move; then he got up.
'I'll be getting along to the office.'
He took his topee and went out.
35 A month passed. Women conceal their feelings better than men and a stranger visiting them would never have guessed that Doris was in any way troubled. But in Guy the strain was obvious; his round, good-natured face was drawn, and in his eyes was a hungry, harassed look. He watched Doris.
40 She was gay and she chaffed him as she had been used to do; they played tennis together; they chatted about one thing and another. But it was evident that she was merely playing a part, and at last, unable to contain himself, he tried to speak again of his connexions with the Malay woman.
45 'Oh, Guy, there's no object in going back on all that,' she answered breezily. 'We've said all we had to say about it and I don't blame you for anything.'
'Why do you punish me then?'

to writhe to twist without stopping

exhausted [ɪgˈzɔːstɪd] very tired

gesture of appeal *eine bittende Geste*

to conceal to hide

strain pressure on sb because they have too much to do or manage; the problems, worry or anxiety that this produces
harassed strained, worried

evident clear
merely *bloß*
to contain oneself to keep one's feelings under control
object reason

interminable lasting a long time and therefore boring and annoying

prahu small boat providing food supplies

to murmur to say sth in a soft and quiet voice that is difficult to understand

aghast filled with horror and surprise

'My poor boy, I don't want to punish you. It's not my fault …' she shrugged her shoulders. 'Human nature is very odd.'

'I don't understand.'

'Don't try.' 5

The words might have been harsh, but she softened them with a pleasant, friendly smile. Every night when she went to bed she leaned over Guy and lightly kissed his cheek. Her lips only touched it. It was as though a moth had just brushed his face in its flight. 10

A second month passed, then a third, and suddenly the six months which had seemed so interminable were over. Guy asked himself whether she remembered. He gave a strained attention now to everything she said, to every look on her face and to every gesture of her hands. She remained im- 15 penetrable. She had asked him to give her six months; well, he had.

The coasting steamer passed the mouth of the river, dropped their mail, and went on its way. Guy busily wrote the letters which it would pick up on the return journey. 20 Two or three days passed by. It was a Tuesday and the prahu was to start at dawn on Thursday to await the steamer. Except at meal time when Doris exerted herself to make conversation they had not of late talked very much togeth- er; and after dinner as usual they took their books and be- 25 gan to read; but when the boy had finished clearing away and was gone for the night Doris put down hers.

'Guy, I have something I want to say to you,' she mur- mured.

His heart gave a sudden thud against his ribs and he felt 30 himself change colour.

'Oh, my dear, don't look like that, it's not so very terrible,' she laughed.

But he thought her voice trembled a little.

'Well?' 35

'I want you to do something for me.'

'My darling, I'll do anything in the world for you.'

He put out his hand to take hers, but she drew it away.

'I want you to let me go home.'

'You?' he cried, aghast. 'When? Why?' 40

'I've borne it as long as I can. I'm at the end of my tether.'

'How long do you want to go for? For always?'

'I don't know. I think so.' She gathered determination. 'Yes, for always.'

'Oh, my God!' 45

His voice broke and she thought he was going to cry.

'Oh, Guy, don't blame me. It really is not my fault. I can't help myself.'

'You asked me for six months. I accepted your terms. You can't say I've made a nuisance of myself.'

'No, no.'

'I've tried not to let you see what a rotten time I was having.'

5 'I know. I'm very grateful to you. You've been awfully kind to me. Listen, Guy, I want to tell you again that I don't blame you for a single thing you did. After all, you were only a boy, and you did no more than the others; I know what the loneliness is here. Oh, my dear, I'm so dreadfully

10 sorry for you. I knew all that from the beginning. That's why I asked you for six months. My common sense tells me that I'm making a mountain out of a molehill. I'm unreasonable; I'm being unfair to you. But, you see, common sense has nothing to do with it; my whole soul is in revolt.

15 When I see the woman and her children in the village I just feel my legs shaking. Everything in this house; when I think of that bed I slept in it gives me goose-flesh … You don't know what I've endured.'

'I think I've persuaded her to go away. And I've applied for

20 a transfer.'

'That wouldn't help. She'll be there always. You belong to them, you don't belong to me. I think perhaps I could have stood it if there'd only been one child, but three; and the boys are quite big boys. For ten years you lived with her.'

25 And now she came out with what she had been working up to. She was desperate. 'It's a physical thing, I can't help it, it's stronger than I am. I think of those thin black arms of hers round you and it fills me with a physical nausea. I think of you holding those little black babies in your arms.

30 Oh, it's loathsome. The touch of you is odious to me. Each night, when I've kissed you, I've had to brace myself up to it. I've had to clench my hands and force myself to touch your cheek.' Now she was clasping and unclasping her fingers in a nervous agony, and her voice was out of control.

35 'I know it's I who am to blame now. I'm a silly, hysterical woman. I thought I'd get over it. I can't, and now I never shall. I've brought it all on myself; I'm willing to take the consequences; if you say I must stay here, I'll stay, but if I stay I shall die. I beseech you to let me go.'

40 And now the tears which she had restrained so long overflowed and she wept broken-heartedly. He had never seen her cry before.

'Of course I don't want do keep you here against your will,' he said hoarsely.

45 Exhausted, she leaned back in her chair. Her features were all twisted and awry. It was horribly painful to see the abandonment of grief on that face which was habitually so placid.

---

nuisance annoyance

to make a mountain out of a molehill (idm) *aus einer Mücke einen Elefanten machen* (molehill – *Maulwurfshügel*)

to apply for to make a formal request
transfer change of place and job

nausea the feeling you have when you are sick or are disgusted by sth and you want to vomit
loathsome disgusting
odious extremely unpleasant
to brace oneself to prepare oneself mentally for doing sth very unpleasant
to clench to squeeze tightly
agony extreme physical or mental pain, fear of death

to beseech, besought, besought to beg
to restrain to hold back

hoarse with a sore throat

awry [ə'raɪ] *schief*

placid not easily excited or irritated, calm and peaceful

'I'm so sorry, Guy. I've broken your life, but I've broken mine too. And we might have been so happy.'
'When do you want to go? On Thursday?'
'Yes.'
She looked at him piteously. He buried his face in his ⁵ hands. At last he looked up.

to mutter to mumble

'I'm tired out,' he muttered.
'May I go?'
'Yes.'
For two minutes perhaps they sat there without a word. She ¹⁰

to start to move suddenly because sth has shocked or surprised you
rail *Geländer*

started when the chik-chak gave its piercing, hoarse, and strangely human cry. Guy rose and went out on to the veranda. He leaned against the rail and looked at the softly flowing water. He heard Doris go into her room.
Next morning, up earlier than usual, he went to her door ¹⁵ and knocked.
'Yes?'

shan't shall not

'I have to go up-river today. I shan't be back till late.'
'All right.'
She understood. He had arranged to be away all day in or- ²⁰ der not to be about while she was packing. It was heartbreaking work. When she had packed her clothes she looked round the sitting-room at the things that belonged to her. It seemed dreadful to take them. She left everything but the photograph of her mother. Guy did not come in till ²⁵ ten o'clock at night.
'I'm sorry I couldn't get back to dinner,' he said. 'The headman at the village I had to go to had a lot of things for

to attend to to take care of

me to attend to.'
She saw his eyes wander about the room and notice that ³⁰ her mother's photograph no longer stood in its place.
'Is everything quite ready?' he asked. 'I've ordered the boatman to be at the steps at dawn.'
'I told the boy to wake me at five.'
'I'd better give you some money.' He went to his desk and ³⁵

drawer *Schublade*

wrote out a cheque. He took some notes from a drawer. 'Here's some cash to take you as far as Singapore and at Singapore you'll be able to change the cheque.'
'Thank you.'
'Would you like me to come to the mouth of the river with ⁴⁰ you?'
'Oh, I think it would be better if we said good-bye here.'
'All right. I think I shall turn in. I've had a long day and

to be dead beat (infml) very tired and exhausted

I'm dead beat.'
He did not even touch her hand. He went into his room. In ⁴⁵ a few minutes she heard him throw himself on his bed. For a little while she sat looking for the last time round that room in which she had been so happy and so miserable.

She sighed deeply. She got up and went into her own room.
Everything was packed except the one or two things she
needed for the night.

It was dark when the boy awakened them. They dressed
5 hurriedly and when they were ready breakfast was waiting
for them. Presently they heard the boat row up to the landing-stage below the bungalow, and then the servants carried
down her luggage. It was a poor pretence they made of eating. The darkness thinned away and the river was ghostly.
10 It was not yet day, but it was no longer night. In the silence
the voices of the natives at the landing-stage were very
clear. Guy glanced at his wife's untouched plate.

'If you've finished we might stroll down. I think you ought
to be starting.'

15 She did not answer. She rose from the table. She went into
her room to see that nothing had been forgotten and then
side by side with him walked down the steps. A little winding path led them to the river. At the landing-stage the native guards in their smart uniform were lined up and they
20 presented arms as Guy and Doris passed. The head boatman gave her his hand as she stepped into the boat. She
turned and looked at Guy. She wanted desperately to say
one last word of comfort, once more to ask for his forgive-
ness, but she seemed to be struck dumb.

25 He stretched out his hand.

'Well, good-bye, I hope you'll have a jolly journey.'

They shook hands.

Guy nodded to the head boatman and the boat pushed off.
The dawn now was creeping along the river mistily, but the
30 night lurked still in the dark trees of the jungle. He stood at
the landing-stage till the boat was lost in the shadows of
the morning. With a sigh he turned away. He nodded absent-mindedly when the guard once more presented arms.
But when he reached the bungalow he called the boy. He
35 went round the room picking out everything that had belonged to Doris.

'Pack all these things up,' he said. 'It's no good leaving
them about.'

Then he sat down on the veranda and watched the day ad-
40 vance gradually like a bitter, an unmerited, and an over-
whelming sorrow. At last he looked at his watch. It was
time for him to go to the office.

In the afternoon he could not sleep, his head ached miserably, so he took his gun and went for a tramp in the jungle.
45 He shot nothing, but he walked in order to tire himself out.
Towards sunset he came back and had two or three drinks,
and then it was time to dress for dinner. There wasn't much
use in dressing now; he might just as well be comfortable;

---

pretence (AmE pretense) the act of behaving in a particular way to make other people believe sth that is not true
to pretend, a pretender

to be struck dumb to be suddenly put into the state of being unable to speak

misty with a lot of light fog; not clear
to lurk *lauern*

unmerited not deserved

tramp walk

to be accustomed to to be used to
listless without energy or enthusiasm

vacant empty

to mock to laugh at
to reverberate to echo

to sidle to move nervously and uncertainly
threshold *Türschwelle*
tattered old and torn
singlet *Unterhemd*

intent showing strong interest and attention

impassive emotionless

he put on a loose native jacket and a sarong. That was what he had been accustomed to wear before Doris came. He was barefoot. He ate his dinner listlessly and the boy cleared away and went. He sat down to read the Tatler. The bungalow was very silent. He could not read and let the paper fall on his knees. He was exhausted. He could not think and his mind was strangely vacant. The chik-chak was noisy that night and its hoarse and sudden cry seemed to mock him.
You could hardly believe that this reverberating sound came from so small a throat. Presently he heard a discreet cough. 'Who's there?' he cried.
There was a pause. He looked at the door. The chik-chak laughed harshly. A small boy sidled in and stood on the threshold.
It was a little half-caste boy in a tattered singlet and a sarong. It was the elder of his two sons.
'What do you want?' said Guy.
The boy came forward into the room and sat down, tucking his legs away under him.
'Who told you to come here?'
'My mother sent me. She says, do you want anything?'
Guy looked at the boy intently. The boy said nothing more. He sat and waited, his eyes cast down shyly. Then Guy in deep and bitter reflection buried his face in his hands. What was the use? It was finished. Finished! He surrendered. He sat back in his chair and sighed deeply.
'Tell your mother to pack up her things and yours. She can come back.'
'When?' asked the boy, impassively.
Hot tears trickled down Guy's funny, round spotty face.
'Tonight.'

George Orwell

Shooting an Elephant

petty small, unimportant
to have the guts (infml) to have courage
riot uproar
to bait to tease
nimble able to move quickly and easily
to trip sb up to catch sb's foot and make them fall or almost fall

In Moulmein, in Lower Burma, I was hated by large numbers of people – the only time in my life that I have been important enough for this to happen to me. I was subdivisional police officer of the town, and in an aimless, petty kind of way anti-European feeling was very bitter. No one had the guts to raise a riot; but if a European woman went through the bazaars alone somebody would probably spit betel juice over her dress. As a police officer I was an obvious target and was baited whenever it seemed safe to do so. When a nimble Burman tripped me up on the football field and the referee (another Burman) looked the other way, the crowd yelled with hideous laughter. This happened more than once. In the end the sneering yellow faces of young men that met me everywhere, the insults hooted after me when I was at a safe distance, got badly on my nerves. The young Buddhist priests were the worst of all. There were several thousands of them in the town and none of them seemed to have anything to do except stand on street corners and jeer at Europeans.

All this was perplexing and upsetting. For at that time I had already made up my mind that imperialism was an evil thing and the sooner I chucked up my job and got out of it the better. Theoretically – and secretly, of course – I was all for the Burmese and all against their oppressors, the British. As for the job I was doing, I hated it more bitterly than I can perhaps make clear. In a job like that you see the dirty work of Empire at close quarters. The wretched prisoners huddling in the stinking cages of the lock-ups, the grey, cowed faces of the long-term convicts, the scarred buttocks of the men who had been flogged with bamboos – all these oppressed me with an intolerable sense of guilt. But I could get nothing into perspective, I was young and ill-educated and I had had to think out my problems in the utter silence that is imposed on every Englishman in the East. I did not even know that the British Empire is dying, still less did I know that it is a great deal better than the younger empires that are going to supplant it. All I knew was that I was stuck between my hatred of the empire I served and my rage against the evil-spirited little beasts who tried to make my job impossible. With one part of my mind I thought of the British Raj as an unbreakable tyranny, as something clamped down, in saecula saeculorum, upon the will of prostrate peoples; with another part I thought that the greatest joy in the world would be to drive a bayonet into a Buddhist priest's guts. Feelings like these are the normal by-products of imperialism; ask any Anglo-Indian official, if you can catch him off duty.

One day something happened which in a roundabout way was enlightening. It was a tiny incident in itself, but it gave me a better glimpse than I had had before of the real nature of imperialism – the real motives for which despotic governments act. Early one morning the sub-inspector at a police station the other end of the town rang me up on the phone and said that an elephant was ravaging the bazaar. Would I please come and do something about it? I did not know what I could do, but I wanted to see what was happening and I got on to a pony and started out. I took my rifle, an old .44 Winchester and much too small to kill an elephant, but I thought

---

hideous very ugly or unpleasant
sneering grinning
to hoot to make a loud noise like a car horn

to jeer to laugh at sb or shout rude remarks at them to show that you do not respect them

to chuck sth up to give up

> **oppressor** a person or group of people that treats sb in a cruel and unfair way, esp by not giving them the same freedom, rights, etc as other people
> **to oppress; oppression**

at close quarters very near
wretched sick, unhappy
to huddle *sich zusammendrängen*
cowed frightened
convict prisoner
scarred *narbig*
buttock *Hinterbacke*
utter *äußerst; -e, -er, -es*
to impose on to force sb to accept sth
to supplant to replace

the Raj British rule in India before 1947
to clamp down to fasten sth very tightly
in saecula saeculorum forever
prostrate lying on the ground and facing downwards
guts (infml) belly

in a roundabout way indirectly
enlighten to give spiritual insight
tiny small
incident happening

to ravage to badly damage sth

to be useful in terrorem
zur Abschreckung dienen

must or **musth** a state of frenzied sexual excitement in the males of certain large mammals, esp elephants [from Urdu *mast*, from Persian: drunk]

to be due *fällig sein*

pursuit act of following or chasing sb
to pursue to follow

to devour to eat quickly and swallow great amounts of food
municipal *städtisch*
to take to one's heels (idm) to escape, to flee
to inflict sth upon sb/sth to make sb/sth suffer sth unpleasant
squalid very dirty, sordid
thatched *strohgedeckt*

invariable never changing

to profess to claim that sth is true or correct, esp when it is not

switch *Rute, Gerte*

to sprawl to sit or lie with one's arms and legs in a disordered way

trench *Graben*

bared not covered

the noise might be useful in terrorem. Various Burmans stopped me on the way and told me about the elephant's doings. It was not, of course, a wild elephant, but a tame one which had gone 'must'. It had been chained up as tame elephants always are when their attack of 'must' is due; but on 5 the previous night it had broken its chain and escaped. Its mahout, the only person who could manage it, when it was in that state, had set out in pursuit, but he had taken the wrong direction and was now twelve hours' journey away, and in the morning the elephant had suddenly reappeared in the 10 town. The Burmese population had no weapons and were quite helpless against it. It had already destroyed somebody's bamboo hut, killed a cow and raided some fruit-stalls and devoured the stock; also it had met the municipal rubbish van, and, when the driver jumped out and took to his heels, 15 had turned the van over and inflicted violences upon it.

The Burmese sub-inspector and some Indian constables were waiting for me in the quarter where the elephant had been seen. It was a very poor quarter, a labyrinth of squalid bamboo huts, thatched with palmleaf, winding all over a 20 steep hillside. I remember that it was a cloudy, stuffy morning at the beginning of the rains. We began questioning the people as to where the elephant had gone, and, as usual, failed to get any definite information. That is invariably the case in the East; a story always sounds clear enough at a 25 distance, but the nearer you get to the scene of events the vaguer it becomes. Some of the people said that the elephant had gone in one direction, some said that he had gone in another, some professed not even to have heard of any elephant. I had almost made up my mind that the whole story 30 was a pack of lies, when we heard yells a little distance away. There was a loud, scandalized cry of 'Go away, child! Go away this instant!' and an old woman with a switch in her hand came round the corner of a hut, violently shooing away a crowd of naked children. Some more women fol- 35 lowed, clicking their tongues and exclaiming; evidently there was something there that the children ought not to have seen. I rounded the hut and saw a man's dead body sprawling in the mud. He was an Indian, a black Dravidian coolie, almost naked, and he could not have been dead many 40 minutes. The people said that the elephant had come suddenly upon him round the corner of the hut, caught him with its trunk, put its foot on his back and ground him into the earth. This was the rainy season and the ground was soft, and his face had scored a trench a foot deep and a couple of 45 yards long. He was lying on his belly with arms crucified and head sharply twisted to one side. His face was coated with mud, the eyes wide open, the teeth bared and grinning

with an expression of unendurable agony. (Never tell me, by the way, that the dead look peaceful. Most of the corpses I have seen looked devilish.) The friction of the great beast's foot had stripped the skin from his back as neatly as one
5 skins a rabbit. As soon as I saw the dead man I sent an orderly to a friend's house near by to borrow an elephant rifle. I had already sent back the pony, not wanting it to go mad with fright and throw me if it smelled the elephant.

The orderly came back in a few minutes with a rifle and five
10 cartridges, and meanwhile some Burmans had arrived and told us that the elephant was in the paddy fields below, only a few hundred yards away. As I started forward practically the whole population of the quarter flocked out of the houses and followed me. They had seen the rifle and were all
15 shouting excitedly that I was going to shoot the elephant. They had not shown much interest in the elephant when he was merely ravaging their homes, but it was different now that he was going to be shot. It was a bit of fun to them, as it would be to an English crowd; besides, they wanted the
20 meat. It made me vaguely uneasy. I had no intention of shooting the elephant – I had merely sent for the rifle to defend myself if necessary – and it is always unnerving to have a crowd following you. I marched down the hill, looking and feeling a fool, with the rifle over my shoulder and an
25 ever-growing army of people jostling at my heels. At the bottom, when you got away from the huts, there was a metalled road and beyond that a miry waste of paddy fields a thousand yards across, not yet ploughed but soggy from the first rains and dotted with coarse grass. The elephant was
30 standing eighty yards from the road, his left side towards us. He took not the slightest notice of the crowd's approach. He was tearing up bunches of grass, beating them against his knees to clean them and stuffing them into his mouth.

I had halted on the road. As soon as I saw the elephant I
35 knew with perfect certainty that I ought not to shoot him. It is a serious matter to shoot a working elephant – it is comparable to destroying a huge and costly piece of machinery – and obviously one ought not to do it if it can possibly be avoided. And at that distance, peacefully eating, the ele-
40 phant looked no more dangerous than a cow. I thought then and I think now that his attack of 'must' was already passing off; in which case he would merely wander harmlessly about until the mahout came back and caught him. Moreover, I did not in the least want to shoot him. I decided that
45 I would watch him for a little while to make sure that he did not turn savage again, and then go home.

But at that moment I glanced round at the crowd that had followed me. It was an immense crowd, two thousand at

---

agony extreme physical or mental pain
corpse dead body

orderly *Ordonnanz*

cartridge bullet, shot
paddy field rice field

to flock out to go and gather together somewhere in large numbers like birds

merely only

jostling closely grouped and fighting for space
metalled made or repaired with small pieces of broken stone
miry muddy
to plough *pflügen*
soggy wet and soft

savage wild

garish very brightly coloured in an unpleasant way

conjurer magician

futility pointlessness
dominion authority to rule; control

puppet *Marionette*

to pose to sit in position for being photographed
sahib used in India, esp in the past, to address a European man, esp one with some social or official status

resolute having or showing great determination

to trail to walk slowly because you are tired or bored, esp behind sb else
feeble weak

preoccupied absorbed appearance or behaviour

to charge to attack

the least and growing every minute. It blocked the road for a long distance on either side. I looked at the sea of yellow faces above the garish clothes – faces all happy and excited over this bit of fun, all certain that the elephant was going to be shot. They were watching me as they would watch a 5 conjurer about to perform a trick. They did not like me, but with the magical rifle in my hands I was momentarily worth watching. And suddenly I realized that I should have to shoot the elephant after all. The people expected it of me and I had got to do it; I could feel their two thousand wills 10 pressing me forward, irresistibly. And it was at this moment, as I stood there with the rifle in my hands, that I first grasped the hollowness, the futility of the white man's dominion in the East. Here was I, the white man with his gun, standing in front of the unarmed native crowd – seemingly 15 the leading actor of the piece; but in reality I was only an absurd puppet pushed to and fro by the will of those yellow faces behind. I perceived in this moment that when the white man turns tyrant it is his own freedom that he destroys. He becomes a sort of hollow, posing dummy, the 20 conventionalized figure of a sahib. For it is the condition of his rule that he shall spend his life in trying to impress the 'natives', and so in every crisis he has got to do what the 'natives' expect of him. He wears a mask, and his face grows to fit it. I had got to shoot the elephant. I had com- 25 mitted myself to doing it when I sent for the rifle. A sahib has got to act like a sahib; he has got to appear resolute, to know his own mind and do definite things. To come all that way, rifle in hand, with two thousand people marching at my heels, and then to trail feebly away, having done noth- 30 ing – no, that was impossible. The crowd would laugh at me. And my whole life, every white man's life in the East, was one long struggle not to be laughed at.

But I did not want to shoot the elephant. I watched him beating his bunch of grass against his knees, with that pre- 35 occupied grandmotherly air that elephants have. It seemed to me that it would be murder to shoot him. At that age I was not squeamish about killing animals, but I had never shot an elephant and never wanted to. (Somehow it always seems worse to kill a *large* animal.) Besides, there was the 40 beast's owner to be considered. Alive, the elephant was worth at least a hundred pounds; dead, he would only be worth the value of his tusks – five pounds, possibly. But I had got to act quickly. I turned to some experienced-looking Burmans who had been there when we arrived, and asked 45 them how the elephant had been behaving. They all said the same thing: he took no notice of you if you left him alone, but he might charge if you went too close to him.

It was perfectly clear to me what I ought to do. I ought to walk up to within, say, twenty-five yards of the elephant and test his behaviour. If he charged I could shoot, if he took no notice of me it would be safe to leave him until the
5 mahout came back. But also I knew that I was going to do no such thing. I was a poor shot with a rifle and the ground was soft mud into which one would sink at every step. If the elephant charged and I missed him, I should have about as much chance as a toad under a steam-roller. But even
10 then I was not thinking particularly of my own skin, only of the watchful yellow faces behind. For at that moment, with the crowd watching me, I was not afraid in the ordinary sense, as I would have been if I had been alone. A white man mustn't be frightened in front of 'natives'; and
15 so, in general, he isn't frightened. The sole thought in my mind was that if anything went wrong those two thousand Burmans would see me pursued, caught, trampled on and reduced to a grinning corpse like that Indian up the hill. And if that happened it was quite probable that some of
20 them would laugh. That would never do. There was only one alternative. I shoved the cartridges into the magazine and lay down on the road to get a better aim.
The crowd grew very still, and a deep, low, happy sigh, as of people who see the theatre curtain go up at last, breathed
25 from innumerable throats. They were going to have their bit of fun after all. The rifle was a beautiful German thing with cross-hair sights. I did not then know that in shooting an elephant one should shoot to cut an imaginary bar running from ear-hole to ear-hole. I ought, therefore, as the
30 elephant was sideways on, to have aimed straight at his ear-hole; actually I aimed several inches in front of this, thinking the brain would be further forward.
When I pulled the trigger I did not hear the bang or feel the kick – one never does when a shot goes home – but I heard
35 the devilish roar of glee that went up from the crowd. In that instant, in too short a time, one would have thought, even for the bullet to get there, a mysterious, terrible change had come over the elephant. He neither stirred nor fell, but every line of his body had altered. He looked suddenly stricken,
40 shrunken, immensely old, as though the frightful impact of the bullet had paralysed him without knocking him down. At last, after what seemed a long time – it might have been five seconds, I dare say – he sagged flabbily to his knees. His mouth slobbered. An enormous senility seemed to have set-
45 tled upon him. One could have imagined him thousands of years old. I fired again into the same spot. At the second shot he did not collapse but climbed with desperate slowness to his feet and stood weakly upright, with legs sagging and

toad *Kröte*
steam-roller *Dampfwalze*

sole single

to shove to push sb/sth in a rough way

cross-hair sights or
cross hairs *Fadenkreuz*
bar line

glee delight

to stir [stɜː(r)] to move
to alter to change
stricken showing the effects of sth
impact effect of hitting

I dare say *ich meine, möchte sagen*

to droop to hang down
to do for to cause the death of
to jolt to shake
remnant rest

mound a small raised area

velvet *Samt*

pretext a false reason that you give for doing sth, usually sth bad, in order to hide the real reason

head drooping. I fired a third time. That was the shot that did for him. You could see the agony of it jolt his whole body and knock the last remnant of strength from his legs. But in falling he seemed for a moment to rise, for as his hind legs collapsed beneath him he seemed to tower upwards like a 5 huge rock toppling, his trunk reaching skyward like a tree. He trumpeted, for the first and only time. And then down he came, his belly towards me, with a crash that seemed to shake the ground even where I lay.

I got up. The Burmans were already racing past me across 10 the mud. It was obvious that the elephant would never rise again, but he was not dead. He was breathing very rhythmically with long rattling gasps, his great mound of a side painfully rising and falling. His mouth was wide open – I could see far down into caverns of pale pink throat. I waited 15 a long time for him to die, but his breathing did not weaken. Finally I fired my two remaining shots into the spot where I thought his heart must be. The thick blood welled out of him like red velvet, but still he did not die. His body did not even jerk when the shots hit him, the tortured breathing continued 20 without a pause. He was dying, very slowly and in great agony, but in some world remote from me where not even a bullet could damage him further. I felt that I had got to put an end to that dreadful noise. It seemed dreadful to see the great beast lying there, powerless to move and yet powerless 25 to die, and not even to be able to finish him. I sent back for my small rifle and poured shot after shot into his heart and down his throat. They seemed to make no impression. The tortured gasps continued as steadily as the ticking of a clock. In the end I could not stand it any longer and went away. I 30 heard later that it took him half an hour to die. Burmans were arriving with dahs and baskets even before I left, and I was told they had stripped his body almost to the bones by the afternoon.

Afterwards, of course, there were endless discussions about 35 the shooting of the elephant. The owner was furious, but he was only an Indian and could do nothing. Besides, legally I had done the right thing, for a mad elephant has to be killed, like a mad dog, if its owner fails to control it. Among the Europeans opinion was divided. The older men said I 40 was right, the younger men said it was a damn shame to shoot an elephant for killing a coolie, because an elephant was worth more than any damn Coringhee coolie. And afterwards I was very glad that the coolie had been killed; it put me legally in the right and it gave me a sufficient pre- 45 text for shooting the elephant. I often wondered whether any of the others grasped that I had done it solely to avoid looking a fool.

Doris Lessing
The Second Hut

Before that season and his wife's illness, he had thought things could get no worse: until then, poverty had meant not to deviate further than snapping point from what he had been brought up to think of as a normal life.

5 Being a farmer (he had come to it late in life, in his forties) was the first test he had faced as an individual. Before he had always been supported, invisibly perhaps, but none the less strongly, by what his family expected of him. He had been a regular soldier, not an unsuccessful one, but his suc-

10 cess had been at the cost of a continual straining against his own inclinations; and he did not know himself what his inclinations were. Something stubbornly unconforming kept him apart from his fellow officers. It was an inward difference: he did not think of himself as a soldier. Even in his

15 appearance, square, close-bitten, disciplined, there had been a hint of softness, or of strain, showing itself in his smile, which was too quick, like the smile of a deaf person afraid of showing incomprehension, and in the anxious look of his eyes. After he left the army he quickly slack-

20 ened into an almost slovenly carelessness of dress and carriage. Now, in his farm clothes there was nothing left to suggest the soldier. With a loose, stained felt hat on the back of his head, khaki shorts a little too long and too wide, sleeves flapping over spare brown arms, his wispy mous-

25 tache hiding a strained, set mouth, Major Carruthers looked what he was, a gentleman farmer going to seed.

The house had that brave, worn appearance of those struggling to keep up appearances. It was a four-roomed shack, its red roof dulling to streaky brown. It was the sort of

30 house an apprentice farmer builds as a temporary shelter till he can afford better. Inside, good but battered furniture stood over worn places in the rugs; the piano was out of tune and the notes stuck; the silver tea things from the big narrow house in England where his brother (a lawyer) now

35 lived were used as ornaments, and inside were bits of paper, accounts, rubber rings, old corks.

The room where his wife lay, in a greenish sun-lanced gloom, was a place of seedy misery. The doctor said it was her heart; and Major Carruthers knew this was true: she

40 had broken down through heart-break over the conditions they lived in. She did not want to get better. The harsh light from outside was shut out with dark blinds, and she turned her face to the wall and lay there, hour after hour, inert and uncomplaining, in a stoicism of defeat nothing could pene-

---

to deviate to go in another direction

to strain to make an effort
inclination tendency, preference
stubborn störrisch, hartnäckig

square fair, honest
hint trace
to slacken to become lazier and less energetic
sloven (dated) messy
carriage here: *Körperhaltung*
stained discoloured, with spots
felt hat *Filzhut*
wispy thin
to go to seed to stop caring about things
to keep up appearances to act as if everything is O.K.
shack *Bude*
to dull to become less bright, clean or sharp
streaky *streifig*
apprentice *in der Lehre, Ausbildung*
battered old and used
rug small carpet
sun-lanced with beams of sunlight cutting through it
gloom 1. a feeling of being sad and without hope
2. almost total darkness
seedy dirty and unpleasant; often connected with immoral or illegal activities
blind *Jalousie*
inert without power to move or act
stoicism the state of not complaining or showing what you are feeling when you are suffering
defeat *Niederlage*

to penetrate to go through

to wash one's hands of sth to refuse to be involved with sth any longer

to wrench to pull or twist sb/sth suddenly and violently

sprightly full of life and energy (esp of older people)

fairness (of skin or hair) a pale colour
wary careful when dealing with sb/sth because you think that there may be danger or problems
solicitude *Besorgtheit, Sorge*

scrupulous *gewissenhaft*

to throb to beat in a strong and often painful way

commodity sth that can be used for trade
efficiency *Leistungsfähigkeit*

trate. Even the children hardly moved her. It was as if she had said to herself: "If I cannot have what I wanted for them, then I wash my hands of life."

Sometimes Major Carruthers thought of her as she had been, and was filled with uneasy wonder and with guilt. That pleasant conventional pretty English girl had been bred to make a perfect wife for the professional soldier she had imagined him to be, but chance had wrenched her on to this isolated African farm, into a life which she submitted herself to, as if it had nothing to do with her. For the first few years she had faced the struggle humorously, courageously: it was a sprightly attitude towards life, almost flirtatious, as a woman flirts lightly with a man who means nothing to her. As the house grew shabby, and the furniture, and her clothes could not be replaced; when she looked into the mirror and saw her drying, untidy hair and roughening face, she would give a quick high laugh and say, "Dear me, the things one comes to!" She was facing this poverty as she would have faced, in England, poverty of a narrowing, but socially accepted kind. What she could not face was a different kind of fear; and Major Carruthers understood that too well, for it was now his own fear.

The two children were pale, fine-drawn creatures, almost transparent-looking in their thin nervous fairness, with the defensive and wary manners of the young who have been brought up to expect a better way of life than they enjoy. Their anxious solicitude wore on Major Carruthers' already over-sensitized nerves. Children had no right to feel the aching pity which showed on their faces whenever they looked at him. They were too polite, too careful, too scrupulous. When they went into their mother's room she grieved sorrowfully over them, and they submitted patiently to her emotion. All those weeks of the school holidays after she was taken ill, they moved about the farm like two strained and anxious ghosts, and whenever he saw them his sense of guilt throbbed like a wound. He was glad they were going back to school soon, for then – so he thought – it would be easier to manage. It was an intolerable strain, running the farm and coming back to the neglected house and the problems of food and clothing, and a sick wife who would not get better until he could offer her hope.

But when they had gone back, he found that after all, things were not much easier. He slept little, for his wife needed attention in the night; and he became afraid for his own health, worrying over what he ate and wore. He learnt to treat himself as if his health was not what he was, what made him, but something apart, a commodity like efficiency, which could be estimated in terms of money at the end of a season. His health stood between them and complete ruin; and soon there were medicine bottles beside his bed, as well as beside his wife's.

5 One day, while he was carefully measuring out tonics for himself in the bedroom, he glanced up and saw his wife's small reddened eyes staring incredulously but ironically at him over the bedclothes. "What are you doing?" she asked. "I need a tonic," he explained awkwardly, afraid to worry
10 her by explanations.

incredulous disbelieving

She laughed, for the first time in weeks; then the slack tears began welling under the lids, and she turned to the wall again.

slack tears the tears are already in her eyes

He understood that some vision of himself had been de-
15 stroyed, finally, for her. Now she was left with an ageing, rather fussy gentleman, carefully measuring medicine after meals. But he did not blame her; he never had blamed her; not even though he knew her illness was a failure of will. He patted her cheek uncomfortably, and said: "It wouldn't
20 do for me to get run down, would it?" Then he adjusted the curtains over the windows to shut out a streak of dancing light that threatened to fall over her face, set a glass nearer to her hand, and went out to arrange for her tray of slops to be carried in.

fussy *pingelig*

run down tired or ill

slop (or **slops**) weak, liquid food without much taste

25 Then he took, in one swift, painful movement, as if he were leaping over an obstacle, the decision he had known for weeks he must take sooner or later. With a straightening of his shoulders, an echo from his soldier past, he took on the strain of an extra burden: he must get an assistant, whether
30 he liked it or not.

to leap to jump
obstacle *Hindernis*

burden load, obligation

So much did he shrink from any self-exposure, that he did not even consider advertising. He sent a note by native bearer to his neighbour, a few miles off, asking that it should be spread abroad that he was wanting help. He
35 knew he would not have to wait long. It was 1931, in the middle of a slump, and there was unemployment, which was a rare thing for this new, sparsely-populated country.

slump recession, economic decline

He wrote the following to his two sons at boarding-school: I expect you will be surprised to hear I'm getting another
40 man on the place. Things are getting a bit too much, and as I plan to plant a bigger acreage of maize this year, I thought it would need two of us. Your mother is better this week, on the whole, so I think things are looking up. She is looking forward to your next holidays, and asks me to say she will
45 write soon. Between you and me, I don't think she's up to writing at the moment. It will soon be getting cold, I think, so if you need any clothes, let me know, and I'll see what I can do …

to form an estimate to judge

to be taken in to be deceived

prey *Beute*

decency honesty and fairness

sturdy robust

obtuse stupid, plain
generous kind
features *Gesichtszüge*

Afrikander person speaking Afrikaans
Afrikaans language that has developed from Dutch spoken in South Africa

obstinate stubborn

reluctance hesitation

salary money that employees receive for doing their job

A week later, he sat on the little verandah, towards evening, smoking, when he saw a man coming through the trees on a bicycle. He watched him closely, already trying to form an estimate of his character by the tests he had used all his life: the width between the eyes, the shape of the skull, the 5 way the legs were set on to the body. Although he had been taken in a dozen times, his belief in these methods never wavered. He was an easy prey for any trickster, lending money he never saw again, taken in by professional adventurers who (it seemed to him, measuring others by his own 10 decency and the quick warmth he felt towards people) were the essence of gentlemen. He used to say that being a gentleman was a question of instinct: one could not mistake a gentleman.

As the visitor stepped off his bicycle and wheeled it to the 15 verandah, Major Carruthers saw he was young, thirty perhaps, sturdily built, with enormous strength in the thick arms and shoulders. His skin was burnt a healthy orange-brown colour. His close hair, smooth as the fur of an animal, reflected no light. His obtuse, generous features were 20 set in a round face, and the eyes were pale grey, nearly colourless.

Major Carruthers instinctively dropped his standards of value as he looked, for this man was an Afrikander, and thus came into an outside category. It was not that he disliked 25 him for it, although his father had been killed in the Boer War, but he had never had anything to do with the Afrikaans people before, and his knowledge of them was hearsay, from Englishmen who had the old prejudice. But he liked the look of the man: he liked the honest and straight- 30 forward face.

As for Van Heerden, he immediately recognized his traditional enemy, and his inherited dislike was strong. For a moment he appeared obstinate and wary. But they needed each other too badly to nurse old hatreds, and Van Heerden 35 sat down when he was asked, though awkwardly, suppressing reluctance, and began drawing patterns in the dust with a piece of straw he had held between his lips.

Major Carruthers did not need to wonder about the man's circumstances: his quick acceptance of what were poor 40 terms spoke of a long search for work.

He said scrupulously: "I know the salary is low and the living quarters are bad, even for a single man. I've had a patch of bad luck, and I can't afford more. I'll quite understand if you refuse." 45

"What are the living quarters?" asked Van Heerden. His was the rough voice of the uneducated Afrikander: because he was uncertain where the accent should fall in each sentence, his speech had a wavering, halting sound, though his look and manner were direct enough.

Major Carruthers pointed ahead of them. Before the house the bush sloped gently down to the fields. "At the foot of
5 the hill there's a hut I've been using as a storehouse. It's quite well-built. You can put up a place for a kitchen."

Van Heerden rose. "Can I see it?"

They set off. It was not far away. The thatched hut stood in uncleared bush. Grass grew to the walls and reached up to
10 meet the slanting thatch. Trees mingled their branches overhead. It was round, built of poles and mud and with a stamped dung floor. Inside there was a stale musty smell because of the ants and beetles that had been at the sacks of grain. The one window was boarded over, and it was quite
15 dark. In the confusing shafts of light from the door, a thick sheet of felted spider web showed itself, like a curtain halving the interior, as full of small flies and insects as a butcher-bird's cache. The spider crouched, vast and glittering, shaking gently, glaring at them with small red eyes, from
20 the centre of the web. Van Heerden did what Major Carruthers would have died rather than do: he tore the web across with his bare hands, crushed the spider between his fingers, and brushed them lightly against the walls to free them from the clinging silky strands and the sticky mush of
25 insect-body.

"It will do fine," he announced.

He would not accept the invitation to a meal, thus making it clear this was merely a business arrangement. But he asked, politely (hating that he had to beg a favour), for a month's
30 salary in advance. Then he set off on his bicycle to the store, ten miles off, to buy what he needed for his living.

Major Carruthers went back to his sick wife with a burdened feeling, caused by his being responsible for another human being having to suffer such conditions. He could
35 not have the man in the house: the idea came into his head and was quickly dismissed. They had nothing in common, they would make each other uncomfortable – that was how he put it to himself. Besides, there wasn't really any room. Underneath, Major Carruthers knew that if his new assis-
40 tant had been an Englishman, with the same upbringing, he would have found a corner in his house and a welcome as a friend. Major Carruthers threw off these thoughts: he had enough to worry him without taking on another man's problems.
45 A person who had always hated the business of organization, which meant dividing responsibility with others, he found it hard to arrange with Van Heerden how the work was to be done. But as the Dutchman was good with cattle,

---

to thatch to cover a roof with dried straw, reeds etc

slanting hanging down at a certain angle

stale *muffig*
musty *moderig*

felted *filzig*

cache hiding place
to crouch to sit very low to the ground with bent legs

merely only
to beg a favour *um einen Gefallen bitten*

burdened bothered

to dismiss to reject an idea

stock farm animals
to nag to worry sb continuously

laconic using only a few words to say sth

dismaying worrying
to prick sb into to drive sb to (do) sth
resentment a feeling of anger or bitterness about sth that you think unfair
to gall to make bitter, to make sb angry esp because sth is unfair
crisp brief and precise
condescension *herablassende Haltung*
to propitiate sb to stop sb from being angry by trying to please them
to stir oneself to move

flaxen pale yellow colour

foliage the leaves of a tree
to dissolve to disappear

tow-headed *flachshaarig*
bleached pale
sapless without vitality
to patch together to put together

Major Carruthers handed over all the stock on the farm to his care, thus relieving his mind of its most nagging care, for he was useless with beasts, and knew it. So they began, each knowing exactly where they stood. Van Heerden would make laconic reports at the end of each week, in the manner of an expert foreman reporting to a boss ignorant of technicalities – and Major Carruthers accepted this attitude, for he liked to respect people, and it was easy to respect Van Heerden's inspired instinct for animals.

For a few weeks Major Carruthers was almost happy. The fear of having to apply for another loan to his brother – worse, asking for the passage money to England and a job, thus justifying his family's belief in him as a failure, was pushed away; for while taking on a manager did not in itself improve things, it was an action, a decision, and there was nothing that he found more dismaying than decisions. The thought of his family in England, and particularly his elder brother, pricked him into slow burning passions of resentment. His brother's letters galled him so that he had grown to hate mail-days. They were crisp, affectionate letters, without condescension, but about money, bank-drafts, and insurance policies. Major Carruthers did not see life like that. He had not written to his brother for over a year. His wife, when she was well, wrote once a week, in the spirit of one propitiating fate.

Even she seemed cheered by the manager's coming; she sensed her husband's irrational lightness of spirit during that short time.

She stirred herself to ask about the farm; and he began to see that her interest in living would revive quickly if her sort of life came within reach again.

But some two months after Van Heerden's coming, Major Carruthers was walking along the farm road towards his lands, when he was astonished to see, disappearing into the bushes, a small flaxen-haired boy. He called, but the child froze as an animal freezes, flattening himself against the foliage. At last, since he could get no reply, Major Carruthers approached the child, who dissolved backwards through the trees, and followed him up the path to the hut. He was very angry, for he knew what he would see.

He had not been to the hut since he handed it over to Van Heerden. Now there was a clearing, and amongst the stumps of trees and the flattened grass, were half a dozen children, each as tow-headed as the first, with that bleached sapless look common to white children in the tropics who have been subjected to too much sun.

A lean-to had been built against the hut. It was merely a roof of beaten petrol tins, patched together like cloth with wire and nails and supported on two unpeeled sticks. There,

holding a cooking pot over an open fire that was dangerously close to the thatch, stood a vast slatternly woman.
She reminded him of a sow among her litter, as she lifted
her head, the children crowding about her, and stared at
5 him suspiciously from pale and white-lashed eyes.
"Where is your husband?" he demanded.
She did not answer. Her suspicion deepened into a glare of
hate: clearly she knew no English.
Striding furiously to the door of the hut, he saw that it was
10 crowded with two enormous native-style beds: strips of
hide stretched over wooden poles embedded in the mud of
the floor. What was left of the space was heaped with the
stained and broken belongings of the family. Major Carruthers strode off in search of Van Heerden. His anger was
15 now mingled with the shamed discomfort of trying to imagine what it must be to live in such squalor.
Fear rose high in him. For a few moments he inhabited the
landscape of his dreams, a grey country full of sucking
menace, where he suffered what he would not allow him-
20 self to think of while awake: the grim poverty that could
overtake him if his luck did not turn, and if he refused to
submit to his brother and return to England.
Walking through the fields, where the maize was now waving over his head, pale gold with a froth of white, the sharp
25 dead leaves scything crisply against the wind, he could see
nothing but that black foetid hut and the pathetic futureless
children. That was the lowest he could bring his own children to! He felt moorless, helpless, afraid; his sweat ran
cold on him. And he did not hesitate in his mind; driven by
30 fear and anger, he told himself to be hard; he was searching
in his mind for the words with which he would dismiss the
Dutchman who had brought his worst nightmares to life,
on his own farm, in glaring daylight, where they were ines-
capable.
35 He found him with a screaming rearing young ox that was
being broken to the plough, handling it with his sure understanding of animals. At a cautious distance stood the natives who were assisting; but Van Heerden, fearless and
purposeful, was fighting the beast at close range. He saw
40 Major Carruthers, let go the plunging horn he held, and the
ox shot away backwards, roaring with anger, into the crowd
of natives, who gathered loosely about it with sticks and
stones to prevent it running away altogether.
Van Heerden stood still, wiping the sweat off his face, still
45 grinning with the satisfaction of the fight, waiting for his
employer to speak.
"Van Heerden," said Major Carruthers, without preliminaries, "why didn't you tell me you had a family?"

---

slatternly sloppy, dirty
sow female pig
litter *Wurf*

hide skin of an animal
to heap *anhäufen*

squalor 1. dirt, foulness
2. immorality

menace threat

to submit to to give in to

froth foam
to scythe *sensen*
foetid or **fetid** stinking
pathetic *erbärmlich*

moorless without support or
hold (to moor *vertäuen*)
to hesitate to falter, to wait

to rear to rise up on hind
legs
plough *Pflug*

to plunge to move suddenly
forwards and/or downwards

without preliminaries *ohne
Umschweife*

As he spoke the Dutchman's face changed, first flushing into guilt, then setting hard and stubborn. "Because I've been out of work for a year, and I knew you would not take me if I told you."

flyaway soft and fine (of hair)
to shamble to walk in an awkward or lazy way, dragging your feet along the ground
defiant showing disobedience
intermission interruption
incessant never stopping

The two men faced each other, Major Carruthers tall, fly- 5 away, shambling, bent with responsibility; Van Heerden stiff and defiant. The natives remained about the ox, to prevent its escape – for them this was a brief intermission in the real work of the farm – and their shouts mingled with the incessant bellowing. It was a hot day; Van Heerden 10 wiped the sweat from his eyes with the back of his hand.

"You can't keep a wife and all those children here – how many children?"

"Nine."

perpetual continual

Major Carruthers thought of his own two, and his perpetual 15 dull ache or worry over them; and his heart became grieved for Van Heerden. Two children, with all the trouble over everything they ate and wore and thought, and what would become of them, were too great a burden; how did this man, with nine, manage to look so young? 20

"How old are you?" he asked abruptly, in a different tone.

"Thirty-four," said Van Heerden suspiciously, unable to understand the direction Major Carruthers followed.

crease wrinkle

The only marks on his face were sun-creases; it was impossible to think of him as the father of nine children and the 25 husband of that terrible broken-down woman. As Major Carruthers gazed at him, he became conscious of the strained lines on his own face; and tried to loosen himself, because he took so badly what this man bore so well.

"You can't keep a wife and children in such conditions." 30

mealie meal South African finely ground maize (**mealies** South African word for maize)

"We were living in a tent in the bush on mealie meal and what I shot for nine months, and that was through the wet season," said Van Heerden drily.

Major Carruthers knew he was beaten. "You've put me in a false position, Van Heerden," he said angrily. "You know I 35 can't afford to give you more money. I don't know where I'm going to find my own children's school fees, as it is. I told you the position when you came. I can't afford to keep a man with such a family."

sullen silent and bad-tempered

"Nobody can afford to have me either," said Van Heerden 40 sullenly.

"How can I have you living on my place in such a fashion? Nine children! They should be at school. Didn't you know there is a law to make them go to school? Hasn't anybody been to see you about them?" 45

"They haven't got me yet. They won't get me unless someone tells them."

appeal plea

Against this challenge, which was also an unwilling appeal,

Major Carruthers remained silent, until he said brusquely: "Remember, I'm not responsible." And he walked off, with all the appearance of anger.

Van Heerden looked after him, his face puzzled. He did not
5 know whether or not he had been dismissed. After a few moments he moistened his dry lips with his tongue, wiped his hand again over his eyes, and turned back to the ox. Looking over his shoulder from the edge of the field, Major Carruthers could see his wiry, stocky figure leaping and
10 bending about the ox whose bellowing made the whole farm ring with anger.

Major Carruthers decided, once and for all, to put the family out of his mind. But they haunted him; he even dreamed of them; and he could not determine whether it was his own
15 or the Dutchman's children who filled his sleep with fear.

It was a very busy time of the year. Harassed, like all his fellow-farmers, by labour difficulties, apportioning out the farm tasks was a daily problem. All day his mind churned slowly over the necessities: this fencing was urgent, that
20 field must be reaped at once. Yet, in spite of this, he decided it was his plain duty to build a second hut beside the first. It would do no more than take the edge off the discomfort of that miserable family, but he knew he could not rest until it was built.

25 Just as he had made up his mind and was wondering how the thing could be managed, the bossboy came to him, saying that unless the Dutchman went, he and his friends would leave the farm.

"Why?" asked Major Carruthers, knowing what the answer
30 would be. Van Heerden was a hard worker, and the cattle were improving week by week under his care, but he could not handle natives. He shouted at them, lost his temper, treated them like dogs. There was continual friction.

"Dutchmen are no good," said the bossboy simply, voicing
35 the hatred of the black man for that section of the white people he considers his most brutal oppressors.

Now, Major Carruthers was proud that at a time when most farmers were forced to buy labour from the contractors, he was able to attract sufficient voluntary labour to run his
40 farm. He was a good employer, proud of his reputation for fair dealing. Many of his natives had been with him for years, taking a few months off occasionally for a rest in their kraals, but always returning to him. His neighbours were complaining of the sullen attitude of their labourers:
45 so far Major Carruthers had kept this side of that form of passive resistance which could ruin a farmer. It was walking on a knife-edge, but his simple human relationship with his workers was his greatest asset as a farmer, and he knew it.

---

to moisten to wet

wiry thin but strong

to haunt to keep coming to one's mind so that you cannot forget

harassed tired and anxious because you have too much to do
to apportion to divide sth among people, to give a share of sth to sb
to churn over *sich um etw. heftig drehen*
to reap to cut and collect a crop, esp corn, from a field

friction *Reibung*

oppressor a person or group of people that treats sb in a cruel and unfair way, esp by not giving them the same freedom, rights, etc as other people
contractor a person or company that has an official written agreement to do work or provide goods or services for another company
labour workers
kraal a hut village in southern Africa esp one surrounded by a stockade
asset sth that is valuable and useful to sb

He stood and thought, while his bossboy, who had been on this farm twelve years, waited for a reply. A great deal was at stake. For a moment Major Carruthers thought of dismissing the Dutchman; he realized he could not bring himself to do it: what would happen to all those children? He 5 decided on a course which was repugnant to him. He was going to appeal to his employee's pity.

"I have always treated you square?" he asked. "I've always helped you when you were in trouble?"

The bossboy immediately and warmly assented. 10

"You know that my wife is ill, and that I'm having a lot of trouble just now? I don't want the Dutchman to go, just now when the work is so heavy. I'll speak to him, and if there is any more trouble with the men, then come to me and I'll deal with it myself." 15

It was a glittering blue day, with a chill edge on the air, that stirred Major Carruthers' thin blood as he stood, looking in appeal into the sullen face of the native. All at once, feeling the fresh air wash along his cheeks, watching the leaves shake with a ripple of gold on the trees down the slope, he 20 felt superior to his difficulties, and able to face anything. "Come," he said, with his rare, diffident smile. "After all these years, when we have been working together for so long, surely you can do this for me. It won't be for very long." 25

He watched the man's face soften in response to his own; and wondered at the unconscious use of the last phrase, for there was no reason, on the face of things, why the situation should not continue as it was for a very long time.

They began laughing together; and separated cheerfully; 30 the African shaking his head ruefully over the magnitude of the sacrifice asked of him, thus making the incident into a joke; and he dived off into the bush to explain the position to his fellow-workers.

Repressing a strong desire to go after him, to spend the 35 lovely fresh day walking for pleasure, Major Carruthers went into his wife's bedroom, inexplicably confident and walking like a young man.

She lay as always, face to the wall, her protruding shoulders visible beneath the cheap pink bed-jacket he had 40 bought for her illness. She seemed neither better nor worse. But as she turned her head his buoyancy infected her a little; perhaps, too, she was conscious of the exhilarating day outside her gloomy curtains.

What kind of miraculous release was she waiting for? he 45 wondered as he delicately adjusted her sheets and pillows and laid his hand gently on her head. Over the bony cage of the skull, the skin was papery and blueish. What was she

---

to be at stake sth that can be won or lost, depending on the success of a particular action

repugnant making you feel strong dislike or disgust
to appeal to to ask for
square fair

to assent to agree

chill coldness

ripple a small wave
slope *Hang*
diffident shy, modest

rueful showing or feeling that you are sad or sorry
incident happening

inexplicable that cannot be explained or understood
to protrude *hervorstehen*

buoyancy cheerfulness
exhilarating thrilling, exciting
gloomy dark

delicately carefully

thinking? He had a vision of her brain as a small frightened animal pulsating under his fingers.

With her eyes still closed, she asked in her querulous thin voice: "Why don't you write to George?"

5 Involuntarily his fingers contracted on her hair, causing her to start and to open her reproachful, red-rimmed eyes. He waited for her usual appeal: the children, my health, our future. But she sighed and remained silent, still loyal to the man she had imagined she was marrying; and he could feel
10 her thinking: *the lunatic stiff pride of men.*

Understanding that for her it was merely a question of waiting for his defeat, as her deliverance, he withdrew his hand, in dislike of her, saying: "Things are not as bad as that yet." The cheerfulness of his voice was genuine, hold-
15 ing still the courage and hope instilled into him by the bright day outside.

"Why, what has happened?" she asked swiftly, her voice suddenly strong, looking at him in hope.

"Nothing," he said; and the depression settled down over
20 him again. Indeed, nothing had happened; and his confidence was a trick of the nerves. Soberly he left the bedroom, thinking: I must get that well built; and when that is done, I must do the drains, and then… He was thinking, too, that all these things must wait for the second hut.
25 Oddly, the comparatively small problem of that hut occupied his mind during the next few days. A slow and careful man, he set milestones for himself and overtook them one by one.

Since Christmas the labourers had been working a seven-
30 day week, in order to keep ahead in the race against the weeds. They resented it, of course, but that was the custom. Now that the maize was grown, they expected work to slack off, they expected their Sundays to be restored to them. To ask even half a dozen of them to sacrifice their
35 weekly holiday for the sake of the hated Dutchman might precipitate a crisis. Major Carruthers took his time, stalking his opportunity like a hunter, until one evening he was talking with his bossboy as man to man, about farm problems; but when he broached the subject of a hut, Major Carru-
40 thers saw that it would be as he feared: the man at once turned stiff and unhelpful. Suddenly impatient, he said: "It must be done next Sunday. Six men could finish it in a day, if they worked hard."

The black man's glance became veiled and hostile. Re-
45 sponding to the authority in the voice he replied simply: "Yes, baas." He was accepting the order from above, and refusing responsibility: his co-operation was switched off: he had become a machine for transmitting orders. Nothing

querulous peevish, complaining

to contract *sich zusammenzie-hen*
reproachful expressing blame or criticism
appeal urgent, worried request

deliverance the state of being rescued from danger or pain

to instil sth in/into sb to gradually make sb feel, think or behave in a particular way over a period of time
swiftly quickly

sober serious

drain *Abflussrohr*

odd strange

to resent to feel bitter or angry about

to slack off to go more slowly

to precipitate to make sth, esp sth bad, happen suddenly or sooner than it should
to stalk to move slowly and quietly towards an animal or person in order to kill, catch or harm it or them
to broach to begin talking about a subject that is difficult to discuss because it is embarrassing
veiled not expressed directly
hostile aggressive

to exasperate to annoy

stern serious, expecting sb to obey you

hoe *Hacke*

fierce angry, aggressive
antagonism feelings of hatred and aggression
compound living area
disproportionate too large or too small
to loom to appear as a large shape that is not clear, esp in a frightening or threatening way
superstitious believing in black magic, ghosts, etc
malignant bad, evil

exuberance energy, excitement, happiness

casual careless
contemptuous showing no respect

irrepressible very strong, impossible to control or stop
to sag to hang down in the middle

fecundity fertility, ability to produce a lot of children
heave a rising and falling movement
matter *Materie*
confiding showing trust

to cuff a light, friendly hit with an open hand

exasperated Major Carruthers more than when this happened. He said sternly: "I'm not having any nonsense. If that hut isn't built, there'll be trouble."

"Yes, baas," said the bossboy again. He walked away, stopped some natives who were coming off the fields with ⁵ their hoes over their shoulders, and transmitted the order in a neutral voice. Major Carruthers saw them glance at him in fierce antagonism; then they turned away their heads, and walked off, in a group, towards their compound.

It would be all right, he thought, in disproportionate relief. ¹⁰ It would be difficult to say exactly what it was he feared, for the question of the hut had loomed so huge in his mind that he was beginning to feel an almost superstitious foreboding. Driven downwards through failure after failure, fate was becoming real to him as a cold malignant force; ¹⁵ the careful balancing of unfriendly probabilities that underlay all his planning had developed in him an acute sensitivity to the future; and he had learned to respect his dreams and omens. Now he wondered at the strength of his desire to see that hut built, and whatever danger it represented be- ²⁰ hind him.

He went to the clearing to find Van Heerden and tell him what had been planned. He found him sitting on a candlebox in the doorway of the hut, playing good-humouredly with his children, as if they had been puppies, tumbling ²⁵ them over, snapping his fingers in their faces, and laughing outright with boyish exuberance when one little boy squared up his fists at him in a moment of temper against this casual, almost contemptuous treatment of them. Major Carruthers heard that boyish laugh with amazement; he ³⁰ looked blankly at the young Dutchman, and then from him to his wife, who was standing, as usual, over a petrol tin that balanced on the small fire. A smell of meat and pumpkin filled the clearing. The woman seemed to Major Carruthers less a human being than the expression of an ele- ³⁵ mental, irrepressible force: he saw her, in her vast sagging fleshiness, with her slow stupid face, her instinctive responses to her children, whether for affection or temper, as the symbol of fecundity, a strong, irresistible heave of matter. She frightened him. He turned his eyes from her and ⁴⁰ explained to Van Heerden that a second hut would be built here, beside the existing one.

Van Heerden was pleased. He softened into quick confiding friendship. He looked doubtfully behind him at the small hut that sheltered eleven human beings, and said that ⁴⁵ it was really not easy to live in such a small space with so many children. He glanced at the children, cuffing them affectionately as he spoke, smiling like a boy. He was proud

of his family, of his own capacity for making children: Major Carruthers could see that. Almost, he smiled; then he glanced through the doorway at the grey squalor of the interior and hurried off, resolutely preventing himself from
5 dwelling on the repulsive facts that such close-packed living implied.

The next Saturday evening he and Van Heerden paced the clearing with tape measure and spirit level, determining the area of the new hut. It was to be a large one. Already the
10 sheaves of thatching grass had been stacked ready for next day, shining brassily in the evening sun; and the thorn poles for the walls lay about the clearing, stripped of bark, the smooth inner wood showing white as kernels.

Major Carruthers was waiting for the natives to come up
15 from the compound for the building before daybreak that Sunday. He was there even before the family woke, afraid that without his presence something might go wrong. He feared the Dutchman's temper because of the labourers' sulky mood.

20 He leaned against a tree, watching the bush come awake, while the sky flooded slowly with light, and the birds sang about him. The hut was, for a long time, silent and dark. A sack hung crookedly over the door, and he could glimpse huddled shapes within. It seemed to him horrible, a stink-
25 ing kennel shrinking ashamedly to the ground away from the wide hall of fresh blue sky. Then a child came out, and another; soon they were spilling out of the doorway, in their little rags of dresses, or hitching khaki pants up over the bony jut of a hip. They smiled shyly at him, offering
30 him friendship. Then came the woman, moving sideways to ease herself through the narrow door-frame – she was so huge it was almost a fit. She lumbered slowly, thick and stupid with sleep, over to the cold fire, raising her arms in a yawn, so that wisps of dull yellow hair fell over her shoul-
35 ders and her dark slack dress lifted in creases under her neck. Then she saw Major Carruthers and smiled at him. For the first time he saw her as a human being and not as something fatally ugly. There was something shy, yet frank, in that smile; so that he could imagine the strong, laughing
40 adolescent girl, with the frank, inviting, healthy sensuality of the young Dutchwoman – so she had been when she married Van Heerden. She stooped painfully to stir up the ashes, and soon the fire spurted up under the leaning patch of tin roof. For a while Van Heerden did not appear; neither
45 did the natives who were supposed to be here a long while since; Major Carruthers continued to lean against a tree, smiling at the children, who nevertheless kept their distance from him unable to play naturally because of his

---

to dwell on to think or talk about sth all the time

to pace to walk up and down in a small area
tape measure *Maßband*
spirit level *Wasserwaage*
sheaf bundle, bunch
brass *Messing*

kernel *Kern*

sulky silent or bad-tempered because you are angry about sth

crooked not straight, bent or twisted
to huddle to gather closely together
kennel a small hut for a dog

rag *Fetzen*
to hitch to pull up
jut *Vorsprung*
to ease here: to move through slowly and carefully
fit the right size or shape
to lumber to move in a slow and awkward way
to yawn *gähnen*
wisp a small, thin peace
crease fold or line in material

frank honest

to stoop to bend down

to file up to walk in a line
incline *Hang*

trench *Graben*
pebble small stone

apologetic, -ally showing that you are sorry for doing sth wrong
to apologize
an apology

to scamp (dated) to do the work in a sloppy way

to linger to stay
to supersede to replace

perfunctory done as duty

bark *Rinde, Borke*

gash cut
to lace to bind

slender thin in an attractive or graceful way

slushy *matschig*
mound a small hill
plaster *Verputz*

presence there, smiling at Mrs. Van Heerden who was throwing handfuls of mealie meal into a petrol tin of boiling water, to make native-style porridge.

It was just on eight o'clock, after two hours of impatient waiting, that the labourers filed up the bushy incline; with 5 the axes and picks over their shoulders, avoiding his eyes. He pressed down his anger: after all it was Sunday, and they had had no day off for weeks; he could not blame them.

They began by digging the circular trench that would 10 hold the wall poles. As their picks rang out on the pebbly ground, Van Heerden came out of the hut, pushing aside the dangling sack with one hand and pulling up his trousers with the other, yawning broadly, then smiling at Major Carruthers apologetically. "I've had my sleep 15 out," he said; he seemed to think his employer might be angry.

Major Carruthers stood close over the workers, wanting it to be understood by them and by Van Heerden that he was responsible. He was too conscious of their resentment, and 20 knew that they would scamp the work if possible. If the hut was to be completed as planned, he would need all his tact and good-humour. He stood there patiently all morning, watching the thin sparks flash up as the picks swung into the flinty earth. Van Heerden lingered nearby, unwilling to 25 be thus publicly superseded in the responsibility for his own dwelling in the eyes of the natives.

When they flung their picks and went to fetch the poles, they did so with a side glance at Major Carruthers, challenging him to say the trench was not deep enough. He 30 called them back, laughingly, saying: "Are you digging for a dog-kennel then, and not a hut for a man?" One smiled unwillingly in response; the others sulked. Perfunctorily they deepened the trench to the very minimum that Major Carruthers was likely to pass. By noon, the poles were 35 leaning drunkenly in place, and the natives were stripping the binding from beneath the bark of nearby trees. Long fleshy strips of fibre, rose-coloured and apricot and yellow, lay tangled over the grass, and the wounded trees showed startling red gashes around the clearing. Swiftly the poles 40 were laced together with this natural rope, so that when the frame was complete it showed up against green trees and sky like a slender gleaming white cage, interwoven lightly with rosy-yellow. Two natives climbed on top to bind the roof poles into their conical shape, while the others stamped 45 a slushy mound of sand and earth to form plaster for the walls. Soon they stopped – the rest could wait until after the midday break.

Worn out by the strain of keeping the balance between the
fiery Dutchman and the resentful workers, Major Carruthers went off home to eat. He had one and a half hour's
break. He finished his meal in ten minutes, longing to be
5 able to sleep for once till he woke naturally. His wife was
dozing, so he lay down on the other bed and at once
dropped off to sleep himself. When he woke it was long
after the time he had set himself. It was after three. He rose
in a panic and strode to the clearing, in the grip of one of
10 his premonitions.
There stood the Dutchman, in a flaring temper, shouting at
the natives who lounged in front of him, laughing openly.
They had only just returned to work. As Major Carruthers
approached, he saw Van Heerden using his open palms in a
15 series of quick swinging slaps against their faces, knocking
them sideways against each other: it was as if he were cuffing his own children in a fit of anger. Major Carruthers broke
into a run, erupting into the group before anything else could
happen. Van Heerden fell back on seeing him. He was beef-
20 red with fury. The natives were bunched together, on the
point of throwing down their tools and walking off the job.
"Get back to work," snapped Major Carruthers to the men:
and to Van Heerden: "I'm dealing with this." His eyes were
an appeal to recognize the need for tact, but Van Heerden
25 stood squarely there in front of him, on planted legs,
breathing heavily. "But Major Carruthers …" he began, im-
plying that as a white with his employer not there, it was
right that he should take the command. "Do as I say," said
Major Carruthers. Van Heerden, with a deadly look at his
30 opponents, swung on his heel and marched off into the hut.
The slapping swing of the grain-bag was as if a door had
been slammed. Major Carruthers turned to the natives.
"Get on," he ordered briefly, in a calm decisive voice.
There was a moment of uncertainty. Then they picked up
35 their tools and went to work.
Some laced the framework of the roof; others slapped the
mud on to the walls. This business of plastering was usually a festival, with laughter and raillery, for there were
gaps between the poles, and a handful of mud could fly
40 through a space into the face of a man standing behind: the
thing could become a game, like children playing snow-
balls. Today there was no pretence at good-humour. When
the sun went down the men picked up their tools and filed
off into the bush without a glance at Major Carruthers. The
45 work had not prospered. The grass was laid untidily over
the roof-frame, still uncut and reaching to the ground in
long swatches. The first layer of mud had been unevenly
flung on. It would be a shabby building.

worn out very tired

resentful feeling bitter or angry
about sth that you think is unfair

to long to to want sth very
much esp. if it does not seem
likely to happen soon

premonition feeling that sth bad
is going to happen
to flare to burn brightly
to lounge to stand, sit or lie in a
lazy way

fit attack

to erupt to break in suddenly
and violently

to bunch to gather together in
a group

raillery Neckerei

pretence false behaviour,
insincerity

to prosper to develop in a
successful way

swatch pieces

to cherish to love sb/sth very much and want to protect them or it

to be keyed up nervous and excited, esp before an important event
grudging reluctant, unwilling
apprehension worry or fear that sth unpleasant may happen
to trim to make sth neater, smaller, better, etc by cutting parts from it
to grain smooth *abschmirgeln*
to elapse to pass

pungent with a strong smell of

to wrench out to pull out with force

to dread to fear
tension *Spannung*

"His own fault," thought Major Carruthers, sending his slow, tired blue glance to the hut where the Dutchman was still cherishing the seeds of wounded pride. Next day, when Major Carruthers was in another part of the farm, the Dutchman got his own back in a fine flaming scene with the plough- ₅ boys: they came to complain to the bossboy, but not to Major Carruthers. This made him uneasy. All that week he waited for fresh complaints about the Dutchman's behaviour. So much was he keyed up, waiting for the scene between himself and a grudging bossboy, that when nothing happened ₁₀ his apprehensions deepened into a deep foreboding.

The building was finished the following Sunday. The floors were stamped hard with new dung, the thatch trimmed, and the walls grained smooth. Another two weeks must elapse before the family could move in, for the place smelled of ₁₅ damp. They were weeks of worry for Major Carruthers. It was unnatural for the Africans to remain passive and sullen under the Dutchman's handling of them, and especially when they knew he was on their side. There was something he did not like in the way they would not meet his eyes and ₂₀ in the over-polite attitude of the bossboy.

The beautiful clear weather that he usually loved so much, May weather, sharpened by cold, and crisp under deep clear skies, pungent with gusts of wind from the drying leaves and grasses of the veld, was spoilt for him this year: ₂₅ something was going to happen.

When the family eventually moved in, Major Carruthers became discouraged because the building of the hut had represented such trouble and worry, while now things seemed hardly better than before: what was the use of two ₃₀ small round huts for a family of eleven? But Van Heerden was very pleased, and expressed his gratitude in a way that moved Major Carruthers deeply; unable to show feeling himself, he was grateful when others did, so relieving him of the burden of his shyness. There was a ceremonial at- ₃₅ mosphere on the evening when one of the great sagging beds was wrenched out of the floor of the first hut and its legs plastered down newly into the second hut.

That very same night he was awakened towards dawn by voices calling to him from outside his window. He started ₄₀ up, knowing that whatever he had dreaded was here, glad that the tension was over. Outside the back door stood his bossboy, holding a hurricane lamp which momentarily blinded Major Carruthers.

"The hut is on fire." ₄₅

Blinking his eyes, he turned to look. Away in the darkness flames were lapping over the trees, outlining branches so that as a gust of wind lifted them patterns of black leaves

showed clear and fine against the flowing red light of the
fire. The veld was illuminated with a fitful plunging glare.
The two men ran off into the bush down the rough road,
towards the blaze.

5 The clearing was lit up, as bright as morning, when they
arrived. On the roof of the first hut squatted Van Heerden,
lifting tins of water from a line of natives below, working
from the water-butt, soaking the thatch to prevent it catch-
ing the flames from the second hut that was only a few
10 yards off. That was a roaring pillar of fire. Its frail skeleton
was still erect, but twisting and writhing incandescently
within its envelope of flame, and it collapsed slowly as he
came up, subsiding in a crash of sparks.
"The children," gasped Major Carruthers to Mrs. Van
15 Heerden, who was watching the blaze fatalistically from
where she sat on a scattered bundle of bedding, the tears
soaking down her face, her arms tight round a swathed child.
As she spoke she opened the cloths to display the smallest
infant. A swathe of burning grass from the roof had fallen
20 across its head and shoulders. He sickened as he looked,
for there was nothing but raw charred flesh. But it was
alive: the limbs still twitched a little.
"I'll get the car and we'll take it in to the doctor."
He ran out of the clearing and fetched the car. As he tore
25 down the slope back again he saw he was still in his pyja-
mas, and when he gained the clearing for the second time,
Van Heerden was climbing down from the roof, which
dripped water as if there had been a storm. He bent over
the burnt child.
30 "Too late," he said.
"But it's still alive."
Van Heerden almost shrugged; he appeared dazed. He continually turned his head to survey the glowing heap that
had so recently sheltered his children. He licked his lips
35 with a quick unconscious movement, because of their burning dryness. His face was grimed with smoke and inflamed
from the great heat, so that his young eyes showed star-
tlingly clear against the black skin.
"Get into the car," said Major Carruthers to the woman.
40 She automatically moved towards the car, without looking
at her husband, who said: "But it's too late, man."
Major Carruthers knew the child would die, but his protest
against the waste and futility of the burning expressed itself
in this way: that everything must be done to save this life,
45 even against hope. He started the car and slid off down the
hill. Before they had gone half a mile he felt his shoulder
plucked from behind, and, turning, saw the child was now
dead. He reversed the car into the dark bush off the road,

fitful happening only for short periods

to squat *hocken*

water-butt water-barrel
to soak to make wet
pillar *Säule*
frail weak, thin
incandescent giving out light

to subside to become calmer or quieter

fatalistic showing a belief in fate and feeling that you cannot con-trol events or stop them from happening
to swathe [sweɪð] to wrap

charred burnt and black as coal

to tear down to run fast

dazed unable to think, esp because of a shock or blow

grimed dirty

futility pointlessness, having no purpose

to pluck to pull

to wail to scream and cry esp due to sadness or pain

to clutch to hold tightly

bereaved [bɪˈriːvd] having lost a relative who has recently died

to stoop to walk with one's head and shoulders bent forward

disgust a strong feeling of dislike or disapproval for sb/sth that you feel is unacceptable, or for sth that looks, smells, etc unpleasant
tense *angespannt*

guileful dishonest, deceitful

humiliation, to humiliate to make sb feel ashamed or stupid and lose the respect of other people

reproach blame or criticism

and drove back to the clearing. Now the woman had begun wailing, a soft monotonous, almost automatic sound that kept him tight in his seat, waiting for the next cry.

The fire was now a dark heap, fanning softly to a glowing red as the wind passed over it. The children were standing ₅ in a half-circle, gazing fascinated at it. Van Heerden stood near them, laying his hands gently, restlessly, on their heads and shoulders, reassuring himself of their existence there, in the flesh and living, beside him.

Mrs. Van Heerden got clumsily out of the car, still wailing, ₁₀ and disappeared into the hut, clutching the bundled dead child.

Feeling out of place among that bereaved family, Major Carruthers went up to his house, where he drank cup after cup of tea, holding himself tight and controlled, conscious ₁₅ of overstrained nerves.

Then he stooped into his wife's room, which seemed small and dark and airless. The cave of a sick animal, he thought, in disgust; then, ashamed of himself, he returned out of doors, where the sky was filling with light. He sent a message for the ₂₀ bossboy, and waited for him in a condition of tensed anger.

When the man came Major Carruthers asked immediately: "Why did that hut burn?"

The bossboy looked at him straight and said: "How should I know?" Then, after a pause, with guileful innocence: "It ₂₅ was the fault of the kitchen, too close to the thatch."

Major Carruthers glared at him, trying to wear down the straight gaze with his own accusing eyes.

"That hut must be rebuilt at once. It must be rebuilt today."

The bossboy seemed to say that it was a matter of indiffer- ₃₀ ence to him whether it was rebuilt or not. "I'll go and tell the others," he said, moving off.

"Stop" barked Major Carruthers. Then he paused, fright- ened, not so much at his rage, but his humiliation and guilt. He had foreseen it! He had foreseen it all! And yet, that ₃₅ thatch could so easily have caught alight from the small incautious fire that sent up sparks all day so close to it.

Almost, he burst out in wild reproaches. Then he pulled himself together and said: "Get away from me." What was the use? He knew perfectly well that one of the Africans ₄₀ whom Van Heerden had kicked or slapped or shouted at had fired that hut; no one could ever prove it.

He stood quite still, watching his bossboy move off, tug- ging at the long wisps of his moustache in frustrated anger. And what would happen now?   ₄₅

He ordered breakfast, drank a cup of tea, and spoilt a piece of toast. Then he glanced in again at his wife, who would sleep for a couple of hours yet.

Again tugging fretfully at his moustache, Major Carruthers set off for the clearing.

Everything was just as it had been, though the pile of black débris looked low and shabby now that morning had be-
5 come and heightened the wild colour of sky and bush. The children were playing nearby, their hands and faces black, their rags of clothing black – everything seemed patched and smudged with black, and on one side the trees hung withered and grimy and the soil was hot underfoot.
10 Van Heerden leaned against the framework of the first hut. He looked subdued and tired, but otherwise normal. He greeted Major Carruthers, and did not move.

"How is your wife?" asked Major Carruthers. He could hear a moaning sound from inside the hut.
15 "She's doing well."

Major Carruthers imagined her weeping over the dead child; and said: "I'll take your baby into town for you and arrange for the funeral."

Van Heerden said: "I've buried her already." He jerked his
20 thumb at the bush behind them.

"Didn't you register its birth?"

Van Heerden shook his head. His gaze challenged Major Carruthers as if to say: Who's to know if no one tells them? Major Carruthers could not speak: he was held in silence
25 by the thought of that charred little body, huddled into a packing-case or wrapped in a piece of cloth, thrust into the ground, at the mercy of wild animals or of white ants.

"Well, one comes and another goes," said Van Heerden at last, slowly, reaching out for philosophy as a comfort,
30 while his eyes filled with rough tears.

Major Carruthers stared: he could not understand. At last the meaning of the words came into him, and he heard the moaning from the hut with a new understanding.

The idea had never entered his head; it had been a com-
35 plete failure of the imagination. If nine children, why not ten? Why not fifteen, for that matter, or twenty? Of course there would be more children.

"It was the shock," said Van Heerden. "It should be next month."
40 Major Carruthers leaned back against the wall of the hut and took out a cigarette clumsily. He felt weak. He felt as if Van Heerden had struck him, smiling. This was an absurd and unjust feeling, but for a moment he hated Van Heerden for standing there and saying: this grey country of poverty
45 that you fear so much, will take on a different look when you actually enter it. You will cease to exist; there is no energy left, when one is wrestling naked, with life, for your kind of fine feelings and scruples and regrets.

---

fretful anxious

débris ['debriː] pieces of wood, metal, brick, etc that are left after sth has been destroyed

to smudge to make dirty
grimy [graɪmɪ] *rußig*

subdued unusually quiet

to moan to make a long deep sound, usually expressing unhappiness or suffering

charred slightly burned or blackened

to be at the mercy of *jdm/etw. ausgeliefert sein*

to cease [siːs] to stop

tentative not done with confidence

"We hope it will be a boy," volunteered Van Heerden, with a tentative friendliness, as if he thought it might be considered a familiarity to offer his private motions to Major Carruthers. "We have five boys and four girls – three girls," he corrected himself, his face contracting.   5

Major Carruthers asked stiffly: "Will she be all right?"

"I do it," said Van Heerden. The last was born in the middle of the night, when it was raining. That was when we were in the tent. It's nothing to her," he added, with pride. He was listening, as he spoke, to the slow moaning from in-   10
side. "I'd better be getting in to her," he said, knocking out his pipe against the mud of the walls. Nodding to Major Carruthers, he lifted the sack and disappeared.

After a while Major Carruthers gathered himself together and forced himself to walk erect across the clearing under   15
the curious gaze of the children. His mind was fixed and

numb taub

numb, but he walked as if moving to a destination. When he reached the house, he at once pulled paper and pen towards him and wrote, and each slow difficult word was a

coffin Sarg

nail in the coffin of his pride as a man.   20

Some minutes later he went in to his wife. She was awake, turned on her side, watching the door for the relief of his coming. "I've written for a job at Home," he said simply, laying his hand on her thin dry wrist, and feeling the slow pulse beat up suddenly against his palm.   25

He watched curiously as her face crumpled and the tears of thankfulness and release ran slowly down her cheeks and soaked the pillow.

Cross-Cultural Experiences

R. K. Narayan

A Horse and Two Goats

The village was so small that it found no mention in any atlas. On the local survey map it was indicated by a tiny dot. It was called Kiritam, which in the Tamil language means "crown" (preferably diamond-studded) – a rather
5 gorgeous conception, readily explained by any local enthusiast convinced beyond doubt that this part of India is the apex of the world. In proof thereof, he could, until quite recently, point in the direction of a massive guardian at the portals of the village, in the shape of a horse moulded out
10 of clay, baked, burnt, and brightly coloured. The horse reared his head proudly, prancing, with his forelegs in the air and his tail looped up with a flourish. Beside the horse stood a warrior with scythe-like moustaches, bulging eyes, and an aquiline nose. The image-makers of old had made
15 the eyes bulge out when they wished to indicate a man of strength, just as the beads around the warrior's neck were meant to show his wealth. Blobs of mud now, before the ravages of sun and rain they had had the sparkle of emerald, ruby, and diamond. The big horse looked mottled, but
20 at one time it was white as a dhobi-washed sheet, its black enveloped in a checkered brocade of pure red and black. The lance in the grip of the warrior had been covered with bands of gay colour, and the multicoloured sash around his waist contrasted with every other colour in these surround-
25 ings. This statue, like scores of similar ones scattered along the countryside, was forgotten and unnoticed, with lantana and cactus growing around it. Even the youthful vandals of the village left the statue alone, hardly aware of its existence. On this particular day, an old man was drowsing in
30 the shade of a nearby cactus and watching a pair of goats graze in this arid soil; he was waiting for the sight of a green bus lumbering down the hill road in the evening, which would be the signal for him to start back home, and he was disturbed by a motorist, who jammed on his brakes
35 at the sight of the statue, and got out of his car, and went up to the mud horse.
"Marvellous!" he cried, pacing slowly around the statue. His face was sunburned and red. He wore a khaki-coloured

---

to indicate to point to, to show

gorgeous beautiful
conception understanding or a belief of what sth is or what it should be
apex the top or highest part of something
to mould to shape
clay *Ton*
to rear (of an animal, esp horse) to raise itself on its back legs
to prance to move with high steps
flourish *Schwung*
scythe *Sense*
to bulge to stick out
aquiline ['ækwɪlaɪn] thin and curved, similar to an eagle's beak
bead [biːd] *Perle*
ravage damage
emerald a bright green stone
ruby ['ruːbɪ] a dark red precious stone
mottled marked with shapes of different colours without a regular colour
dhobi washerman (in India, Malaya, East Africa, etc esp formerly)
checkered *kariert*
gay bright, cheerful
sash *Schärpe*
lantana shrub or plant having spikes of yellow or orange flowers
to lumber to move in a slow and awkward way
to jam on to push with force
to pace to walk up and down in a small area

shirt and shorts. Noticing the old man's presence, he said politely in English, "How do you do?"

means of *Mittel*

The old man replied in pure Tamil, his only means of communication, "My name is Muni, and the two goats are mine and mine only; no one can gainsay it, although the village ₅ is full of people ready to slander a man."

to gainsay to disagree
to slander *verleumden*

The red-faced man rested his eyes for a moment in the direction of the goats and the rocks, took out a cigarette, and asked, "Do you smoke?"

"I never even heard of it until yesterday," the old man re- ₁₀ plied nervously, guessing that he was being questioned about a murder in the neighbourhood by this police officer from the government, as his khaki dress indicated.

The red-faced man said, "I come from New York. Have you heard it? Have you heard of America?" ₁₅

The old man would have understood the word "America" (though not "New York") if the name had been pronounced as he knew it – "A Meh Rikya" – but the red-faced man pronounced it very differently, and the old man did not know what it meant. He said respectfully, "Bad characters ₂₀ everywhere these days. The cinema has spoiled the people and taught them how to do evil things. In these days anything may happen."

ingratiating trying too hard to
please sb

"I am sure you must know when this horse was made," said the red-faced man, and smiled ingratiatingly. ₂₅

The old man reacted to the relaxed atmosphere by smiling himself, and pleaded, "Please go away, sir. I know nothing. I promise I will hold him for you if I see any bad character around, but our village has always had a clean record. Must be the other village." ₃₀

record account

"Please, please, I will speak slowly. Please try to understand me," the red-faced man said. "I arrived three weeks ago and have travelled five thousand miles since, seeing your wonderful country."

The old man made indistinct sounds in his throat and shook ₃₅ his head. Encouraged by this, the other went on to explain at length, uttering each syllable with care and deliberation, what brought him to this country, how much he liked it, what he did at home, how he had planned for years to visit India, the dream of his life and so forth – every now and ₄₀ then pausing to smile affably. The old man smiled back and said nothing, whereupon the red-faced man finally said, "How old are you? You have such wonderful teeth. Are they real? What's your secret?"

to utter *äußern*
deliberation careful, slow consideration

affable pleasant, easy to talk to

The old man knitted his brow and said mournfully, "Some- ₄₅ times our cattle, too, are lost; but then we go and consult our astrologer.

mournful very sad

He will look at a camphor flame and tell us in which direc-

camphor *Kampfer*

tion to search for the lost animals. … I must go home now."
And he turned to go.
The other seized his shoulder and said earnestly, "Is there
no one – absolutely no one – here to translate for me?" He
5 looked up and down the road, which was deserted on this
hot afternoon. A sudden gust of wind churned up the dust
and the dead leaves on the roadside into a ghostly column
and propelled it toward the mountain road. "Is this statue
yours? Will you sell it to me?"
10 The old man understood that the other was referring to the
horse. He thought for a second and said, "I was an urchin
of this height when I heard my grandfather explain this
horse and warrior, and my grandfather himself was of
this height when he heard his grandfather, whose grandfa-
15 ther …" Trying to indicate the antiquity of the statue, he
got deeper and deeper into the bog of reminiscence, and
then pulled himself out by saying, "But my grandfather's
grandfather's uncle had first-hand knowledge, although I
don't remember him."
20 "Because I really do want this statue," the red-faced man
said, "I hope you won't drive a hard bargain."
"This horse," the old man continued, "will appear as the
tenth avatar at the end of the Yuga."
The red-faced man nodded. He was familiar with the word
25 "avatar."
"At the end of this Kali Yuga, this world will be destroyed,
and all the worlds will be destroyed, and it is then that the
Redeemer will come, in the form of a horse called Kalki, and
help the good people, leaving the evil ones to perish in the
30 great deluge. And this horse will come to life then, and that
is why this is the most sacred village in the whole world."
"I am willing to pay any price that is reasonable –"
This statement was cut short by the old man, who was now
lost in the visions of various avatars. "God Vishnu is the
35 highest god, so our pandit at the temple has always told us,
and He has come nine times before, whenever evil-minded
men troubled this world."
"But please bear in mind that I am not a millionaire."
"The first avatar was in the shape of a fish," the old man
40 said, and explained the story of how Vishnu at first took the
form of a little fish, which grew bigger each hour and became gigantic, and supported on its back the holy scrip-
tures, which were about to be lost in the ocean. Having
launched on the first avatar, it was inevitable that he should
45 go on with the second one, a tortoise, and the third, a boar
on whose tusk the world was lifted up when it had been
carried off and hidden at the bottom of the ocean by an
extraordinary vicious conqueror of the earth.

to desert to leave, to abandon
to churn sth up to move sth around violently

urchin (old-fashioned) orphan

bog wet soft ground formed out of decaying plants
reminiscence memory

bargain deal, business

avatar (in Hinduism) the manifestation of a deity, notably Vishnu, in human, superhuman, or animal form

Redeemer *der Erlöser*
to perish to die esp in a sudden and violent way
deluge flood

pandit or **pundit** (Hinduism) scholar or expert

to launch on to start with
tortoise ['tɔːtəs] *Schildkröte*
boar *Eber*

vicious [vɪʃəs] evil, devilish

station wagon *Kombi*
to lend sb a hand to help

mutual shared by two or more people
debit a sum of money taken from a bank account
progeny a person's children

nothing ventured, nothing gained (saying) used to say that you have to take risks, if you want to achieve things and be successful

currency *Währung*

to peer to look closely at

to flourish [flʌrɪʃ] to wave sth around in a way that makes people look at it

lakh or **lac** (in India) the number 100 000

"Transportation will be my problem, but I will worry about that later. Tell me, will you accept a hundred rupees for the horse only? Although I am charmed by the moustached soldier, I will have to come next year for him. No space for him now." 5

"It is God Vishnu alone who saves mankind each time such a thing has happened. He incarnated himself as Rama, and He alone could destroy Ravana, the demon with ten heads who shook all the worlds. Do you know the story of Ramayanar?" 10

"I have my station wagon, as you see. I can push the seat back and take the horse in. If you'll just lend me a hand with it."

"Do you know Mahabharata? Krishna was the eighth avatar of Vishnu, incarnated to help the Five Brothers regain their 15 kingdom. When Krishna was a baby, he danced on the thousand-hooded, the giant serpent, and trampled it to death … "

At this stage the mutual mystification was complete. The old man chattered away in a spirit of balancing off the 20 credits and debits of conversational exchanges, and said, in order to be on the credit side, "Oh, honourable one, I hope God has blessed you with numerous progeny. I say this because you seem to be a good man, willing to stay beside an old man and talk to him, while all day I have none to talk 25 to except when somebody stops to ask for a piece of tobacco … How many children have you?"

"Nothing ventured, nothing gained," the red-faced man said to himself. And then, "Will you take a hundred rupees for it?" Which encouraged the other to go into details. 30

"How many of your children are boys and how many girls? Where are they? Is your daughter married? Is it difficult to find a son-in-law in your country also?"

The red-faced man thrust his hand into his pocket and brought forth his wallet, from which he took a hundred ru- 35 pee currency note.

The old man now realized that some financial element was entering their talk. He peered closely at the currency note, the like of which he had never seen in his life; he knew the five and ten by their colours, although always in other 40 people's hands. His own earning at any time was in coppers and nickels. What was this man flourishing the note for? Perhaps for change. He laughed to himself at the notion of anyone's coming to him to change a thousand- or ten-thousand-rupee note. He said with a grin, "Ask our village 45 headman, who is also a money-lender; he can change even a lakh of rupees in gold sovereigns if you prefer it that way.

He thinks nobody knows, but dig the floor of his *puja* room and your head will reel at the sight of the hoard. The man disguises himself in rags just to mislead the public."

"If that's not enough, I guess I could go a little higher," the red-faced man said.

"You'd better talk to him yourself, because he goes mad at the sight of me. Someone took away his pumpkins with the creeper and he thinks it was me and my goats. That's why I never let my goats be seen anywhere near the farms," the old man said, with his eyes travelling to his goats as they were nosing about, attempting to wrest nutrition out of minute greenery peeping out of rock and dry earth.

The red-faced man followed his look and decided it would be a sound policy to show an interest in the old man's pets. He went up to them casually and stroked their backs.

Now the truth dawned on the old man. His dream of a lifetime was about to be realized: the red-faced man was making him an offer for the goats. He had reared them up in the hope of selling them some day and with the capital opening a small shop on this very spot; under a thatched roof he would spread out a gunny sack and display on it fried nuts, coloured sweets, and green coconut for thirsty and hungry wayfarers on the highway. He needed for this project a capital of twenty rupees, and he felt that with some bargaining he could get it now; they were not prize animals worthy of a cattle show, but he had spent his occasional savings to provide them some fancy diet now and then, and they did not look too bad.

Saying, "It is all for you, or you may share it if you have a partner," the red-faced man placed on the old man's palm one hundred and twenty rupees in notes.

The old man pointed at the station wagon.

"Yes, of course," said the other.

The old man said, "This will be their first ride in a motor car. Carry them off after I get out of sight; otherwise they will never follow you but only me, even if I am travelling on the path to the Underworld." He laughed at his own joke, brought his palms together in a salute, turned round, and was off and out of sight beyond a clump of bushes.

The red-faced man looked at the goats grazing peacefully and then perched himself on the pedestal of the horse, as the westerly sun touched off the ancient faded colours of the statue with a fresh splendour. "He must be gone to fetch some help," he remarked, and settled down to wait.

---

puja room Indian room where statues of Gods and Godesses are kept and worshipped by sacrificing and praying to them
to reel to seem to be spinning around and around
to disguise [dɪsˈgaɪz] to change your appearance so that people cannot recognize you
rag a piece of old, often torn, cloth used esp for cleaning things
to wrest obtain with difficulty
nutrition food
minute very tiny

sound here: wise
casual in a carefree, relaxed way
to stroke *streicheln*
to dawn to become obvious or easy to understand
to rear sb/sth up to feed and care for
thatch dried straw, reeds for making a roof
gunny sack a large bag made from rough material and used to store flour, potatoes, etc

fancy expensive

to perch oneself on to sit on sth, esp on the edge of it
pedestal *Podest*
faded weak, grown pale

Chinua Achebe

Dead Men's Path

Michael Obi's hopes were fulfilled much earlier than he had expected. He was appointed headmaster of Ndume Central School in January 1949. It had always been an unprogressive school, so the Mission authorities decided to send a young and energetic man to run it. Obi accepted this 5 responsibility with enthusiasm. He had many wonderful ideas and this was an opportunity to put them into practice. He had had sound secondary school education which designated him a 'pivotal teacher' in the official records and set him apart from the other headmasters in the mission 10 field. He was outspoken in his condemnation of the narrow views of these older and often less-educated ones.

"We shall make a good job of it, shan't we?" he asked his young wife when they first heard the joyful news of his promotion. 15

"We shall do our best," she replied. "We shall have such beautiful gardens and everything will be just *modern* and delightful …" In their two years of married life she had become completely infected by his passion for 'modern methods' and his denigration of 'these old and superannu- 20 ated people in the teaching field who would be better employed as traders in the Onitsha market'. She began to see herself already as the admired wife of the young headmaster, the queen of the school.

The wives of the other teachers would envy her position. 25 She would set the fashion in everything … Then, suddenly, it occurred to her that there might not be other wives. Wavering between hope and fear, she asked her husband, looking anxiously at him.

"All our colleagues are young and unmarried," he said with 30 enthusiasm which for once she did not share. "Which is a good thing," he continued.

"Why?"

"Why? They will give all their time and energy to the school." 35

Nancy was downcast. For a few minutes she became sceptical about the new school; but it was only for a few minutes. Her little personal misfortune could not blind her to her husband's happy prospects. She looked at him as he sat folded up in a chair. He was stoop-shouldered and looked 40 frail. But he sometimes surprised people with sudden bursts of physical energy. In his present posture, however, all his bodily strength seemed to have retired behind his deep-set eyes, giving them an extraordinary power of penetration.

---

sound good and thorough
pivotal of great importance

condemnation very strong disapproval
to condemn to express very strong disapproval of sb/sth, usually for moral reasons

shan't we? shall we not?
promotion a move to a more important job or rank in a company or organization

denigration *Verunglimpfung*
superannuated out-of-date
Onitsha town in southern Nigeria

to envy to wish to have the same qualities, possessions, opportunities, etc as sb else
to occur to to become obvious

downcast sad
misfortune bad luck
prospects (pl) chances of being successful
stoop *krummer Rücken*
frail weak and thin
posture the position in which you hold your body

penetration going into or through sth

He was only twenty-six, but looked thirty or more. On the whole, he was not unhandsome.

"A penny for your thoughts, Mike," said Nancy after a while, imitating the woman's magazine she read.

5 "I was thinking what a grand opportunity we've got at last to show these people how a school should be run." Ndume School was backward in every sense of the word. Mr Obi put his whole life into the work, and his wife hers too. He had two aims. A high standard of teaching was insisted 10 upon, and the school compound was to be turned into a place of beauty. Nancy's dream-gardens came to life with the coming of the rains, and blossomed. Beautiful hibiscus and allamanda hedges in brilliant red and yellow marked out the carefully tended school compound from the rank 15 neighbourhood bushes.

One evening as Obi was admiring his work he was scandalized to see an old woman from the village hobble right across the compound, through a marigold flower-bed and the hedges. On going up there he found faint signs of an 20 almost disused path from the village across the school compound to the bush on the other side.

"It amazes me," said Obi to one of his teachers who had been three years in the school, "that you people allowed the villagers to make use of this footpath. It is simply incredi- 25 ble." He shook his head.

"The path," said the teacher apologetically, "appears to be very important to them. Although it is hardly used, it connects the village shrine with their place of burial."

"And what has that got to do with the school?" asked the 30 headmaster.

"Well, I don't know," replied the other with a shrug of the shoulders. "But I remember there was a big row some time ago when we attempted to close it."

"That was some time ago. But it will not be used now," 35 said Obi as he walked away. "What will the Government Education Officer think of this when he comes to inspect the school next week? The villagers might, for all I know, decide to use the schoolroom for a pagan ritual during the inspection."

40 Heavy sticks were planted closely across the path at the two places where it entered and left the school premises. These were further strengthened with barbed wire.

Three days later the village priest, or *Ani*, called on the headmaster. He was an old man and walked with a slight 45 stoop. He carried a stout walking-stick which he usually tapped on the floor, by way of emphasis, each time he made a new point in his argument.

---

compound area surrounded by a wall or other boundary

to blossom *blühen*

hedge *Hecke*

rank growing too thickly

to hobble to walk with difficulty, esp because your feet hurt

marigold *Sumpfdotterblume*

faint that cannot be clearly seen

disused hardly used any more

apologetic, -ally showing that you are sorry for doing sth wrong

row [raʊ] quarrel, fight

pagan [peɪgən] *heidnisch*

premises (pl) area, compound

barbed wire *Stacheldraht*

stout strong and thick

cordiality warm friendliness

> **ancestral** belonging to the family or the race of people that you are descended from, e.g. your grandparents (= **ancestors** forefathers)

to eradicate to destroy or get rid of sth completely, esp sth bad
to require to need
fantastic difficult to believe

to perch (of birds) to land or sit on a branch
thoroughfare ['θʌrəfeə] a main road in a city or town with busy traffic
to skirt to go around

detour a longer route you take to avoid sth that is blocking your way
burdensome causing worry or hard work
diviner fortune-teller
to propitiate to stop sb from being angry by trying to please them

zeal great energy or enthusiasm for reaching esp a personal aim

"I have heard," he said after the usual exchange of cordialities, "that our ancestral footpath has recently been closed …"

"Yes," replied Mr Obi. "We cannot allow people to make a highway of our school compound." 5

"Look here, my son," said the priest bringing down his walking-stick, "this path was here before you were born and before your father was born. The whole life of this village depends on it. Our dead relatives depart by it and our ancestors visit us by it. But most important, it is the path of 10 children coming in to be born …"

Mr Obi listened with a satisfied smile on his face.

"The whole purpose of our school," he said finally, "is to eradicate just such beliefs as that. Dead men do not require footpaths. The whole idea is just fantastic. Our duty is to 15 teach your children to laugh at such ideas."

"What you say may be true," replied the priest, "but we follow the practices of our fathers. If you re-open the path we shall have nothing to quarrel about. What I always say is: let the hawk perch and let the eagle perch." He rose to go. 20

"I am sorry," said the young headmaster. "But the school compound cannot be a thoroughfare. It is against our regulations. I would suggest your constructing another path, skirting our premises. We can even get our boys to help in building it. I don't suppose the ancestors will find the little 25 detour too burdensome."

"I have no more words to say," said the old priest, already outside.

Two days later a young woman in the village died in childbed. A diviner was immediately consulted and he pre- 30 scribed heavy sacrifices to propitiate ancestors insulted by the fence.

Obi woke up next morning among the ruins of his work. The beautiful hedges were torn up not just near the path but right round the school, the flowers trampled to death and 35 one of the school buildings pulled down … That day, the white Supervisor came to inspect the school and wrote a nasty report on the state of the premises but more seriously about the 'tribal-war situation developing between the school and the village, arising in part from the misguided 40 zeal of the new headmaster'.

Ngugi wa Thiong'o
A Meeting in the Dark

He stood at the door of the hut and saw his old, frail but energetic father coming along the village street, with a rather dirty bag made out of a strong calico swinging by his side. His father always carried this bag. John knew what it
5 contained: a Bible, a hymn-book and probably a notebook and a pen. His father was a preacher. He knew it was he who had stopped his mother from telling him stories when be became a man of God. His mother had stopped telling him stories long ago. She would say to him, 'Now, don't
10 ask for any more stories. Your father may come.' So he feared his father. John went in and warned his mother of his father's coming. Then his father entered. John stood aside, then walked towards the door. He lingered there doubtfully, then he went out.
15 'John, hei, John!'
'Baba!'
'Come back.'
He stood doubtfully in front of his father. His heart beat faster and there was that anxious voice within him asking:
20 Does he know?
'Sit down. Where are you going?'
'For a walk, Father,' he answered evasively.
'To the village?'
'Well-yes-no. I mean, nowhere in particular.' John saw his
25 father look at him hard, seeming to read his face. John sighed, a very slow sigh. He did not like the way his father eyed him. He always looked at him as though John was a sinner, one who had to be watched all the time. 'I am,' his heart told him. John guiltily refused to meet the old man's
30 gaze and looked past him appealingly to his mother who was quietly peeling potatoes. But she seemed oblivious of everything around her.
'Why do you look away? What have you done?'
John shrank within himself with fear. But his face remained
35 expressionless. He could hear the loud beats of his heart. It was like an engine pumping water. He felt no doubt his father knew all about it. He thought: 'Why does he torture me? Why does he not at once say he knows?' Then another voice told him: 'No, he doesn't know, otherwise he would
40 have already jumped at you.' A consolation. He faced his thoughtful father with courage.
'When is the journey?'
Again John thought: Why does he ask? I have told him many times.

frail weak and thin

to linger to stay

evasive not willing to give clear answers to a question

gaze a long, steady look
oblivious not aware of

to shrink, shrank, shrunk to become smaller

to torture to hurt sb physically or mentally in order to punish them or make them tell you sth

consolation comfort

'Next week, Tuesday,' he said.
'Right. Tomorrow we go to the shops, hear?'
'Yes, Father.'
'Then be prepared.'
'Yes, Father.'   5
'You can go.'
'Thank you, Father.' He began to move.
'John!'
'Yes?' John's heart almost stopped beating.

to loiter to hang around

'You seem to be in a hurry. I don't want to hear of you loi- 10
tering in the village. I know young men, going to show off
just because you are going away? I don't want to hear of
trouble in the village.'

relieved feeling happy because sth unpleasant has stopped or has not happened
to persecute to deliberately annoy sb all the time and make their life unpleasant
tough strict

Much relieved, he went out. He could guess what his father
meant by not wanting trouble in the village.   15
'Why do you persecute the boy so much?' Susana spoke
for the first time. Apparently she had carefully listened to
the whole drama without a word. Now was her time to
speak. She looked at her tough old preacher who had been
a companion for life. She had married him a long time ago. 20
She could not tell the number of years. They had been happy. Then the man became a convert. And everything in the
home put on a religious tone.
He even made her stop telling stories to the child. 'Tell him
of Jesus. Jesus died for you. Jesus died for the child. He 25
must know the Lord.' She, too, had been converted. But she
was never blind to the moral torture he inflicted on the boy

to inflict on to make sb suffer sth unpleasant

(that was how she always referred to John), so that the boy
had grown up mortally afraid of his father. She always
wondered if it was love for the son. Or could it be a resent- 30
ment because, well, they two had 'sinned' before marriage?

resentment a feeling of anger or unhappiness about sth that you think is unfair

John had been the result of that sin. But that had not been
John's fault. It was the boy who ought to complain. She
often wondered if the boy had … but no. The boy had been
very small when they left Fort Hall. She looked at her hus- 35
band. He remained mute though his left hand did, rather
irritably, feel about his face.

mute silent
irritable getting annoyed easily

'It is as if he was not your son. Or do you …'

to plead to beg

'Hm, Sister.' The voice was pleading. She was seeking a
quarrel but he did not feel equal to one. Really, women 40
could never understand. Women were women, whether
saved or not. Their son had to be protected against all evil
influences. He must be made to grow in the footsteps of the

to frown die Stirn runzeln

Lord. He looked at her, frowning a little. She had made him
sin but that had been a long time ago. And he had been 45

to tread to step on

saved. John must not tread the same road.
'You ought to tell us to leave. You know I can go away. Go
back to Fort Hall. And then everybody …'

'Look, Sister,' he hastily interrupted. He always called her
sister. Sister-in-Lord, in full. But he sometimes wondered if
she had been truly saved. In his heart he prayed: Lord, be
with our sister Susana. Aloud, he continued, 'You know I
5 want the boy to grow in the Lord.'
'But you torture him so! You make him fear you!'
'Why! He should not fear me. I have really nothing against
him.'
'It is you. You. You have always been cruel to him ...' She
10 stood up. The peelings dropped from her frock and fell in a
heap on the floor. 'Stanley!'
'Sister.' He was startled by the vehemence in her voice. He
had never seen her like this. Lord, take the devil out of her.
Save her this minute. She did not say what she wanted to
15 say. Stanley looked away from her. It was a surprise, but it
seemed he feared his wife. If you had told the people in the
village about this, they would not have believed you. He
took his Bible and began to read. On Sunday he would
preach to a congregation of brethren and sisters.
20 Susana, a rather tall, thin woman, who had once been beautiful, sat down again and went on with her work. She did
not know what was troubling her son. Was it the coming
journey? Still, she feared for him.
Outside, John was strolling aimlessly along the path that
25 led from his home. He stood near the wattle tree which was
a little way from his father's house and surveyed the whole
village. They lay before his eyes, crammed, rows and rows
of mud and grass huts, ending in sharply defined sticks that
pointed to heaven. Smoke was coming out of various huts.
30 It was an indication that many women had already come
from the shambas. Night would soon fall. To the west, the
sun – that lone day-time traveller – was hurrying home behind the misty hills. Again, John looked at the crammed
rows and rows of huts that formed Makeno Village, one of
35 the new mushroom 'towns' that grew up all over the country during the Mau Mau war. It looked so ugly. A pain rose
in his heart and he felt like crying – I hate you, I hate you!
You trapped me alive. Away from you, it would never have
happened. He did not shout. He just watched.
40 A woman was coming towards where he stood. A path into
the village, was just near there. She was carrying a big load
of Kuni which bent her into an Akamba-bow shape. She
greeted him. 'Is it well with you, Njooni (John)?'
'It is well with me, Mother.' There was no trace of bitter-
45 ness in his voice. John was by nature polite. Everyone
knew this. He was quite unlike the other proud, educated
sons of the tribe – sons who came back from the other side
of the waters with white or Negro wives who spoke Eng-

frock (old-fashioned) dress

to be startled by sth to be
surprised by sth

to stroll to walk slowly
wattle tree *Goldakazie*

crammed unpleasantly full

indication sign
shamba (E. Africa) field used for
growing crops
mist light fog

mushroom town a town that
appears suddenly and expands
quickly

to trap sb/sth to catch or keep
sb/sth in a place and prevent
them or it from escaping

Akamba-bow a hunting bow
used by the Akamba tribe

trace *Spur*

humility submissiveness, modesty

to betray to give information about sb/sth to an enemy

lish. And they behaved just like Europeans! John was a favourite, a model of humility and moral perfection. Everyone knew that though a clergyman's son, John would never betray the tribe. They still talked of the tribe and its ways.
'When are you going to – to –'   5
'Makerere?'
'Makelele.' She laughed. The way she pronounced the name was funny. And the way she laughed, too. She enjoyed it. But John felt hurt. So everyone knew of this.
'Next week.'   10
'I wish you well.'
'Thank you, Mother.'
She said quietly, as if trying to pronounce it better 'Makelele'. She laughed at herself again but she was tired. The load was heavy.   15
'Stay well, Son.'
'Go well and in peace, Mother.'
And the woman who all the time had stood, moved on, panting like a donkey, but she was obviously pleased with John's politeness.   20

to pant to breathe heavily

John remained long, looking at her. What made such a woman live on day to day, working hard, yet happy? Had she much faith in life? Or was her faith in the tribe? She and her kind, who had never been touched by ways of the whiteman, looked as though they had something to cling   25
to. As he watched her disappear, he felt proud that they should think well of him. He felt proud that he had a place in their esteem. And then came the pang. *Father will know.*
They will know. He did not know what he feared most; the action his father would take when he found out, or the loss   30
of the little faith the simple villagers had placed in him, when they knew. He feared to lose everything.
He went down to the small local tea-shop. He met many people who wished him well at the college. All of them knew that the priest's son had finished all the whiteman's   35
learning in Kenya.
He would now go to Uganda. They had read this in the *Baraya,* the Swahili Weekly. John did not stay long at the shop. The sun had already gone to rest and now darkness was coming. The evening meal was ready. His tough father   40
was still at the table reading his Bible. He did not look up when John entered. Strange silence settled in the hut.
'You look unhappy.' His mother first broke the silence.
John laughed. It was a nervous little laugh. 'No, Mother,' he hastily replied, nervously looking at his father. He se-   45
cretly hoped that Wamuhu had not blabbed.
'Then I am glad.'
She did not know. He ate his dinner and went out to his hut.

faith trust, belief

to cling to to hold tight to

esteem great respect and admiration
pang a sudden sharp pain

to blab to tell sb information that should be kept secret

A man's hut. Every young man had his own hut. John was never allowed to bring any girl visitor in there. Stanley did not want 'trouble'. Even to be seen standing with one was a crime. His father could easily thrash him. He feared his
5 father, though sometimes he wondered why he feared him. He ought to have rebelled like the other educated young men. He lit the lantern. He took it in his hand. The yellow light flickered dangerously and then went out. He knew his hands were shaking. He lit it again and hurriedly took his
10 big coat and a huge Kofia which were lying on the unmade bed. He left the lantern burning, so that his father would see it and think he was in. John bit his lower lip spitefully. He hated himself for being so girlish. It was unnatural for a boy of his age.
15 Like a shadow, he stealthily crossed the courtyard and went on to the village street.
He met young men and women lining the streets. They were laughing, talking, whispering. They were obviously enjoying themselves. John thought, they are more free than I am.
20 He envied their exuberance. They clearly stood outside or above the strict morality that the educated ones had to be judged by. Would he have gladly changed places with them? He wondered. At last, he came to the hut. It stood at the very heart of the village. How well he knew it – to his sor-
25 row. He wondered what he should do! Wait for her outside? What if her mother came out instead? He decided to enter.
'Hodi!'
'Enter. We are in.'
John pulled down his hat before he entered. Indeed they
30 were all there – all except she whom he wanted. The fire in the hearth was dying. Only a small flame from a lighted lantern vaguely illuminated the whole hut. The flame and the giant shadow created on the wall seemed to be mocking him. He prayed that Wamuhu's parents would not recog-
35 nize him. He tried to be 'thin', and to disguise his voice as he greeted them. They recognized him and made themselves busy on his account. To be visited by such an edu- cated one, who knew all about the whiteman's world and knowledge and who would now go to another land beyond,
40 was not such a frequent occurrence that it could be taken lightly. Who knew but he might be interested in their daughter? Stranger things had happened. After all, learning was not the only thing. Though Wamuhu had no learning, yet she had charms and could be trusted to captivate any
45 young man's heart with her looks and smiles.
'You will sit down. Take that stool.'
'No!' He noticed with bitterness that he did not call her Mother'.

to thrash to beat

Kofia type of African hat

spiteful having or showing hatred and a desire to harm or hurt sb or their feelings

stealthy quietly

to envy to wish to have the same qualities, possessions, opportunies, etc as sb else
exuberance energy, cheerful- ness

hearth floor of the fireplace

to mock to laugh at sb

to disguise to change the appearance of

beyond on the further side of sth
occurrence event, happening

to captivate to catch and keep

glance a quick look

to bolt to run away quickly

to mutter to mumble
inaudible that cannot be heard

circumcised *beschnitten*

virtuous morally good, honest,
decent
to initiate sb in sth to make sb
a member of a particular group,
esp as part of a secret ceremony

clay *Ton*
to poke to dig into with a stick

numbness *Taubheit*
to tremble to shiver

to mourn to grieve for
to crumble to break
into pieces

'Where is Wamuhu?'
The mother threw a triumphant glance at her husband.
They exchanged a knowing look. John bit his lip again and
felt like bolting. He controlled himself with difficulty.
'She has gone out to get some tea leaves. Please sit down. 5
She will cook you some tea when she comes.'
'I am afraid ...' he muttered some inaudible word and went
out. He almost collided with Wamuhu.
In the hut: 'Didn't I tell you? Trust a woman's eye!'
'You don't know these young men.' 10
'But you see John is different. Everyone speaks well of
him and he is a clergyman's son.'
'Y-e-e-s! A clergyman's son! You forget your daughter is circumcised.' The old man was remembering his own day. He
had found for himself a good virtuous woman, initiated in 15
all the tribe's ways. And she had known no other man. He
had married her. They were happy. Other men of his Rika
had done the same. All the girls had been virgins, it being a
taboo to touch a girl in that way, even if you slept in the
same bed, as indeed so many young men and girls did. Then 20
the white men had come, preaching a strange religion,
strange ways, which all men followed. The tribe's code of
behaviour was broken. The new faith could not keep the
tribe together. How could it? The men who followed the new
faith would not let the girls be circumcised. And they would 25
not let their sons marry circumcised girls. Puu! Look at
what was happening. Their young men went away to the
land of the whitemen. What did they bring? White women.
Black women who spoke English. Aaa – bad. And the
young men who were left just did not mind. They made un- 30
married girls their wives and then left them with fatherless
children.
'What does it matter?' his wife was replying. 'Is Wamuhu
not as good as the best of them? Anyway, John is different.'
'Different! Different! Puu! They are all alike. Those coated 35
with the white clay of the whiteman's ways are the worst.
They have nothing inside. Nothing – nothing here.' He took
a piece of wood and nervously poked the dying fire. A
strange numbness came over him. He trembled. And he
feared; he feared for the tribe. For now he saw it was not 40
only the educated men who were coated with strange ways,
but the whole tribe. The old man trembled and cried inside
mourning for a tribe that had crumbled. The tribe had nowhere to go to. And it could not be what it was before. He
stopped poking and looked hard at the ground. 45
'I wonder why he came. I wonder.' Then he looked at his
wife and said, 'Have you seen strange behaviour with your
daughter?'

His wife did not answer. She was preoccupied with her own great hopes.

John and Wamuhu walked on in silence. The intricate streets and turns were well known to them both. Wamuhu
5 walked with quick light steps; John knew she was in a happy mood. His steps were heavy and he avoided people, even though it was dark. But why should he feel ashamed? The girl was beautiful, probably the most beautiful girl in the whole of Limuru. Yet he feared being seen with her. It
10 was all wrong. He knew that he could have loved her; even then he wondered if he did not love her. Perhaps it was hard to tell but, had he been one of the young men he had met, he would not have hesitated in his answer.

Outside the village he stopped. She, too, stopped. Neither
15 had spoken a word all through. Perhaps the silence spoke louder than words. Both of them were only too conscious of each other.

'Do they know?' Silence. Wamuhu was probably considering the question. 'Don't keep me waiting. Please answer
20 me,' he implored. He felt weary, very weary, like an old man who had suddenly reached his journey's end.

'No. You told me to give you one more week. A week is over today.'

'Yes. That's why I came!' John whispered hoarsely.

25 Wamuhu did not speak. John looked at her. Darkness was now between them. He was not really seeing her; before him was the image of his father – haughtily religious and dominating. Again he thought: I, John, a priest's son, respected by all and going to college, will fall, fall to the
30 ground. He did not want to contemplate the fall.

'It was your fault.' He found himself accusing her. In his heart he knew he was lying.

'Why do you keep on telling me that? Don't you want to marry me?'

35 John sighed. He did not know what to do. He remembered a story his mother used to tell him. *Once upon a time there was a young girl ... she had no home to go to and she could not go forward to the beautiful land and see all the good things because the Irimu was on the way ...*

40 'When will you tell them?'

'Tonight.'

He felt desperate. Next week he would go to the college. If he could persuade her to wait, he might be able to get away and come back when the storm and consternation had abat-
45 ed. But then the government might withdraw his bursary. He was frightened and there was a sad note of appeal as he turned to her and said, 'Look, Wamuhu, how long have you been pre- ... I mean, like this?'

---

preoccupied absorbed

intricate ['ɪntrɪkət] complex

to hesitate to wait because of doubts or feelings of insecurity about sth

to implore to ask intensively
weary ['wɪərɪ] old and tired

hoarse with a sore throat

haughty arrogant

consternation a feeling of great surprise, shock or anxiety
to abate to become less strong
bursary scholarship
appeal request

deliberate intentional
to blackmail sb to force sb to do sth by threatening them
profusely in large amounts

Calvinistic having very strict moral attitudes

to blaspheme to speak about God or the holy things of a particular religion in an offensive way: to swear using the names of God or holy things
to crush to press or squeeze sth so hard that it is damaged
to blanket to cover completely like a blanket *(Decke)*

to console sb/yourself to give comfort or sympathy to sb who is unhappy or disappointed
trial an act of testing the ability, quality, performance, etc, esp before a final decision is reached about them
to defy to resist
prospects (pl) chances of being successful
to consent to allow, give permission

'I have told you over and over again, I have been pregnant for three months and mother is being suspicious. Only yesterday she said I breathed like a woman with a child.'
'Do you think you could wait for three weeks more?'
She laughed. Ah! the little witch! She knew his trick. Her ₅ laughter always aroused many emotions in him.
'All right,' he said. 'Give me just tomorrow. I'll think up something. Tomorrow I'll let you know.'
'I agree. Tomorrow. I cannot wait any more unless you mean to marry me.' ₁₀
Why not marry her? She is beautiful! Why not marry? Do I love her or don't I?
She left. John felt as if she was deliberately blackmailing him. His knees were weak and lost strength. He could not move but sank on the ground in a heap. Sweat poured pro- ₁₅ fusely down his cheeks, as if he had been running hard under a strong sun. But this was cold sweat. He lay on the grass; he did not want to think. Oh, no! He could not possibly face his father. Or his mother. Or Reverend Carstone who had had such faith in him. John realized that, though ₂₀ he was educated, he was no more secure than anybody else. He was no better than Wamuhu. Then why don't you marry her? He did not know. John had grown up under a Calvinistic father and learnt under a Calvinistic headmaster – a missionary! John tried to pray. But to whom was he pray- ₂₅ ing? To Carstone's God? It sounded false. It was as if he was blaspheming. Could he pray to the God of the tribe? His sense of guilt crushed him.
He woke up. Where was he? Then he understood. Wamuhu had left him. She had given him one day. He stood up; he ₃₀ felt good. Weakly, he began to walk back home. It was lucky that darkness blanketed the whole earth and him in it. From the various huts, he could hear laughter, heated talks or quarrels. Little fires could be seen flickering red through the open doors. Village stars, John thought. He raised up ₃₅ his eyes. The heavenly stars, cold and distant, looked down on him impersonally. Here and there, groups of boys and girls could be heard laughing and shouting. For them life seemed to go on as usual. John consoled himself by thinking that they, too, would come to face their day of ₄₀ trial.
John was shaky. Why! Why could he not defy all expectations, all prospects of a future, and marry the girl? No. No. It was impossible. She was circumcised and he knew that his father and the church would never consent to such a ₄₅ marriage. She had no learning – or rather she had not gone beyond standard four. Marrying her would probably ruin his chances of ever going to a university.

He tried to move briskly. His strength had returned. His imagination and thought took flight. He was trying to explain his action before an accusing world – he had done so many times before, ever since he knew of this. He still
5 wondered what he could have done. The girl had attracted him. She was graceful and her smile had been very bewitching. There was none who could equal her and no girl in the village had any pretence to any higher standard of education. Women's education was very low. Perhaps that
10 was why so many Africans went 'away' and came back married. He too wished he had gone with the others, especially in the last giant student airlift to America. If only Wamuhu had learning … and she was uncircumcised … then he might probably rebel.
15 The light still shone in his mother's hut. John wondered if he should go in for the night prayers. But he thought against it; he might not be strong enough to face his parents. In his hut the light had gone out. He hoped his father had not noticed it.
20 John woke up early. He was frightened. He was normally not superstitious, but still he did not like the dreams of the night. He dreamt of circumcision; he had just been initiated in the tribal manner. Somebody – he could not tell his face, came and led him because he took pity on him. They went,
25 went into a strange land. Somehow, he found himself alone. The somebody had vanished. A ghost came. He recognized it as the ghost of the home he had left. It pulled him back; then another ghost came. It was the ghost of the land he had come to. It pulled him forward. The two contested.
30 Then came other ghosts from all sides and pulled him from all sides so that his body began to fall into pieces. And the ghosts were insubstantial. He could not cling to any. Only they were pulling him and he was becoming nothing, nothing … he was now standing a distance away. It had not
35 been him. But he was looking at the girl, the girl in the story. She had nowhere to go. He thought he would go to help her; he would show her the way. But as he went to her, he lost his way … he was all alone … something destructive was coming towards him, coming, coming … He woke
40 up. He was sweating all over.
Dreams about circumcision were no good. They portended death. He dismissed the dream with a laugh. He opened the window only to find the whole country clouded in mist. It was perfect July weather in Limuru. The hills, ridges, val-
45 leys and plains that surrounded the village were lost in the mist. It looked such a strange place. But there was almost a magic fascination in it. Limuru was a land of contrasts and evoked differing emotions at different times. Once John

brisk quick, busy

pretence claim

airlift an operation to take people, etc from an area by plane, esp in an emergency

superstitious believing in magic, ghosts, etc

to vanish to disappear

to contest to struggle to gain control or power

insubstantial not real or solid

destructive causing destruction or damage

to portend to be a sign or warning of sth
to dismiss to decide that sth is not important
ridge Gebirgskamm

to evoke to bring sth to mind

to yearn to want sth very much, esp when it is difficult to get

to repel to drive, keep or push sth away

pot-hole *Schlagloch*

vice the opposite of virtue

betrayal act of giving information to an enemy

odd strange

the day of reckoning *Tag der Abrechnung*

to shudder to shiver

unfortunate caused by bad luck

scar *Narbe*

lanky having long thin limbs and moving in an awkward way

wistful melancholy

vigour energy

to be destined for having a future which has been decided or planned at an earlier time, esp by fate

observance the practice of obeying a law

pharisaical very proud of the fact that one has high religious and moral standards, but not caring enough for other people

to shepherd to take care of sheep

to be liable to [ˈlaɪəbl] to be likely to

to expel to drive away

prejudicial [ˌpredʒʊˈdɪʃl] harming or likely to harm sb/sth

disintegration gradual loss of strength or unity

due to because of

would be fascinated and would yearn to touch the land, embrace it or just be on the grass. At another time he would feel repelled by the dust, the strong sun and the pot-holed roads. If only his struggle were just against the dust, the mist, the sun and the rain, he might feel content. Content to 5 live here. At least he thought he would never like to die and be buried anywhere else but at Limuru. But there was the human element whose vices and betrayal of other men were embodied in the new ugly villages. The last night's incident rushed into his mind like a flood, making him weak again. 10 He got out of his blankets and went out. Today he would go to the shops. He was uneasy. An odd feeling was coming to him – in fact had been coming – that his relationship with his father was perhaps unnatural. But he dismissed the thought. Tonight would be the day of reckoning. 15 He shuddered to think of it. It was unfortunate that this scar had come into his life at this time, when he was going to Makerere and it would have brought him closer to his father.

They went to the shops. All day long, John remained quiet 20 as they moved from shop to shop buying things from the lanky but wistful Indian traders. And all day long, John wondered why he feared his father so much. He had grown up fearing him, trembling whenever he spoke or gave commands. John was not alone in this. 25
Stanley was feared by all.
He preached with great vigour, defying the very gates of hell. Even during the Emergency, he had gone on preaching, scolding, judging and condemning. All those who were not saved were destined for hell. Above all, Stanley was 30 known for his great and strict moral observances – a bit too strict, rather pharisaical in nature. None noticed this; certainly not the sheep he shepherded. If an elder broke any of the rules, he was liable to be expelled, or excommunicated. Young men and women, seen standing together 'in a man- 35 ner prejudicial to church and God's morality' (they were one anyway) were liable to be excommunicated. And so, many young men tried to serve two masters by seeing their girls at night and going to church by day. The alternative was to give up church-going altogether. 40
Stanley took a fatherly attitude to all the people in the village. You must be strict with what is yours. And because of all this he wanted his house to be a good example of this to all. That is why he wanted his son to grow upright. But motives behind many human actions may be mixed. He could 45 never forget that he had also fallen before his marriage. Stanley was also a product of the disintegration of the tribe due to the new influences.

The shopping did not take long. His father strictly observed the silences between them and neither by word nor by hint did he refer to last night. They reached home and John was thinking that all was well when his father called him.

5 'John.'

'Yes, Father.'

'Why did you not come for prayers last night?'

'I forgot …'

'Where were you?'

10 Why do you ask me? What right have you to know where I was? One day I am going to revolt against you. But, immediately, John knew that this act of rebellion was something beyond him – unless something happened to push him into it. It needed someone with something he lacked.

15 'I – I – I mean, I was …'

'You should not sleep so early before prayers. Remember to turn up tonight.'

'I will.'

Something in the boy's voice made the father look up. John 20 went away relieved. All was still well.

Evening came. John dressed like the night before and walked with faltering steps towards the fatal place. The night of reckoning had come. And he had not thought of anything. After this night all would know. Even Reverend 25 Carstone would hear of it. He remembered Reverend Carstone and the last words of blessing he had spoken to him. No! he did not want to remember. It was no good remembering these things; and yet the words came. They were clearly written in the air, or in the darkness of his 30 mind. 'You are going into the world. The world is waiting even like a hungry lion, to swallow you, to devour you. Therefore, beware of the world. Jesus said, Hold fast unto …' John felt a pain – a pain that wriggled through his flesh as he remembered these words. He contemplated the com-35 ing fall. Yes! He, John, would fall from the Gates of Heaven down through the open waiting Gates of Hell. Ah! He could see it all, and all that people would say. All would shun his company, all would give him oblique looks that told so much. The trouble with John was that his imagina-40 tion magnified the fall from the heights of 'goodness' out of all proportion. And fear of people and consequences ranked high in the things that made him contemplate the fall with so much horror.

John devised all sorts of punishment for himself. And when 45 it came to thinking of a way out, only fantastic and impossible ways of escape came into his head. He simply could not make up his mind. And because he could not, and because he feared Father and people and did not know his

hint indirect suggestion

to falter to become weaker, less confident

blessing benediction

to devour to eat eagerly

to wriggle to twist and turn
to contemplate to think about

to shun to avoid
oblique indirect

to devise to think up

true attitude to the girl, he came to the agreed spot having nothing to tell her. Whatever he did looked fatal to him. Then suddenly he said:

'Look, Wamuhu. Let me give you money. You might then say that someone else was responsible. Lots of girls have ₅ done this. Then that man may marry you. For me, it is impossible. You know that.'

'No. I cannot do that. How can you, you …'

'I will give you two hundred shillings.'

'No!'   10

'Three hundred.'

'No!' She was almost crying. It pained her to see him so.

'Four hundred, five hundred, six hundred.' John had begun calmly but now his voice was running high. He was excited. He was becoming more desperate. Did he know what he ₁₅ was talking about? He spoke quickly, breathlessly, as if he was in a hurry. The figure was rapidly rising – nine thousand, ten thousand, twenty thousand … He is mad. He is foaming. He is quickly moving towards the girl in the dark. He has lain his hands on her shoulders and is madly ₂₀ imploring her in a hoarse voice. Deep inside him, something horrid that assumes the threatening anger of his father and the village seems to be pushing him. He is violently shaking Wamuhu, while his mind tells him that he is patting her gently. Yes, he is out of his mind. The figure has now ₂₅ reached fifty thousand shillings and is increasing. Wamuhu is afraid. She extricates herself from him, the mad, educated son of a religious clergyman, and runs. He runs after her and holds her, calling her by all sorts of endearing words. But he is shaking her, shake, shake, her, her – he tries to ₃₀ hug her by the neck, presses. … She lets out one horrible scream and then falls on the ground. And so all of a sudden, the struggle is over, the figures stop, and John stands there trembling like the leaf of a tree on a windy day.

Soon everyone will know that he has created and then ₃₅ killed.

to foam (infml) to be very angry so that bubbles come out of one's mouth
to implore to beg
to assume to take on, absorb

to pat to touch sb/sth gently several times with your flat hand, esp as a sign of affection

to extricate oneself to free oneself from sb/sth

endearing causing people to feel affection

to hug to embrace

Postcolonial Consequences

Muriel Spark
The Black Madonna

When the Black Madonna was installed in the Church of
the Sacred Heart the Bishop himself came to consecrate it.
His long purple train was upheld by the two curliest of the
choir. The day was favoured suddenly with thin October
5 sunlight as he crossed the courtyard from the presbytery to
the church, as the procession followed him chanting the
Litany of the Saints: five priests in vestments of white
heavy silk interwoven with glinting threads, four lay officials with straight red robes, then the confraternities and
10 the tangled columns of the Mothers' Union.
The new town of Whitney Clay had a large proportion of
Roman Catholics, especially among the nurses at the new
hospital; and at the paper mills, too, there were many Catholics, drawn inland from Liverpool by the new housing es-
15 tate; likewise, with the canning factories.
The Black Madonna had been given to the church by a recent convert. It was carved out of bog oak.
'They found the wood in the bog. Had been there hundreds
of years. They sent for the sculptor right away by phone.
20 He went over to Ireland and carved it there and then. You
see, he had to do it while it was still wet.'
'Looks a bit like contemporary art.'
'Nah, that's not contemporary art, it's old-fashioned. If
you'd ever seen contemporary work you'd *know* it was old-
25 fashioned.'
'Looks like contemp-'
'It's old-*fashioned.* Else how'd it get sanctioned to be put up?'
'It's not so nice as the Immaculate Conception at Lourdes.
That lifts you up.'
30 Everyone got used, eventually, to the Black Madonna with
her square hands and straight carved draperies. There was
a movement to dress it up in vestments, or at least a lace
veil.
'She looks a bit gloomy, Father, don't you think?'
35 'No,' said the priest, 'I think it looks fine. If you start dressing it up in cloth you'll spoil the line.'
Sometimes people came from London especially to see the
Black Madonna, and these were not Catholics; they were,

to consecrate to state officially
in a religious ceremony that sth
is holy
train *Schleppe*
curly *lockig*
presbytery a house where a
Roman Catholic priest lives
to chant to sing
vestment a piece of clothing
worn by a priest during services
thread Faden
lay *Laien-*
confraternity *Bruderschaft*
tangled muddled
column a long moving line of
people
can metal container in which
food and drink is stored/
preserved; BrE also tin
to carve to make objects,
patterns, etc by cutting away
material from wood
bog oak *Sumpfgehölz*

contemporary modern

Immaculate Conception *unbe-
fleckte Empfängnis*
to lift sb up to raise sb to a
higher (here: spiritual) level
eventually finally
drapery loose clothing hanging
in folds like a curtain
lace veil *Spitzenschleier*
gloomy dark, sad and without
hope

said the priest, probably no religion at all, poor souls, though gifted with faculties. They came, as if to a museum, to see the line of the Black Madonna which must not be spoiled by vestments.

The new town of Whitney Clay had swallowed up the old 5 village. One or two cottages with double dormer windows, an inn called 'The Tyger', a Methodist chapel and three small shops represented the village; the three shops were already threatened by the Council; the Methodists were fighting to keep their chapel. Only the double dormer cot- 10 tages and the inn were protected by the Nation and so had to be suffered by the Town Planning Committee.

The town was laid out like geometry in squares, arcs (to allow for the by-pass) and isosceles triangles, breaking off, at one point, to skirt the old village which, from the aerial 15 view, looked like a merry doodle on the page.

Manders Road was one side of a parallelogram of green-bordered streets. It was named after one of the founders of the canning concern, Manders' Figs in Syrup, and it comprised a row of shops and a long high block of flats named 20 Cripps house after the late Sir Stafford Cripps who had laid the foundation stone. In flat twenty-two on the fifth floor of Cripps House lived Raymond and Lou Parker. Raymond Parker was a foreman at the motor works, and was on the management committee. He had been married for fifteen 25 years to Lou, who was thirty-seven at the time that the miraculous powers of the Black Madonna came to be talked of.

Of the twenty-five couples who lived in Cripps House five were Catholics. All, except Raymond and Lou Parker, had 30 children. A sixth family had recently been moved by the Council into one of the six-roomed houses because of the seven children besides the grandfather.

Raymond and Lou were counted lucky to have obtained their three-roomed flat although they had no children. 35 People with children had priority; but their name had been on the waiting list for years, and some said Raymond had a pull with one of the Councillors who was a director of the motor works.

The Parkers were among the few tenants of Cripps House 40 who owned a motor car. They did not, like most of their neighbours, have a television receiver, for being childless they had been able to afford to expand themselves in the way of taste, so that their habits differed slightly and their amusements considerably, from those of their neighbours. 45 The Parkers went to the pictures only when the *Observer* had praised the film; they considered television not their

---

gifted talented

dormer window *Mansardenfenster*

to be suffered by (passive) to be tolerated by

isosceles triangle *gleichschenkliges Dreieck*
aerial view view from a plane
merry (infml, esp BrE) slightly drunk
doodle lines, shapes, etc one draws when bored or thinking about sth else
to comprise to have sth as parts, to consist of

miraculous magical

to obtain to get

to have a pull with to have a useful connection to

tenant a person who pays rent for the use of a room, etc

to expand in the way of taste to spend a lot of money on stylish or high quality objects and amusements
considerably much, a lot

sort of thing; they adhered to their religion; they voted Labour; they believed that the twentieth century was the best so far; they assented to the doctrine of original sin; they frequently applied the word 'Victorian' to ideas and people

5 they did not like – for instance, when a local Town Councillor resigned his office Raymond said, 'He had to go. He's Victorian. And far too young for the job'; and Lou said Jane Austen's books were too Victorian; and anyone who opposed the abolition of capital punishment was Vic-

10 torian. Raymond took the *Reader's Digest,* a magazine called *Motoring* and the *Catholic Herald.* Lou took the *Queen, Woman's Own* and *Life.* Their daily paper was the *News Chronicle.* They read two books apiece each week. Raymond preferred travel books; Lou liked novels.

15 For the first five years of their married life they had been worried about not having children. Both had submitted themselves to medical tests as a result of which Lou had a course of injections. These were unsuccessful. It had been a disappointment since both came from large sprawling

20 Catholic families. None of their married brothers and sisters had less than three children. One of Lou's sisters, now widowed, had eight; they sent her a pound a week. Their flat in Cripps House had three rooms and a kitchen. All round them their neighbours were saving up to buy

25 houses. A council flat, once obtained, was a mere platform in space to further the progress of the rocket. This ambition was not shared by Raymond and Lou; they were not only content, they were delighted, with these civic chambers, and indeed took something of an aristocratic view of them,

30 not without a self-conscious feeling of being free, in this particular, from the prejudices of that middle class to which they as good as belonged. 'One day; said Lou, 'it will be the thing to live in a council flat.' They were eclectic as to their friends. Here, it is true, they

35 differed slightly from each other. Raymond was for inviting the Ackleys to meet the Farrells. Mr Ackley was an accountant at the Electricity Board. Mr and Mrs Farrell were respectively a sorter at Manders' Figs in Syrup and an usherette at the Odeon.

40 'After all,' argued Raymond, 'they're all Catholics.' 'Ah well,' said Lou, 'but now, their interests are different. The Farrells wouldn't know what the Ackleys were talking about. The Ackleys like politics. The Farrells like to tell jokes. I'm not a snob, only sensible.'

45 'Oh, please yourself.' For no one could call Lou a snob, and everyone knew she was sensible. Their choice of acquaintance was wide by reason of their active church membership: that is to say, they were mem-

---

to adhere to to stick firmly to

to assent to to agree to

to resign to officially tell sb that you are leaving your job

abolition the official ending of a law, a system or an institution
to abolish

to submit to agree to undergo

sprawling spreading in an untidy way

ambition wish to succeed

civic chambers *Sozialwohnung*

eclectic not following one style or set of ideas but choosing from or using a wide variety
accountant *Buchhalter*

respectively in the order that they were just mentioned
usherette a woman whose job is to lead people to their seats in a theatre or cinema

acquaintance friends

sidesman *Kirchendiener*

talkative liking to talk a lot

chap (BrE, infml, becoming old-fashioned) used to talk about a man in a friendly way
them darkies (non-standard/derog) those darkies

bewildered confused

defiant openly refusing to obey
objection reason to be against sth
to cease [siːs] to stop, to end
to take up with to start going out with

bers of various guilds and confraternities. Raymond was a sidesman, and he also organized the weekly football lottery in aid of the Church Decoration Fund. Lou felt rather out of things when the Mother's Union met and had special Masses, for the Mothers' Union was the only group she did 5 not qualify for. Having been a nurse before her marriage she was, however, a member of the Nurses' Guild.

Thus, most of their Catholic friends came from different departments of life. Others, connected with the motor works where Raymond was a foreman, were of different 10 social grades to which Lou was more alive than Raymond. He let her have her way, as a rule, when it came to a question of which would mix with which.

A dozen Jamaicans were taken on at the motor works. Two came into Raymond's department. He invited them to the 15 flat one evening to have coffee. They were unmarried, very polite and black. The quiet one was called Henry Pierce and the talkative one, Oxford St John. Lou, to Raymond's surprise and pleasure, decided that all their acquaintance, from top to bottom, must meet Henry and Oxford. All 20 along he had known she was not a snob, only sensible, but he had rather feared she would consider the mixing of their new black and their old white friends not sensible.

'I'm glad you like Henry and Oxford,' he said. 'I'm glad we're able to introduce them to so many people.' For the 25 dark pair had, within a month, spent nine evenings at Cripps House; they had met accountants, teachers, packers and sorters. Only Tina Farrell, the usherette, had not seemed to understand the quality of these occasions: 'Quite nice chaps, them darkies, when you get to know them.' 30 'You mean Jamaicans,' said Lou. 'Why shouldn't they be nice? They're no different from anyone else.'

'Yes, yes, that's what I mean,' said Tina.

'We're all equal,' stated Lou. 'Don't forget there are black Bishops.' 35

'Jesus, I never said we were the equal of a Bishop,' Tina said, very bewildered.

'Well, don't call them darkies.'

Sometimes, on summer Sunday afternoons Raymond and Lou took their friends for a run in their car, ending up at a 40 riverside roadhouse. The first time they turned up with Oxford and Henry they felt defiant; but there were no objections, there was no trouble at all. Soon the dark pair ceased to be a novelty. Oxford St John took up with a pretty red-haired bookkeeper, and Henry Pierce, missing his companion, spent more of his time at the Parker's flat. Lou and 45 Raymond had planned to spend their two weeks' summer holiday in London. 'Poor Henry,' said Lou. 'He'll miss us.'

Once you brought him out he was not so quiet as you thought at first. Henry was twenty-four, desirous of knowledge in all fields, shining very much in eyes, skin, teeth, which made him seem all the more eager. He called out the
5 maternal in Lou, and to some extent the avuncular in Raymond: Lou used to love him when he read out lines from his favourite poems which he had copied into an exercise book.

> Haste thee, nymph, and bring with thee
> Jest and youthful jollity,
> 10 Sport that ...

Lou would interrupt: 'You should say jest, jollity – not yest, yollity.'
'Jest,' he said carefully. 'And laughter holding both his sides,' he continued. '*Laughter* – hear that, Lou? – *laugh-*
15 *ter.* That's what the human race was made for. Those folks that go round gloomy, Lou, they ...'
Lou loved this talk. Raymond puffed his pipe benignly. After Henry had gone Raymond would say what a pity it was such an intelligent young fellow had lapsed. For Henry had
20 been brought up in a Roman Catholic mission. He had, however, abandoned religion. He was fond of saying, 'The superstition of today is the science of yesterday.'
'I can't allow,' Raymond would say, 'that the Catholic Faith is superstition. I can't allow that.'
25 'He'll return to the Church one day' – this was Lou's contribution, whether Henry was present or not. If she said it in front of Henry he would give her an angry look. These were the only occasions when Henry lost his cheerfulness and grew quiet again.
30 Raymond and Lou prayed for Henry, that he might regain his faith. Lou said her rosary three times a week before the Black Madonna.
'He'll miss us when we go on our holidays.'
Raymond telephoned to the hotel in London. 'Have you a
35 single room for a young gentleman accompanying Mr and Mrs Parker?' He added, 'A coloured gentleman.' To his pleasure a room was available, and to his relief there was no objection to Henry's colour.
They enjoyed their London holiday, but it was somewhat
40 marred by a visit to that widowed sister of Lou's to whom she allowed a pound a week towards the rearing of her eight children. Lou had not seen her sister Elizabeth for nine years. They went to her one day towards the end of their holiday. Henry sat at the back of the car beside a large suitcase
45 stuffed with old clothes for Elizabeth. Raymond at the wheel kept saying, 'Poor Elizabeth – eight kids,' which irritated Lou, though she kept her peace.

---

avuncular behaving like an uncle

jest joke
jollity cheerfulness, happiness

benign [bɪˈnaɪn] kind and gentle

to lapse to stop believing in or practising your religion
to abandon to leave/to give up
to be fond of to like
superstition belief in magic and forebodings, etc

> **contribution** *Beitrag*
> **to contribute** *beitragen*

rosary *Rosenkranz*

to be available free for use

marred damaged, spoilt
to rear a child to bring up

to irritate to make angry
to keep one's peace to keep silent

Outside the underground station at Victoria Park, where they stopped to ask the way, Lou felt a strange sense of panic. Elizabeth lived in a very downward quarter of Bethnal Green, and in the past nine years since she had seen her Lou's memory of the shabby ground-floor rooms ₅ with their peeling walls and bare boards, had made a kinder nest for itself. Sending off the postal order to her sister each week she had gradually come to picture the habitation at Bethnal Green in an almost monastic light; it would be bare but well-scrubbed, spotless, and shining with Brasso ₁₀ and holy poverty. The floor-boards gleamed. Elizabeth was grey-haired, lined, but neat. The children were well-behaved, sitting down betimes to their broth in two rows along an almost refectory table. It was not till they had reached Victoria Park that Lou felt the full force of the fact ₁₅ that everything would be different from what she had imagined. 'It may have gone down since I was last there,' she said to Raymond who had never visited Elizabeth before. 'What's gone down?'
'Poor Elizabeth's place.' ₂₀
Lou had not taken much notice of Elizabeth's dull little monthly letters, almost illiterate, for Elizabeth, as she herself always said, was not much of a scholar.

> *James is at another job I hope that's the finish of the bother I had my blood pressure there was a* ₂₅ *Health visitor very nice. Also the assistance they sent my Dinner all the time and for the kids at home they call it meals on Wheels. I pray to the Almighty that James is well out of his bother he never lets on at sixteen their all the same never* ₃₀ *open his mouth but Gods eyes are not shut. Thanks for P.O. you will be rewarded your affect sister Elizabeth.*

Lou tried to piece together in her mind the gist of nine years' such letters. James was the eldest; she supposed he ₃₅ had been in trouble.
'I ought to have asked Elizabeth about young James,' said Lou. 'She wrote to me last year that he was in a bother, there was talk of him being sent away, but I didn't take it in at the time, I was busy.' ₄₀
'You can't take everything on your shoulders,' said Raymond. 'You do very well by Elizabeth.' They had pulled up outside the house where Elizabeth lived on the ground floor. Lou looked at the chipped paint, the dirty windows and torn grey-white curtains and was reminded with start- ₄₅

---

bare not covered

habitation accommodation
monastic *mönchisch*
to scrub to clean by rubbing
spotless without any marks of dirt
to gleam to shine
broth thick soup made by boiling meat or fish and vegetables in water
refectory *Speisesaal*

dull boring
illiterate showing no or only poor command of writing skills and reading ability

gist the main or general meaning of a piece of writing, etc

to chip here: *abblättern*

ling clarity of her hopeless childhood in Liverpool from which, miraculously, hope had lifted her, and had come true, for the nuns had got her that job; and she had trained as a nurse among white-painted beds, and white shining
5 walls, and tiles, hot water everywhere and Dettol without stint. When she had first married she had wanted all white-painted furniture that you could wash and liberate from germs; but Raymond had been for oak, he did not understand the pleasure of hygiene and new enamel paint, for his
10 upbringing had been orderly, he had been accustomed to a lounge suite and autumn tints in the front room all his life. And now Lou stood and looked at the outside of Elizabeth's place and felt she had gone right back.

On the way back to the hotel Lou chattered with relief that
15 it was over. 'Poor Elizabeth, she hasn't had much of chance. I liked little Francis, what did you think of little Francis, Ray?'
Raymond did not like being called Ray, but he made no objection for he knew that Lou had been under a strain. Eli-
20 zabeth had not been very pleasant. She had expressed admiration for Lou's hat, bag, gloves and shoes which were all navy blue, but she had used an accusing tone. The house had been smelly and dirty. 'I'll show you round,' Elizabeth had said in a tone of mock refinement, and they were
25 forced to push through a dark narrow passage behind her skinny form till they came to the big room where the children slept. A row of old iron beds each with a tumble of dark blanket rugs, no sheets. Raymond was indignant at the sight and hoped that Lou was not feeling upset. He knew
30 very well Elizabeth had a decent living income from a number of public sources, and was simply a slut, one of those who would not help themselves.
'Ever thought of taking a job, Elizabeth?' he had said, and immediately realized his stupidity. But Elizabeth took her
35 advantage. 'What d'you mean? *I'm* not going to leave my kids in no nursery. *I'm* not going to send them to no home. What kids need these days is a good home life and that's what they get.' And she added, 'God's eyes are not shut,' in a tone which was meant for him, Raymond, to get at him
40 for doing well in life.
Raymond distributed half-crowns to the younger children and deposited on the table half-crowns for those who were out playing in the street.
'Goin' already?' said Elizabeth in her tone of reproach. But
45 she kept eyeing Henry with interest, and the reproachful tone was more or less a routine affair.
'You from the States?' Elizabeth said to Henry.

---

startling surprising

tile *Fliese*
Dettol (brand name) antiseptic
without stint without restriction

enamel *Emaille*
to be accustomed to to be used to
lounge suite a group of matching sofas and armchairs
tint a shade or particular colour

strain stress

mock false, artificial
refinement good manners
skinny very thin
tumble mess
indignant angry and shocked

decent good enough
slut lazy, untidy woman who has many sexual partners

nursery *Kindergarten*

reproach criticism

sticky *klebrig*
to wink at to close one eye and open it again quickly, esp as a private signal, or to show sth is a joke

to cheek up to sb to behave in a nasty and rude manner towards sb, lacking in respect
to jerk to shake
lopsided having one side lower than the other
to clutter to fill with too many things
erroneous [ɪˈrəʊniəs] AmE [ɪˈroʊ-] based on wrong information
contraceptive *Verhütungsmittel*
to distress to worry

bleached made blonde by using chemicals

tubercular turn to fall ill with tuberculosis, a serious infectious lung disease

Henry sat on the edge of his sticky chair and answered, no, from Jamaica, while Raymond winked at him to cheer him. 'During the war there was a lot of boys like you from the States,' Elizabeth said, giving him a sideways look.
Henry held out his hand to the second youngest child, a girl 5 of seven, and said, 'Come talk to me.'
The child said nothing, only dipped into the box of sweets which Lou had brought.
'Come talk,' said Henry.
Elizabeth laughed. 'If she does talk you'll be sorry you 10 ever asked. She's got a tongue in her head, that one. You should hear her cheeking up to the teachers.' Elizabeth's bones jerked with laughter among her loose clothes. There was a lopsided double bed in the corner, and beside it a table cluttered with mugs, tins, a comb and brush, a number 15 of hair curlers, a framed photograph of the Sacret Heart, and also Raymond noticed what he thought erroneously to be a box of contraceptives. He decided to say nothing to Lou about this; he was quite sure she must have observed other things which he had not; possibly things of a more 20 distressing nature.
Lou's chatter on the way back to the hotel had a touch of hysteria. 'Raymond, dear,' she said in her most chirpy West End voice, 'I simply *had* to give the poor dear *all* my next week's housekeeping money. We shall have to starve, dar- 25 ling, when we get home, That's *simply* what we shall have to do.'
'OK,' said Raymond.
'I ask you,' Lou shrieked, 'what else could I do, what *could* I do?' 30
'Nothing at all,' said Raymond, 'but what you've done.'
'My own *sister*, my dear,' said Lou; 'and did you see the way she had her hair bleached? – All streaky, and she used to have a lovely head of hair.'
'I wonder if she tries to raise herself?' said Raymond, 'with 35 all those children she could surely get better accommodation if only she –'
'That sort,' said Henry, leaning forward from the back of the car, 'never moves. It's the slum mentality, man. Take some folks I've seen back home –' 40
'There's no comparison,' Lou snapped suddenly, 'this is quite a different case.'
Raymond glanced at her in surprise; Henry sat back, offended. Lou was thinking wildly, what a cheek *him* talking like a snob. At least Elizabeth's white. 45

Their prayers for the return of faith to Henry Pierce were so far answered in that he took a tubercular turn which was followed by a religious one. He was sent off to a sanatorium in Wales with a promise from Lou and Raymond to visit him before Christmas. Meantime, they applied themselves to Our Lady for the restoration of Henry's health.

5 Oxford St John, whose love affair with the red-haired girl had come to grief, now frequented their flat, but he could never quite replace Henry in their affections. Oxford was older and less refined than Henry. He would stand in front of the glass in their kitchen and tell himself: 'Man, you just

10 a big black bugger.' He kept referring to himself as black, which of course he was, Lou thought, but it was not the thing to say. He stood in the doorway with his arms and smile thrown wide: 'I am black but comely, O ye daughters of Jerusalem.' And once, when Raymond was out, Oxford

15 brought the conversation round to that question of being black *all over*, which made Lou very uncomfortable and she kept looking at the clock and dropped stitches in her knitting.

Three times a week when she went to the black Our Lady

20 with her rosary to ask for the health of Henry Pierce, she asked also that Oxford St John would get another job in another town, for she did not like to make objections, telling her feelings to Raymond; there were no objections to make that you could put your finger on. She could not very

25 well complain that Oxford was common; Raymond despised snobbery, and so did she, it was a very delicate question. She was amazed when, within three weeks, Oxford announced that he was thinking of looking for a job in Manchester.

30 Lou said to Raymond, 'Do you know, there's something *in* what they say about the bog-oak statue in the church.'
'There may be,' said Raymond. 'People say so.'
Lou could not tell him how she had petitioned the removal of Oxford St John. But when she got a letter from Henry

35 Pierce to say he was improving, she told Raymond, 'You see, we asked for Henry to get back the Faith, and so he did. Now we ask for his recovery and he's improving.'
'He's having good treatment at the sanatorium,' Raymond said. But he added, 'Of course we'll have to keep up the

40 prayers.' He himself, though not a rosary man, knelt before the Black Madonna every Saturday evening after Benediction to pray for Henry Pierce.

Whenever they saw Oxford he was talking of leaving Whitney Clay. Raymond said, 'He's making a big mistake going

45 to Manchester. A big place can be very lonely. I hope he'll change his mind.'
'He won't,' said Lou, so impressed was she now by the powers of the Black Madonna. She was good and tired of

to apply oneself to sth/sb to work at/for sth or study sth very hard
restoration recovery
to come to grief to have an unpleasant end
to frequent to visit a particular place often
glass mirror

comely attractive

to knit *stricken*

to despise to hate
delicate embarrassing

to petition to beg, to ask for

Oxford St John with his feet up on her cushions, and calling himself a nigger.

'We'll miss him,' said Raymond, 'he's such a cheery big soul.'

'We will,' said Lou. She was reading the parish magazine; 5 which she seldom did, although she was one of the voluntary workers who sent them out, addressing hundreds of wrappers every month. She had vaguely noticed, in previous numbers, various references to the Black Madonna, how she had granted this or that favour. Lou had heard that 10 people sometimes came from neighbouring parishes to pray at the Church of the Sacred Heart because of the statue. Some said they came from all over England, but whether this was to admire the art-work or to pray, Lou was not sure. She gave her attention to the article in the parish 15 magazine:

> While not wishing to make excessive claims ... many prayers answered and requests granted to the Faithful in an exceptional way ... two remarkable cures effected, but medical evidence is, of course, still in reserve, a certain 20 lapse of time being necessary to ascertain permanency of cure. The first of these cases was a child of twelve suffering from leukaemia ... The second ... While not desiring to create a *cultus* where none is due, we must remember it is always our duty to honour Our Blessed Lady, the dis- 25 penser of all graces, to whom we owe ...
> Another aspect of the information received by the Father Rector concerning our 'Black Madonna' is one pertaining to childless couples of which three cases have come to his notice. In each case the couple claim to have offered con- 30 stant devotion to the 'Black Madonna', and in two of the cases specific requests were made for the favour of a child. In *all* cases the prayers were answered. The proud parents ... It should be the loving duty of every parishioner to make a special thanksgiving ... The Father Rector 35 will be grateful for any further information ...

'Look, Raymond,' said Lou. 'Read this.'
They decided to put in for a baby to the Black Madonna.
The following Saturday, when they drove to the church for Benediction Lou jangled her rosary. Raymond pulled up 40 outside the church. 'Look here, Lou,' he said, 'do you want a baby in any case?' – for he partly thought she was only putting the Black Madonna to the test – 'Do you want a child, after all these years?'
This was a new thought to Lou. She considered her neat flat 45 and tidy routine, the entertaining with her good coffee cups,

parish *Kirchengemeinde*

to grant a favour to give sb sth that they have wished for

to grant to to give as a gift

evidence proof
in reserve expressed with a certain caution
lapse of time period of time
to ascertain to make sure
due deserved
dispenser of all graces *Gnadenspender*

to pertain to to be related to

devotion love

to put in for sth (esp BrE) to officially ask for sth
to jangle to rattle

the weekly papers and the library books, the tastes which they would not have been able to cultivate had they had a family of children. She thought of her nice young looks which everyone envied, and her freedom of movement.

5 'Perhaps we should try,' she said. 'God won't give us a child if we aren't meant to have one.'

'We have to make some decisions for ourselves,' he said. 'And to tell you the truth if *you* don't want a child, *I* don't.'

'There's no harm in praying for one,' she said.

10 'You have to be careful what you pray for,' he said. 'You mustn't tempt Providence.'

She thought of her relatives, and Raymond's, all married with children. She thought of her sister Elizabeth with her eight, and remembered that one who cheeked up to the

15 teachers, so pretty and sulky and shabby, and she remembered the fat baby Francis sucking his dummy and clutching Elizabeth's bony neck.

'I don't see why I shouldn't have a baby,' said Lou.

Oxford St John departed at the end of the month. He prom-

20 ised to write, but they were not surprised when weeks passed and they had no word. 'I don't suppose we shall ever hear from him again,' said Lou. Raymond thought he detected satisfaction in her voice, and would have thought she was getting snobbish as women do as they get older,

25 losing sight of their ideals, had she not gone on to speak of Henry Pierce. Henry had written to say he was nearly cured, but had been advised to return to the West Indies.

'We must go and see him,' said Lou. 'We promised. What about the Sunday after next?'

30 'OK,' said Raymond.

It was the Saturday before that Sunday when Lou had her first sick turn. She struggled out of bed to attend Benediction, but had to leave suddenly during the service and was sick behind the church in the presbytery yard. Raymond

35 took her home, though she protested against cutting out her rosary to the Black Madonna.

'After only six weeks!' she said, and she could hardly tell whether her sickness was due to excitement or nature. 'Only six weeks ago,' she said – and her voice had a touch of

40 its old Liverpool – 'did we go to that Black Madonna and the prayer's answered, see.'

Raymond looked at her in awe as he held the bowl for her sickness. 'Are you sure?' he said.

She was well enough next day to go to visit Henry in the

45 sanatorium. He was fatter and, she thought, a little coarser: and tough in his manner, as if once having been nearly disembodied he was not going to let it happen again. He was leaving the country very soon. He promised to come and

---

to tempt to attract sb or make sb want to do or have sth, even though they know it is wrong
temptation the desire to do or have sth that you know is bad or wrong

Providence *Vorsehung*
sulky offended, bad-tempered
dummy *Schnuller*
to clutch to hold sth tightly

sick turn a sudden fit of sickness, esp in pregnancy
Benediction Christian prayer of blessing

awe feeling of respect and slight fear

coarse rough, rude, vulgar
disembodied separated from the body

to skim through to read sth quickly in order to find a particular point or the main points

lest *damit nicht, aus Furcht, dass*

promotion a move to a more important job or rank in a company

cot small bed with high sides for a baby

cradle *Wiege*
to trim to decorate
frill *Rüsche*

to require to need

delivery process of giving birth to a baby

see them before he left. Lou barely skimmed through his next letter before handing it over to Raymond.

Their visitors, now, were ordinary white ones. 'Not so colourful,' Raymond said, 'as Henry and Oxford were.' Then he looked embarrassed lest he should seem to be making a 5 joke about the word coloured.

'Do you miss the niggers?' said Tina Farrell, and Lou forgot to correct her.

Lou gave up most of her church work in order to sew and knit for the baby. Raymond gave up the *Reader's Digest*. 10 He applied for promotion and got it; he became a departmental manager. The flat was now a waiting-room for next summer, after the baby was born, when they would put down the money for a house. They hoped for one of the new houses on a building site on the outskirts of the town. 15 'We shall need a garden,' Lou explained to her friends. 'I'll join the Mothers' Union,' she thought. Meantime the spare bedroom was turned into a nursery. Raymond made a cot, regardless that some of the neighbours complained of the hammering. Lou prepared a cradle, trimmed it with frills. She 20 wrote to her relatives; she wrote to Elizabeth, sent her five pounds, and gave notice that there would be no further weekly payments, seeing that they would now need every penny.

'She doesn't require it, anyway,' said Raymond. 'The Welfare State looks after people like Elizabeth.' And he told 25 Lou about the contraceptives he thought he had seen on the table by the double bed. Lou became very excited about this. 'How did you know they were contraceptives? What did they look like? Why didn't you tell me before? What a cheek, calling herself a Catholic, do you think she has a 30 man, then?'

Raymond was sorry he had mentioned the subject.

'Don't worry, dear, don't upset yourself, dear.'

'And she told me she goes to Mass every Sunday, and all the kids go excepting James. No wonder he's got into trouble 35 with an example like that. I might have known, with her peroxide hair. A pound a week I've been sending up to now, that's fifty-two pounds a year. I would never have done it, calling herself a Catholic with birth control by her bedside.'

'Don't upset yourself, dear.' 40

Lou prayed to the Black Madonna three times a week for a safe delivery and a healthy child. She gave her story to the Father Rector who announced it in the next parish magazine. 'Another case has come to light of the kindly favour of our 'Black Madonna' towards a childless couple ...' 45 Lou recited her rosary before the statue until it was difficult for her to kneel, and, when she stood, could not see her feet. The Mother of God with her black bog-oaken drapery, her high black cheekbones and square hands looked more virginal than ever to Lou as she stood counting her beads in front of her stomach.

She said to Raymond, 'If it's a girl we must have Mary as
5 one of the names. But not the first name, it's too ordinary.'

'Please yourself, dear,' said Raymond. The doctor had told him it might be a difficult birth.

'Thomas, if it's a boy,' she said, 'after my uncle. But if it's a girl I'd like something fancy for a first name.'

10 He thought, Lou's slipping, she didn't used to say that word, fancy.

'What about Dawn?' she said. 'I like the sound of Dawn. Then Mary for a second name. Dawn Mary Parker, it sounds sweet.'

15 'Dawn! That's not a Christian name,' he said. Then he told her, 'Just as you please, dear.'

'Or Thomas Parker,' she said.

She had decided to go into the maternity wing of the hospital like everyone else. But near the time she let Raymond
20 change her mind, since he kept saying, 'At your age, dear, it might be more difficult than for the younger women. Better book a private ward, we'll manage the expense.'

In fact, it was a very easy birth, a girl. Raymond was allowed in to see Lou in the late afternoon. She was half
25 asleep. 'The nurse will take you to see the baby in the nursery ward,' she told him. 'She's lovely, but terribly red.'

'They're always red at birth,' said Raymond.

He met the nurse in the corridor. 'Any chance of seeing the baby? My wife said …

30 She looked flustered. 'I'll get the Sister,' she said.

'Oh, I don't want to give any trouble, only my wife said –'

'That's all right. Wait here, Mr Parker.'

The Sister appeared, a tall grave woman. Raymond thought her to be short-sighted for she seemed to look at him fairly
35 closely before she bade him follow her.

The baby was round and very red, with dark curly hair.

'Fancy her having hair. I thought they were born bald,' said Raymond.

'They sometimes have hair at birth,' said the Sister.

40 'She's very red in colour.' Raymond began comparing his child with those in the other cots. 'Far more so than the others.'

'Oh, that will wear off.'

Next day he found Lou in a half-stupor. She had been
45 given a strong sedative following an attack of screaming hysteria. He sat by her bed, bewildered. Presently a nurse beckoned him from the door. 'Will you have a word with Matron?'

---

fancy extraordinary
to slip to slide, to fall down to a lower level

flustered nervous, confused

grave very serious

to bid, bade, bade to ask

to fancy to imagine
bald having (almost) no hair

stupor a state in which you are unable to think, hear, etc because of a shock
sedative a drug that makes sb go to sleep or makes them feel calm and relaxed
to beckon to give a signal with your finger or hand to call sb nearer

'Your wife is upset about her baby,' said the matron. 'You see, the colour. She's a beautiful baby, perfect. It's a question of the colour.'

'I noticed the baby was red,' said Raymond, 'but the nurse said –' 'Oh, the red will go. It changes, you know. But the 5 baby will certainly be brown, if not indeed black, as indeed we think she will be. A beautiful healthy child.'

'Black?' said Raymond.

'Yes, indeed we think so; indeed I must say, certainly so,' said the matron. 'We did not expect your wife to take it so 10 badly when we told her. We've had plenty of dark babies here, but most of the mothers expect it.'

'There must be a mix-up. You must have mixed up the babies,' said Raymond.

'There's no question of mix-up,' said the matron sharply. 15 'We'll soon settle that. We've had some of *that* before.'

'But neither of us are dark, 'said Raymond. 'You've seen my wife. You see me –'

'That's something you must work out for yourselves. I'd have a word with the doctor if I were you. But whatever 20 conclusion you come to, please don't upset your wife at this stage. She has already refused to feed the child, says it isn't hers, which is ridiculous.'

'Was it Oxford St John?' said Raymond.   25

'Raymond, the doctor told you not to come here upsetting me. I'm feeling terrible.'

'Was it Oxford St John?'

'Clear out of here, you swine, saying things like that.'

He demanded to be taken to see the baby, as he had done 30 every day for a week. The nurses were gathered round it, neglecting the squalling whites in the other cots for the sight of their darling black. She was indeed quite black, with a woolly crop and tiny negroid nostrils. She had been baptized that morning, though not in her parents' presence. 35 One of the nurses had stood as godmother.

The nurses dispersed in a flurry as Raymond approached. He looked hard at the baby. It looked back with its black button eyes. He saw the name-tab round its neck, 'Dawn Mary Parker.' He got hold of a nurse in the corridor. 'Look here, you just 40 take that name Parker off that child's neck. The name's not Parker, it isn't my child.'

The nurse said, 'Get away, we're busy.'

'There's just a *chance,*' said the doctor to Raymond, 'that if there's ever been black blood in your family or your wife's, 45 it's coming out now. It's a very long chance. I've never known it happen in my experience, but I've heard of cases, I could read them up.'

---

to settle sth to sort sth out

to squall to shriek

crop short hairstyle
nostrils openings at the end of the nose
to baptize *taufen*
godmother *Patin*
to disperse to hurry away in all directions
flurry excited hurry
name-tab *Namensband*

'There's nothing like that in my family,' said Raymond. He thought of Lou, the obscure Liverpool antecedents. The parents had died before he had met Lou.

'It could be several generations back,' said the doctor.

5 Raymond went home, avoiding the neighbours who would stop him to inquire after Lou. He rather regretted smashing up the cot in his first fury. That was something low coming out in him. But again, when he thought of the tiny black hands of the baby with their pink fingernails he did not re-
10 gret smashing the cot.

He was successful in tracing the whereabouts of Oxford St John. Even before he heard the result of Oxford's blood test he said to Lou, 'Write and ask your relations if there's been any black blood in the family.'

15 'Write and ask *yours,*' she said.

She refused to look at the black baby. The nurses fussed round it all day, and came to report its progress to Lou.

'Pull yourself together, Mrs Parker, she's a lovely child.'

'You must care for your infant,' said the priest.

20 'You don't know what I'm suffering,' Lou said.

'In the name of God,' said the priest, 'if you're a Catholic Christian you've got to expect to suffer.'

'I can't go against my nature,' said Lou. 'I can't be ex-pected to –'

25 Raymond said to her one day in the following week, 'The blood tests are all right, the doctor says,'

'What do you mean, all right?'

'Oxford's blood and the baby's don't tally, and –'

'Oh, shut up,' she said. 'The baby's black and your blood
30 tests can't make it white.'

'No,' he said. He had fallen out with his mother, through his inquiries whether there had been coloured blood in his family. 'The doctor says,' he said, 'that these black mix-tures sometimes occur in seaport towns. It might have been
35 generations back.'

'One thing,' said Lou. 'I'm not going to take that child back to the flat.'

'You'll have to,' he said.

Elizabeth wrote her a letter which Raymond intercepted:

40 *'Dear Lou Raymond is asking if we have any blacks in the family well that's funny you have a coloured God is not asleep. There was that Flinn cousin Tommy at Liverpool he was very dark they put it down to the past a nigro off a ship that would
45 be before our late Mothers Time God rest her soul she would turn in her grave you shoud have kept up your bit to me whats a pound a Week to you. It was*

---

obscure not well-known
antecedent forefather

to inquire to ask about

whereabouts (pl) the place where sb is

to fuss around to pay too much attention to

infant child

to tally to fit together

to intercept to stop sth/sb that is going from one place to another from arriving

on our fathers side the colour and Mary Flinn you remember at the dairy was dark remember her hare was like nigro hare it must be back in the olden days the nigro some ansester but it is only nature. I thank the almighty it has missed my kids and your hubby must think it was that nigro you was showing off when you came to my place. I wish you all the best as a widow with kids you should send my money as per usual your affec sister Elizabeth.'

dairy a place or a farm where milk products are stored and processed
hare here: wrong spelling of hair
ansester here: wrong spelling of ancestor
hubby (infml) husband

'I gather from Elizabeth,' said Raymond to Lou, 'that there was some element of colour in your family. Of course, you couldn't be expected to know about it. I do think, though, that some kind of record should be kept.'
'Oh, shut up,' said Lou. 'The baby's black and nothing can make it white.'

Two days before Lou left the hospital she had a visitor, although she had given instructions that no one except Raymond should be let in to see her. This lapse she attributed to the nasty curiosity of the nurses, for it was Henry Pierce come to say goodbye before embarkation. He stayed less than five minutes.

lapse mistake

'Why, Mrs Parker, your visitor didn't stay long,' said the nurse.
'No, I soon got rid of him. I thought I made it clear to you that I didn't want to see anyone. You shouldn't have let him in.'
'Oh, sorry, Mrs Parker, but the young gentleman looked so upset when we told him so. He said he was going abroad and it was his last chance, he might never see you again. He said, "How's the baby?", and we said, "Tip-top."'
'I know what's in your mind,' said Lou. 'But it isn't true. I've got the blood tests.'
'Oh, Mrs Parker, I wouldn't suggest for a minute …'

they niggers (non-standard) those niggers

'She must have went with one of they niggers that used to come.'
Lou could never be sure if that was what she heard from the doorways and landings as she climbed the stairs of Cripps House, the neighbours hushing their conversation as she approached.
'I can't take to the child. Try as I do, I simply can't even like it.'
'Nor me,' said Raymond. 'Mind you, if it was anyone else's child I would think it was all right. It's just the thought of it being mine, and people thinking it isn't.'
'That's just it,' she said.
One of Raymond's colleagues had asked him that day how his friends Oxford and Henry were getting on. Raymond had to look twice before he decided that the question was

landing *Treppenabsatz*
to hush to (suddenly) stop talking

innocent. But one never knew … Already Lou and Raymond had approached the adoption society. It was now only a matter of waiting for word.

'If that child was mine,' said Tina Farrell, 'I'd never part
5 with her. I wish we could afford to adopt another. She's the loveliest little darkie in the world.'

'You wouldn't think so,' said Lou, 'if she really was yours. Imagine it for yourself, waking up to find you've had a black baby that everyone thinks has a nigger for its father.'
10 'It *would* be a shock,' Tina said, and tittered.   **to titter** to laugh nervously

'We've got the blood tests,' said Lou quickly.

Raymond got a transfer to London. They got word about the adoption very soon.

'We've done the right thing,' said Lou. 'Even the priest had
15 to agree with that, considering how strongly we felt against keeping the child.'

'Oh, he said it was a good thing?'

'No, not a *good* thing. In fact he said it would have been a good thing if we could have kept the baby. But failing that,   **failing that** since that was not
20 we did the *right* thing. Apparently, there's a difference.'   possible

Qaisra Shahraz
A Pair of Jeans

Miriam slid off the bus seat and glanced quickly at her watch. They were coming! And she was very late. Murmuring her goodbye to her two university friends, she made her way to the door and waited for her bus stop to approach.
25 Once there she got off the bus and hurriedly waved goodbye to her friends again. She pulled the jacket close to her body, becoming suddenly very self-conscious about her jean-clad legs and the short vest she wore beneath it. It had, unfortunately, shrunk in the wash. All day she had kept
30 pulling it down to cover her midriff. Strange but she felt odd in her clothing. Yet they were just the type of clothes she needed to wear today; for hill walking in the peak dis-   **midriff** middle part of the body
trict, in the North West of England. Somehow here, in the   **peak** pointed top of a mountain
vicinity of her home, however, she felt different. As she
35 crossed the road and headed for her own street, she was   **vicinity** neighbourhood
very conscious of her appearance and hoped that she would not meet anyone she knew. She tugged at the hemline of her vest; it had ridden up yet again. With the other hand,   **hemline** ['hemlaɪn] *Saum*
she held onto the jacket front as it had no buttons.   **outing** short trip
40 Her mind turned to the outing. It had been a wonderful day, but her legs ached after climbing all those green hills – still

pace speed of walking
to anticipate to expect

semi-detached house *Doppelhaus*

to falter to become weaker

wits the ability to think quickly and clearly and to make a good decision

to scurry to run with quick short steps

to survey to examine

frail weak and thin
shalwar a pair of light loose trousers with a tight fit around the ankles
kameze (kameez) a long tunic
chadar a cloth used as a head covering by Muslim and Hindu women

poise *Haltung*

surreptitious secret and quick

skimpy small and tight-fitting

off guard not carefully prepared

stride one long step
in a daze in a confused state

mortification act of making sb feel very ashamed or embarrassed
to mortify (usually passive)

it was worth it. Her eye on her watch she hastened her pace. It was much later than she had anticipated. She remembered the phone call of yesterday evening. They said they were coming today. What if they had already arrived? She glanced down at her tightly jean-clad legs. As soon as she got home she must discreetly make her way to her room and quickly get changed. 5

Just as Miriam reached the gate of her semi-detached house, she heard a car pull up behind her. Nervously she swept round to see who it was. On spotting the colour of the car and the person behind the wheel her step faltered – colour ebbing from her face. On pretence of opening the gate she turned round and tried to collect her wits about her. Too late! They were already here. Her heart was now rocking madly against her chest and the clothes burned her. She wanted to quickly rush inside her home and peel them off. She clutched at her jacket front, covering her waist. 10 15

She braced her shoulders. She could not scurry inside. That was not the way things were done, no matter what the circumstances. Calmly, she let go of the gate and turned round to greet the two people who had by now stepped out of the car and were surveying her. She didn't realise that she had let go of her jacket too. It fell wide open, revealing the short vest underneath. Their eyes fell straight to the inch of her waist flesh. The woman was her future mother-in-law, a slightly frail woman dressed in shalwar and kameze with a chadar around her shoulders. The elderly man, behind the wheel earlier, was the woman's husband. He seemed to tower behind his wife. 20 25

Miriam found herself unable to look either of them in the eye. A watery, hesitant smile played around her mouth. She did not know what to do, or how to act. Her cheeks burnt in embarrassment; poise now very much lost. And yet these were the very people she wanted to impress. All she was aware of was the surreptitious glances they darted at her. In fact not at her as Miriam, but at the figure, the appearance she presented clad in a pair of Levis and a skimpy leather jacket to top it up. This was not the Miriam they knew, but a stranger; a western version of Miriam. She immediately sensed their awkwardness. They too were caught off guard and did not know what to do with themselves – in particular with their eyes. The father-in-law was bent on avoiding eye contact with her, by studiously looking above her head. He pushed the gate open and in two strides had crossed the driveway and was now solidly knocking on the front door. 30 35 40

Miriam stepped aside to let the woman pass, silently walking behind her husband. Miriam followed them in a semi daze. As she closed the gate behind her she remembered with mortification that while the woman had accepted her 45

mumbled greeting, by her reply 'Wa laikum Assalam', the father-in-law had ignored it. That was not like him at all. Miriam's mother, Fatima, opened the door to her expected guests, beaming in pleasure and warmth as she beheld them.
5 She had not expected Miriam to come with them, however. When she saw her daughter hovering behind the two guests, Fatima received a shock. Never before in her life had Miriam glimpsed such a dramatic change in her mother's face. Normally she wouldn't have batted an eyelid if her daughter
10 had turned up at her door at 11 o'clock at night, as long as she knew where she was and with whom and at what time she was returning home. Today, however, she was viewing her daughter's arrival and appearance through a different set of lenses. In fact, through the lenses of Miriam's future in-
15 laws – the view just didn't look very good.
In one glance she took in her daughter's appearance. The jeans which wouldn't have normally aroused her interest, today stood out brazenly on Miriam's body, tightly moulded against her full legs. Fatima couldn't quite make herself
20 understand why she felt ashamed of her daughter's clothing and why she was suddenly angry with her, for being seen like this. Her eyes gaped at Miriam's midriff showing through. Heat was now rushing through Fatima's cheeks. An inch of her daughter's flesh was visible! Her mind reel-
25 ing and the urge to usher her out of sight strong, Fatima communicated her displeasure and desperately signalled with her eyebrows, to her daughter to go up and change into something more respectable. Miriam understood and was only too glad to oblige.
30 Squeezing past her mother and out of sight of their guests who had now entered their living room, Miriam almost ran up the stairs to her bedroom. Once there, she shut the door behind her and breathed out deeply. Her earlier feeling of tiredness and exhilaration from the hill walking had van-
35 ished – instead discontent had taken its place. Two mere steps into her home had led to another world. The other she had left behind with her friends on the bus. She shrugged the feeling aside. What mattered now were the two people downstairs. And they mattered! Her future lay
40 with them.
Going further into the room she peeled off her jacket, vest and tight pair of jeans, and let them fall, lying in a clutter on the woollen carpet. She looked down at them with dis-taste. Her mouth twisted into a cynical line. "Damn it!"
45 Her mind shouted – rebelling. "They are only clothes. I am still the same young woman they visited regularly – the person that they have happily chosen as a bride for their son in their household."

to behold, beheld, beheld (old use or literary) to look at or see sb/sth
to hover to stay close to sth

to glimpse to see
not to bat an eyelid to show no surprise or embarrassment when sth unusual happens

brazen open and without shame, esp about sth that people find shocking
moulded against fitting

to gape to stare at sb/sth with an open mouth because of a surprise or a shock
to reel to seem to be spinning around and around
urge strong wish
to usher to take sb where they should go

to oblige to obey

exhilaration excitement, hap-piness
to vanish to disappear
discontent dissatisfaction

contrivance a clever plan or trick
to contrive to manage to do sth in spite of difficulties

maroon dark reddish-brown
sari traditional long Indian dress

composure the state of being calm and in control of your feelings or behaviour
sway influence

docile quiet and easy to control

hoyden girl who behaves in a wild and noisy manner

hanger *Kleiderbügel*
to rear to raise

to swathe in to wrap or cover in

draped covered with long loosely hanging clothes

to scuttle to scurry

hypocrisy *Heuchelei*
to gall to make sb feel upset and angry
demure composed and reserved, not attracting attention
to traipse to walk somewhere slowly when you are tired and unwilling
wellingtons rubber-boots

"Deny it as much as you like, Miriam", her heart whispered back. "It's no use. They have seen another side of you – your other persona."

The other 'persona' had apparently, by either sheer accident or mere contrivance, remained hidden from them from ₅ the very beginning. When they first saw her at a party, she was dressed in a maroon chiffon sari and later on each occasion she was always smartly but discreetly and respectably dressed in a traditional shalwar kameze suit. Never at any time had they glimpsed a tightly jean-clad ₁₀ Miriam with an inch of midriff showing! In fact, judging by her mother's expression and lack of composure, it must have been a nasty shock! For now, they were seeing her as a young college woman who was very much under the sway of western fashion and by extension its moral values. ₁₅ Muslim girls do not go outdoors dressed like that, especially in the short jacket, which hardly covered her hips and a skimpy vest. She had heard of stories about in-laws who were prejudiced against such girls. For they weren't the docile, the obedient and sweet daughter-in-laws that they ₂₀ preferred. On the contrary, they were seen as a threat and portrayed as rebellious *hoydens,* who did not respect either their husbands or their in-laws. Miriam was all too familiar with such stereotyped views of women.

From her wardrobe she pulled off a blue crepe shalwar ₂₅ kameze suit from a hanger. As she put it on, her rebellious spirit reared its head again. 'They are only clothes!' her mind hissed in anger.

She could not deny the fact, however, that having them on her back she had embraced a new set of values. In fact a ₃₀ new personality. Her body was now modestly swathed in an elegant long tunic and baggy trousers. The curvy contours of her female body were discreetly draped. With a quick glance in the mirror she left her room. It was a confident woman gliding down the stairs. She was now in full control ₃₅ of herself. There was to be no scuttling down the stairs, her poise was back. Her long dupatta scarf was draped around her shoulders and one edge of it was over her head.

Once downstairs in the hallway, outside the sitting room door, she halted, her hypocrisy galling her. She was neatly ₄₀ acting out a role, the one that her future in-laws preferred. A role of a demure and elegant bride and daughter-in-law – dressed modestly, with her body properly covered. Yet she was the same person who had earlier traipsed the Pennine countryside in a tight pair of jeans and wellingtons and who ₄₅ was now dressed in the height of Pakistani fashion. The difference lay in what her in-laws regarded and termed as an acceptable mode of dress. Or was she the same person? She

didn't know. Perhaps it was true that there were two sides to her character. A person who spontaneously switched from one setting to another, from one mode of dress into another – in short swapping one identity for another. Now, dressed
5 as she was, she was part and parcel of another identity, of another world, that of a Muslim Asian environment. Ensconced now in the other home ground, her thoughts, actions and feelings had seamlessly altered accordingly.

Her head held high, Miriam entered the living room. Once
10 inside, she felt four pairs of eyes turn in her direction. She stared ahead knowing instinctively that apart from her father's, those eyes were busy comparing her present demure appearance with her earlier one. It was amazing how she was able to move around the room at ease, in her shal-
15 war kameze suit, in a manner that she could never have done in her earlier clothes amongst these people. She sat down beside her mother, acutely aware of her mother-in-law's eyes; discreetly appraising both her appearance and her movements.
20 After a while, the conversation flagged. Fatima was doing her very best at entertaining and trying to revive a number of topics of interest to the other couple. The two guests, however, seemed to shy away. In particular from the one concerning their children's marriage in six month's time.
25 Miriam sat up, noticing that they were ill at ease and had made no direct eye contact with her. This was so unlike their usual behaviour. There were moments too, when husband and wife had exchanged surreptitious glances. Fatima was now quite anxious. From the moment her guests had
30 stepped into their home her instinct told her that something was wrong. She was ready to discuss the subject with them. But first she requested her daughter to bring in some refreshments. The dinner had already been prepared and laid out on the dining table in the kitchen.
35 Miriam was only too happy to leave the room; behind her a hushed silence reigned. She pottered around the kitchen, collecting bits and pieces of crockery from the cupboards. Her own hunger had vanished. The appearance of those two people had done a miraculous thing to her metabolic
40 system. She was arranging the plates and glasses on the tray when she heard their voices in the hallway. They sounded as if they were saying goodbye to her parents in the hallway. Miriam was surprised. Miriam hastened and picked up the tray. Were they going already? They hadn't
45 eaten anything! The table was laid for dinner. She called "Auntie" addressing her future mother-in-law. She turned and smiled. They were in a hurry to get home, because they had guests staying in their home, she informed.

---

part and parcel an important element

ensconced safe and relaxed

seamless smooth

to alter to change

to appraise to evaluate

to flag to become weak

to be ill at ease to feel uncomfortable, nervous and embarrassed

hushed unusually quiet, depressed

to potter around (in) the kitchen (fam) *in der Küche werkeln*

crockery *Geschirr*

metabolic system *Stoffwechsel*

to dwell on sth to think a lot about sth

fairly to some extent but not totally

to revise (BrE) to prepare for an exam by looking again at work that you have done

autocratic expecting obedience

newscaster newsreader

blur a shape that cannot be seen clearly
gaze a long steady look at sb/sth

implication sth that is suggested or indirectly stated
to imply; to be implied

reckoning a time when sb's actions will be judged to be right or wrong and they may be punished
to prevaricate *ausweichen*
to peep at to look quickly and secretly at sb/sth

'That is a lousy excuse', Miriam thought. If they had guests at home, why did they bother to come in the first place, anyway? Still dwelling on the subject she returned to the kitchen and put the tray back on the table; what a waste of time! The two parents-in-law walked to their car in silence – both ₅ were lost in their own thoughts. The silence continued during their journey. There was no need for communication. Somehow they could guess what the other was thinking about and read each other's thoughts fairly accurately. On reaching home, the so-called guests to whom Begum re- ₁₀ ferred to earlier, had apparently gone. Their elder son, Farook was not yet in. The younger was upstairs, studying for his 'GCSE' examinations. They could hear the music from the CD disc blaring away. He loved listening to songs as he revised. ₁₅
Ayub shed his jacket and hung it in the hallway and went straight to the living room. Begum followed behind, also taking off her coat and outdoor shawl. Switching on the television, Ayub sat down in his armchair. Begum hovered listlessly near his armchair for a minute, looking down at ₂₀ her husband – waiting. Then mechanically folding her woollen shawl into its customary neat folds, she left the room and went upstairs to her bedroom to place it in her drawer. For a few moments she stood lost in her thoughts, looking out of the bedroom window. Mrs Williams had an- ₂₅ other car. This was the third in six months. What did she do with them? Then she heard her husband call her name, his voice supremely autocratic.
Mrs Williams and her love of cars put aside, Begum returned to the living room and sat down on the sofa opposite her hus- ₃₀ band, waiting for him to begin. Her heartbeat had automatically quickened. The seconds were ticking away into minutes, and her husband, however, still had made no move to say anything, his gaze on the newscaster. Instead she picked up the Urdu national newspaper 'Daily Jang' from the coffee ₃₅ table, and began to read it. More precisely she was pretending to read it, the words were a blur in front of her eyes.
Ayub, at last, stood up, stretching out his legs. Striding across the room, he switched off the television. Returning to his chair, his pointed gaze now fell on his wife. ₄₀
"Well", he began softly.
It was now her turn to play; she pretended not to hear him or understand the implication of his exclamation "well". Now that the moment of reckoning had come, she absurdly wanted to prevaricate – to put the discussion off. ₄₅
"Well, what?" she responded coldly, buying time, peeping at her unsmiling husband over the edge of the newspaper.

"You know very well what I mean! Don't pretend to misunderstand me, Begum." He rasped under his breath, not at all amused by her manner, tone or her words.

5 Begum calmly examined the harsh outlines of her husband's unsmiling face. She was lost. She did not know what to say, or how to say it, although she knew the subject he was referring to. Thus her lips would not open, she simply stared at him.

"Well, what do you think of your future daughter-in-law? I
10 thought you told me that she was a very "sharif", a very modest girl. Was that naked waist what you would call modest?" He lanced at her.

"I am sure she is." Begum defensively volunteered, feeling hedged. After all she was the one who had originally taken
15 a liking to Miriam.

"Huh!" Ayub grunted. "Sharif! dressed like that! God knows who has seen her. Would you like any of your friends and relatives to have seen her as she appeared today, would you Begum?" The voice was cutting.

20 "But she's a college student – college students do dress like that. Haven't you yourself joked about tatty jean-clad university students?" Begum boldly persisted.

She wanted to excuse Miriam's mode of dress to herself and to him, she knew she was not going to make a success
25 of it because, secretly in her own heart, she very much agreed with her husband.

"Tell me, in those clothes of hers, would you be proud to have her as your daughter-in-law? I know I am not. You talk about her being a university student. Well, have
30 you any idea what sort of company she might be keeping with that lot. You've only seen her at odd times, and always at home. Do you know what she is really like? Have you thought of the effect she could have in your household? With their lifestyle, such girls also want a
35 lot of freedom. In fact, they want to lead their lives the way their English college friends do. Did you notice what time she came in? She knew we were coming, yet that had not made any difference to her lifestyle. Do you expect her to change overnight in order to suit us. People
40 form habits, Begum, do you understand? Are you prepared for a daughter-in-law who goes in and out of the house whenever she feels like it, dressed like that and returns home as late as that? Don't your cheeks burn at the thought of that bit of flesh you saw? Imagine how our
45 son will feel about her! I hope shame! And what if she has a boyfriend already – have you thought of that? What if she has a boyfriend already? What if she takes drugs? What if … What if … So many questions to ask our-

to lance at *scharf entgegnen*
to volunteer to reply
to feel hedged to feel driven into a corner

tatty (infml, esp BrE) shabby
bold brave and confident

selves! Do you know, we do not know this girl at all, Begum! Can you guarantee that she will make our son happy?"

He strategically paused, waiting for her to say something. Begum, bemused, had nothing to add. The talking had be- 5 come his arena not hers. He continued.

"You know of a number of cases where the educated, the so-called *modern* girls have twined their husbands around their little fingers, and expected them to dance to their tunes. Are you prepared for that to happen to your beloved 10 son? To lose him to such a daughter-in-law? Have you the heart for that?"

Begum just stared, listening quietly to her husband's angry lecture. Deep down, however, in her own heart she agreed with much of what he had said. Rattled by his tone and his 15 words, she, however, was reluctant to voice her agreement. She hadn't quite anticipated the direction towards which the conversation was heading. After 25 years of marriage, she could read him like a book – his words, their nuance, the tilt of his eyebrow, the authorative swing of his hand, 20 the thin line of his mouth spelled only one message.

She had already jumped ahead. With a sinking heart she had guessed correctly the conclusion, the outcome of this discussion. She did not know how to react in front of him, nor did she disagree with him over anything he said. Not one jot. 25 Her own thoughts had run in a similar direction. When she saw Miriam standing near the garden gate with her jacket open similar thoughts had whizzed through her mind too, although she would not have voiced them in such a harsh way. Her perception of what her daughter-in-law should be 30 like did not quite tally with the picture that Miriam presented to them or to the clear picture that Ayub's words had conjured up. Why did that stupid girl have to wear those jeans and that vest today of all days? She angrily groaned inside her head. And why did Ayub have to see her like that? 35

She had always reckoned on a conventional sort of daughter-in-law – the epitome of tradition. Definitely not one who was so strongly influenced by western form of dress, culture and probably feminist ideas as Miriam. The mad girl had no qualms about blatantly showing a part of her 40 body in a public place, Begum shuddered.

What about Farook, their son? How would they deal with him? Luckily, it was not Farook who had initially befriended Miriam, but she herself. A glimpse of Miriam at a Mehndi party (hen party), had tugged at Begum's heart. 45 From the first moment she had fitted the epitome of what her future daughter-in-law should be like – young, beautiful and well educated. She had just obtained three 'A' levels,

---

rattled worried
reluctant unwillig

tilt *Neigung*

not one jot used to mean 'not even a small amount'

to tally with to match up
to conjure up to bring to mind
today of all days *ausgerechnet heute*

epitome of sth a perfect example of sth

qualm [kwaːm] doubt
blatant impudent, without any attempt to hide

at high grades from school, and was now doing a geography course at the university.

Begum had liked the way Miriam had behaved – ever so correctly and gracefully. Above all, she had liked the way
5 she dressed herself. How ironic that assumption was after today's event. It was the way the black chiffon sari had hugged her slender figure, and how her hair was elegantly wound up in a knot at the top of her head – just perfect. She was neither over-dressed nor over-decked in jewels nor
10 over made-up as some of her peers were wont to be. Nor for that matter was she over-boisterous or making a spectacle of herself as some of her friends did. In short, she had viewed her as the epitome of perfection, everything that was correct and appealing. She definitely had stood out
15 from amongst the other girls. Looking back now, two years later, Begum was sure that, not her son, but she herself had fallen in love with Miriam at first sight, and not just that. Her name 'Miriam' wove a magic spell around her. It had a special ring to it and she had loved using it.
20 And there was more – Begum had taken a real liking to Miriam's parents too, especially her mother. And, liking one's child's in-laws, particularly the mother was an important part of the equation. She knew of cases where the two mother-in-laws hated each other's guts and never quite got
25 on with each other. Begum and Miriam's mother Fatima met for the first time at the Mehndi party. After that they became warm friends and were seen to be in and out of each other's homes. With the subject of their growing children's futures looming in their domestic horizons, the two
30 mothers had, as a matter of course, discussed and dwelled at length on the subject of their children's marriage prospects. Farook and Miriam had also met each other soon afterwards. Often, accompanied by their parents they too, took a liking to each other. They found they were very compatible
35 in their interests and personalities and had a lot to laugh about – often giggling together. When their parents suggested the idea of marriage – both heartily agreed. Farook just couldn't help grinning all over. Miriam was struck with sudden shyness, her cheeks burning. Soon afterwards an
40 engagement party was held for the two. In order to let them complete their respective courses, the wedding was to be postponed for a year or so.

That was a year ago. Today Farook's parents went to meet Miriam's, in order to discuss the arrangements for the
45 forthcoming wedding in six months time. They were to decide on the date and discuss possible venues for the two receptions. Instead they had returned home, without even mentioning the word wedding. Yet their thoughts were very

---

assumption belief

peer a person who is the same age or has the same social status as you
to be wont to to be used to
boisterous noisy and full of energy
appealing attractive

equation mathematical calculation
to hate sb's guts to strongly dislike sb

to loom to appear important or threatening and likely to happen soon

to be compatible to fit together

engagement *Verlobung*

to postpone to put off

venue location, place

to prompt to urge

to rasp to say sth in an unpleasant and harsh voice

to utter *äußern*

to clutch to hold on tight to

tentative hesitant

to resign yourself to sth to accept sth unpleasant that cannot be changed or avoided

modesty chasteness

to dread to be worried about sth unpleasant
traitor a person who betrays their friends, their country, etc

to dash to hurry

much centred on that subject. However, more importantly on Miriam herself – her clothes and her body!

"Well," Ayub's cold prompting brought his wife to the present.

Begum turned to look at her husband once more and calm- 5
ly waited for him to finish what he was going to say. There was a speculative gleam in his eyes.

"What are you going to do?" he rasped.

This time she could not pretend to misunderstand him.

She faced him squarely – poised for a battle. Yet as she was 10
about to utter the words her heart sank. For she saw her Miriam fast disappearing from the horizon. But then as she tried to clutch onto her image in her mind, there arose that one of her in that silly pair of faded jeans, and that ridiculously short vest. Her heart sank. It had to be. It was better 15
to face the matter now than regret it later. The problem was, how she, Begum, was going to deal with it. She did not have the heart nor the courage to play the role demanded of her, or the one that she inevitably had to play in this drama. Knowing her husband, she knew for sure, that he 20
would leave it to her – to sort out the situation with the two parties; her son and Miriam and her family.

Once again she looked her husband directly in the eye.

"You truly don't want the wedding to take place then?" she tentatively asked, still desperate to hold onto Miriam.   25
Begum's gaze fell. His eyes crushed.

"I thought I had already made myself obvious! What do you think?" He was enraged and he let her know it.

"I suppose I agree with what you say, but how are we going to go about it?" Begum stammered, the boldness gone, now 30
very much resigned to both her and Miriam's fates.

"I leave that entirely to you – especially as you were the one so hot on the girl. I am sure we can find lots of other women for our son, women who have a more discreet taste in clothing and a good understanding of female modesty. 35
Similarly, I am sure, her parents will find a man more suited to her lifestyle than our son, a man who has the capacity to tolerate her particular mode of dressing, for the want of a better word."

They heard the front door open. That must be their son Fa- 40
rook. They stopped talking and stared at each other. Begum's heart was thumping away, dreading talking to him about Miriam. She felt like a traitor. Quickly getting up she went into the kitchen to get his dinner. She hoped he would go straight to his room first. Ayub picked up the newspaper 45
and began to read it.

Miriam had just got in from university, when she heard the phone ringing. She dashed down from her room to answer it. She faltered – it was Aunt Begum. She quickly obliged Begum in her request to speak to her mother and called her mother. Leaving the phone she went into the living room and sat down to watch television.

5 Fatima left the meal she was preparing and went to speak to Begum. They talked for nearly five minutes. There were several moments of awkward pauses on either side of the telephone receivers. By the time the conversation ended a pinched look had settled around Fatima's mouth.

10 Begum had nervously said her 'Salam'. Fatima had quite literally forgotten to return the greeting at the end, but silently put the receiver down. Her eyes stared at the wall.

At the other end, with her head bent over her legs, Begum thanked Allah that it was over and done with. She sank 15 down against the banister of the stairs. She felt bad, oh God, terribly bad. She had hated herself every minute of that conversation and the role she had been forced to play. Putting herself in Fatima's position, she realised how painful it must be for her. How would she feel if she had 20 found out that her daughter was to be jilted at the last minute?

Mechanically, as if in a daze, and with her hand held against her temple, Fatima, for her part, went into the living room. Going to the sofa, she sat down and pushed the 25 cushion aside absent-mindedly and stared in front of her, at the fireplace.

Miriam did not notice anything unusual about her mother until she realised that her mother had not said a word since she entered the room. "What did Aunt Begum say?" she 30 asked quietly – her heart's rhythm had altered for some reason.

"I – I," Fatima stalled as she sought to answer her daughter's question. She was not yet ready to divulge what she had learnt. She was still reeling from the shock herself. 35 What would it do to her daughter? She turned her face away from her daughter.

"What is it, mother?" Miriam's heart had now gained a steady sharp beat. Dread entered. "What did Aunt Begum say?" she asked again.

40 Unable to control herself any longer Fatima bitterly burst out with, "She said that your engagement had to be broken off!" Miriam paled. Her heart had now sunk to the pit of her stomach. "Why, mother?" she said quietly. She was amazed at how clearly her mind was functioning, although a buzz-45 ing sound seemed to hammer in her head.

"She said that they came yesterday to inform us, but found it impossible to get around to doing so. Begum says that her sister insists that her daughter was betrothed to Farook.

pinched pale and thin, esp because of illness, cold or worry

banister *Geländer*

to jilt [dʒɪlt] (often passive) to end a romantic relationship with sb in a sudden and unkind way

temple *Schläfe*

to stall to try to avoid answering a question so that you have more time
to divulge to reveal a secret

dread fear

betrothed *verlobt*

well-matched well-suited to each other

to purchase ['pɜːtʃəs] to buy

premonition a feeling that sth (bad) is going to happen

to be bound to certain or likely to happen

to rummage to move things around carelessly

repugnant making you feel strong dislike or disgust

to mesmerize to fascinate

vicious brutal

nonchalantly here: innocently

blissful extremely happy

havoc disorder

That they were well-matched together. She says she is very sorry and apologises, but apparently her sister comes first."
"Liars! What a lousy excuse!" Miriam's mind screamed, but she uttered not a word – instead left the room.
She ran upstairs to her bedroom, and closed the door be- 5
hind her. Standing in the middle, she drew in a deep breath. Where did this sister come from? Why was it she was never heard of before.
"Not to marry Farook?" Miriam voiced loudly. Why, only yesterday she was planning how they were going to lead 10
their lives together. In fact deciding on which area they were going to purchase their house from, after they got married and had jobs.
Her mouth twisted into a cynical line. In her heart she knew. From that first moment she saw them that night in 15
her jeans and short vest, she had a dreadful premonition. She had known, although she had denied it emphatically to herself, that something was wrong or bound to go wrong. Their faces, their body language had told the whole story.
The buzzing sound was still hammering in her head. Going 20
to her wardrobe she pulled it open and looked inside. Her eyes sought wildly and her hands rummaged through the clothes and the hangers, until she found what she was seeking.
She pulled off from the hanger the repugnant looking art- 25
icle and threw it on the floor, as if it burned her to hold it. She stared at it as if mesmerised by it. Then with her foot she gave it a vicious kick. Her mouth resumed its cynical twist. Her friends would never believe her if she told them.
The shabby-looking and much worn pair of jeans lay non- 30
chalantly near the end of the bed, blissfully unaware of the havoc it had created in the life of its wearer.

New Ending to "A Pair of Jeans"

to scrutinise (AmE -ize) to examine closely

tell-tale *verräterisch*

turmoil confusion

haggard tired

ordeal torture

to jolt to jump

to vie with sb for sth to compete strongly with sb in order to obtain or achieve sth

She stepped over the pair of jeans and looked at herself in the long mirror on the wall. Eyes widening, she scrutinised her face and body for any tell-tale signs of her inner tur- 35
moil. Her face looked haggard. The mouth, which was normally full-lipped, was now a thin, sharp, pinkish line. There was a certain stiffness about her, the way her shoulders sloped down; as if carrying her body was an immense ordeal.
40
Angrily she swept away from the mirror and went to the window to look down at the lawn and flower beds in the rear garden. Ideas and thoughts jolted and formed in her head, each vying with the other for attention. One idea,

however, lodged itself firmly in her mind: Farook and his
parents weren't going to get away with it!

"They can't do this to me!", her mind screamed. She didn't
know whether Farook knew about this matter, but she was
5 going to make sure that he definitely did and there was only one way of finding out if he didn't! She noticed below
that the flowers were in full bloom. The colour of those
roses reminded her of the bridal bouquet she was planning
for herself. All of a sudden her body relaxed and she felt a
10 certain calmness descend over her as she closed her bedroom door behind her.

There was no rushing. She simply glided down the stairs
and began to dial Farook's phone number on her mobile by
the time she reached the hallway. As the phone bell pipped
15 away at the other end, her heart skipped a beat for a frac-
tion of a second. What if his mother or father picked up the
phone? What would she say to them? She was about to
snap her mobile shut when rebellion surfaced again.
She shook her fears aside. So what if they answered the
20 phone! She would deal with them and the situation as it
arose. To her dismay, nobody answered the phone at the
other end. She tried again, defiantly letting it ring for two
minutes – somebody was going to answer it one way or
another.

25 Her mother came out of the kitchen and saw Miriam with
her mobile phone held fast to her ear. Miriam heard her
mother's approach, turned and caught her eye. Fatima shot
her a questioning glance. Who was she ringing? A worried
look entering her face.

30 At last somebody picked up the receiver. The ringing
stopped and the word "hello" was audible to Miriam's ear.
Relief shot through her. It was her Farook. She greeted him
first with "hello" and then with the Arabic "Assalam-a-
Alaikum", "Peace be upon you!". She then reverted to
35 speaking in English.

"Farook, it's Miriam." She tried to control the rhythm of
her heartbeat and keep her voice steady.

"How are you, Miriam?"

"I am fine …" She was staring at her mother. Fatima was
40 desperately signalling her to end the call.

Miriam ignored her mother's shaking hand and turned to
look instead at the picture of a landscape on the wall opposite, concentrating on what she was saying.

"Are you alone at home, Farook, or are your parents with
45 you? If they are there, I want us to meet in the Student Union." Tone brusque.

"Usman is with me. Mum and dad have gone out. They'll
be back soon though; did you want to speak to them?"

---

to get away with sth to do sth
bad and not be punished

to surface to come up

dismay shock
defiant [dɪˈfaɪənt]
openly refusing to obey sb/sth
sometimes in an aggressive way

to revert to to return to

intrigued very interested in sth/sb and wanting to know more about it/them

to break sth to sb to give news or information to sb

riddle puzzle

to fret about to be worried about

mutinous [ˈmjuːtənəs] rebellious

to bruise to affect sb badly (a bruise: *Bluterguss*)

to ejaculate to exclaim
to sting, stung, stung *stechen*

blunder a stupid or careless mistake
to placate to calm and comfort

seemly appropriate for a social situation

fiancé *Verlobter*

to flush to become red in the face
irritated angry

"No, it's you … I wanted to speak to you, Farook." She paused for a few seconds, her heart thudding again, and then continued, still in control.

"Have you heard anything about us, Farook?"

"Us? No. What do you mean Miriam?" He was now quite ₅ intrigued.

"Just as I thought." Her voice hardened. A bitter laughing in her head. "It's probably too soon for them to break it to you. They are probably deciding what to do and how to put it to you." ₁₀

"Miriam, you've got me all puzzled now. Come on girl, what is going on?" He nervously laughed.

"I am sorry Farook – just talking to myself. I know it's all in riddles to you, isn't it? Look, I can't say much more over the phone, but can I come and see you at home, and then ₁₅ we can talk together with your parents?"

"Of course you can, Miriam, but really, you've now got me all worried, I must say."

"It's nothing to fret about. I'll tell you in a short while. Hudah Hafiz." Her voice and thoughts were calm again. ₂₀

Miriam switched off her phone and faced her mother. Fatima noted the distinct mutinous line of her daughter's mouth. She struggled to say the right thing but did not want to bruise her daughter's ego further. She had a duty, however, to advise her as a mother, but the right words ₂₅ just failed to spring to her aid. Finally, she softly offered: "Miriam, that wasn't the right thing to do or say."

"The right thing to do?" Miriam ejaculated – stung. "Do you think Farook's parents have done the right thing by me?" She hissed, her betrayed eyes darting an angry beam ₃₀ of light at her mother.

Fatima realised her blunder. It was a mighty wrong thing to say under the circumstances. Of course her daughter had the right to feel as she did. So Fatima attempted to placate her with her next words. ₃₅

"I am sorry, Miriam, I didn't mean that. It's just that I thought that instead of you contacting Farook, it should be us, your parents, doing it in the first place – that is the seemly thing to do."

"Oh mother! There you go on again about 'seemly' things. ₄₀ There is nothing 'unseemly' about me contacting my own fiancé." She laid extra stress on the word "own". "After all, I am engaged to him, am I not? Or have you forgotten that too?" Angry heat was rushing out of her cheeks.

"No I haven't forgotten! There is no need for your sar- ₄₅ casm." Fatima snapped back also now quite flushed, beginning to get irritated with her daughter and the situation in which she presently found herself.

"I just mean that your father and I should go firstly to visit Farook and his parents to discuss the matter. Do you think that we don't care about you – about how they have jilted you, and on what grounds? After all, it's a matter of our
5 *Izzat*, our honour, the way we are being treated so shabbily – that our daughter is dropped like a sack of potatoes. I was under a great deal of shock when I listened to Begum earlier today on the phone, but now the shock has worn off, and like you I am very, very angry." She passionately end-
10 ed, hoping to clarify her own feelings and position to her daughter.

Miriam shrugged. "You can sort that out with father, Farook and his parents, but I am going to see Farook personally and right now, mother!" A defiant tilt arched her eye-
15 brows above her flashing eyes. Hoping that her mother had understood the message Miriam swept round and went upstairs to her bedroom.

Fatima stared after her daughter helplessly – she was in a real dilemma. She wanted to tell and advise Miriam that
20 she shouldn't meet Farook, until they themselves had met his parents. At the same time she felt deeply for her daughter and wanted to support her in any way that she could. Never before had she felt the gulf between Miriam's generation and her own so keenly. The generation and culture
25 gap lay between them as wide as the ocean. She never did this sort of thing in her youth. Unthinkable! No matter what happened, the parents saw to everything. It was they who resolved problems; children did not take things into their own hands.

30 Pakistan was so far from Britain, it was another place and she was thinking of another time. As her daughter had said it wasn't a matter of what was the right thing to do conventionwise, but it was time for positive action. If Miriam thought she had a right to consult Farook about this matter, then she
35 had every right to do so, and she, as her mother, would support her! Times had indeed changed. They lived and were brought up in different worlds, traditions and cultures. Above all the world was quickly changing around them.

Returning to the lounge, she stood listlessly in the middle.
40 It was a pity that her husband was not in. He would have seen to everything. What would have happened if, instead of her, her husband had picked up the phone? She wondered wryly would Begum have said the same to her husband what she had said to herself? Probably not, she
45 thought cynically.

Inside, her blood raged, feeling so terribly bitter. What had their daughter done, to deserve to be treated in such a fashion? It was a great insult for all of them.

keenly strongly

lounge a room for waiting, sitting and relaxing

wry being both amused and disappointed or annoyed, feeling irony

to rage [reɪdʒ] to rush wildly, furiously

jaunty feeling confident and
pleased with yourself

She herself had so liked Begum. Up till this evening she
had prided herself on gaining a good *kourmani*, a mother-
in-law for her daughter. They had also become good friends
over the time they had known each other. And now this!
She heard her daughter's thudding steps on the stairs – light ₅
and jaunty. Miriam entered the room. Fatima turned to look
at her daughter. Her eyes widened ever so slightly as they
swept over Miriam's body. Then her gaze met Miriam's
and was held there. There was a challenging look in her
daughter's eyes. Fatima registered the look and accepted it ₁₀
wordlessly. Miriam waited for her mother to make some
comment about her appearance. Under her mother's
shocked gaze she held herself tall and erect; the mutinous
line of her mouth very much prominent.
"I am going to see Farook, mother" she softly informed ₁₅
and waited, giving her mother sufficient time to say something. Fatima said nothing, her gaze dropped. Miriam then
turned and left the room.
The outside door clicked shut behind her. Fatima moved to
the window. It looked onto the front garden and its drive- ₂₀
way. She saw her daughter shut the garden gate behind her.
Then placing one hand in the pocket of her faded pair of
jeans, while the other held the short jacket tightly against
her chest, Miriam began to walk away.

Hanif Kureishi

My Son the Fanatic

surreptitious done secretly or
quickly, in the hope that other
people will not notice
to rouse to get up
clue an object, a fact or some
information that helps sb to
discover the answer to
a problem
tangle confused mess
bat *Schläger*
initially at the beginning

Surreptitiously, the father began going into his son's bed- ₂₅
room. He would sit there for hours, rousing himself only to
seek clues. What bewildered him was that Ali was getting
tidier. The room, which was usually a tangle of clothes,
books, cricket bats and video games, was becoming neat
and ordered; spaces began appearing where before there ₃₀
had been only mess.
Initially, Parvez had been pleased: his son was outgrowing
his teenage attitudes. But one day, beside the dustbin,
Parvez found a torn shopping bag that contained not only
old toys but computer disks, videotapes, new books, and ₃₅
fashionable clothes the boy had bought a few months before. Also without explanation, Ali had parted from the
English girlfriend who used to come around to the house.
His old friends stopped ringing.

For reasons he didn't himself understand, Parvez was unable to bring up the subject of Ali's unusual behaviour. He was aware that he had become slightly afraid of his son, who between his silences, was developing a sharp tongue.
5 One remark Parvez did make – "You don't play your guitar anymore" – elicited the mysterious but conclusive reply, "There are more important things to be done."

Yet Parvez felt his son's eccentricity as an injustice. He had always been aware of the pitfalls that other men's sons had
10 stumbled into in England. It was for Ali that Parvez worked long hours; he spent a lot of money paying for Ali's education as an accountant. He had bought Ali good suits, all the books he required, and a computer. And now the boy was throwing his possessions out! The TV, video-player and
15 stereo system followed the guitar. Soon the room was practically bare. Even the unhappy walls bore pale marks where Ali's pictures had been removed.

Parvez couldn't sleep; he went more often to the whisky bottle, even when he was at work. He realised it was im-
20 perative to discuss the matter with someone sympathetic.

Parvez had been a taxi-driver for twenty years. Half that time he'd worked for the same firm. Like him, most of the other drivers were Punjabis. They preferred to work at night, when the roads were clearer and the money better.
25 They slept during the day, avoiding their wives. They led almost a boy's life together in the cabbies' office, playing cards and setting up practical jokes, exchanging lewd stories, eating takeaways from local *balti* houses, and discussing politics and their own problems.
30 But Parvez had been unable to discuss the subject of Ali with his friends. He was too ashamed. And he was afraid, too, that they would blame him for the wrong turning his boy had taken, just as he had blamed other fathers whose sons began running around with bad girls, skipping school and joining gangs.
35 For years, Parvez had boasted to the other men about how Ali excelled in cricket, swimming and football, and what an attentive scholar he was, getting As in most subjects. Was it asking too much for Ali to get a good job, marry the right girl, and start a family? Once this happened, Parvez
40 would be happy. His dreams of doing well in England would have come true. Where had he gone wrong?

One night, sitting in the taxi office on busted chairs with his two closest friends, watching a Sylvester Stallone film, Parvez broke his silence.
45 "I can't understand it!" he burst out. "Everything is going from his room. And I can't talk to him any more. We were

---

to elicit sth from sb to provoke sb to give information or to react
conclusive final

pitfall trap

accountant *Buchhalter*
to require to need

bare empty

imperative urgent
sympathetic *mitfühlend*

Punjabi person living in the province of Punjab in Pakistan
cabby (infml) taxidriver
practical joke *Streich*
lewd [luːd] indecent, obscene

balti Indian dish made and served in a pan

to boast to talk proudly
to excel to be very good at doing sth

busted broken

account story

glance quick look

scrupulous careful about paying attention to every detail

severe here: strict

to stagger out to walk with weak, unsteady steps

bloodshot *blutunterlaufen*

dilated widened

to be liable to to tend to

vigil [ˈvɪdʒɪl] (night) watch

not father and son – we were brothers! Where has he gone? Why is he torturing me?" And Parvez put his head in his hands.

Even as he poured out his account, the men shook their heads and gave one another knowing glances.   5

"Tell me what is happening!" he demanded.

The reply was almost triumphant. They had guessed something was going wrong. Now it was clear: Ali was taking drugs and selling his possessions to pay for them. That was why his bedroom was being emptied.   10

"What must I do, then?"

Parvez's friends instructed him to watch Ali scrupulously and to be severe with him, before the boy went mad, overdosed, or murdered someone.

Parvez staggered out into the early-morning air, terrified   15
that they were right. His boy – the drug-addict killer!

To his relief, he found Bettina sitting in his car.

Usually the last customers of the night were local "brasses", or prostitutes. The taxi-drivers knew them well and often drove them to liaisons. At the end of the girls' night, the   20
men would ferry them home, though sometimes they would join the cabbies for a drinking session in the office. Occasionally, the drivers would go with the girls. "A ride in exchange for a ride," it was called.

Bettina had known Parvez for three years. She lived outside   25
the town and, on the long drives home, during which she sat not in the passenger seat but beside him, Parvez had talked to her about his life and hopes, just as she had talked about hers. They saw each other most nights.

He could talk to her about things he'd never be able to   30
discuss with his own wife. Bettina, in turn, always reported on her night's activities. He liked to know where she had been and with whom. Once, he had rescued her from a violent client, and since then they had come to care for each other.   35

Though Bettina had never met Ali, she heard about the boy continually. That night, when Parvez told Bettina that he suspected Ali was on drugs, to Parvez's relief, she judged neither him nor the boy, but said. "It's all in the eyes." They might be bloodshot; the pupils might be dilated; Ali might   40
look tired. He could be liable to sweats, or sudden mood changes. "OK?"

Parvez began his vigil gratefully. Now that he knew what the problem might be, he felt better. And surely, he figured, things couldn't have gone too far?   45

He watched each mouthful the boy took. He sat beside him at every opportunity and looked into his eyes. When he could, he took the boy's hand, checked his temperature. If

the boy wasn't at home, Parvez was active, looking under the carpet, in Ali's drawers, and behind the empty wardrobe – sniffing, inspecting, probing. He knew what to look for: Bettina had drawn pictures of capsules, syringes, pills,
5 powders, rocks.

Every night, she waited to hear news of what he'd witnessed. After a few days of constant observation, Parvez was able to report that although the boy had given up sports, he seemed healthy. His eyes were clear. He didn't
10 – as Parvez expected he might – flinch guiltily from his father's gaze. In fact, the boy seemed more alert and steady than usual: as well as being sullen, he was very watchful. He returned his father's long looks with more than a hint of criticism, of reproach, even – so much so that Parvez began
15 to feel that it was he who was in the wrong, and not the boy.

"And there's nothing else physically different?" Bettina asked.

"No!" Parvez thought for a moment. "But he is growing a
20 beard."

One night, after sitting with Bettina in an all-night coffee shop, Parvez came home particularly late. Reluctantly, he and Bettina had abandoned the drug theory, for Parvez had found nothing resembling any drug in Ali's room. Besides,
25 Ali wasn't selling his belongings. He threw them out, gave them away, or donated them to charity shops.

Standing in the hall, Parvez heard the boy's alarm clock go off. Parvez hurried into his bedroom, where his wife, still awake, was sewing in bed. He ordered her to sit down and
30 keep quiet, though she had neither stood up nor said a word. As she watched him curiously, he observed his son through the crack of the door.

The boy went into the bathroom to wash. When he returned to his room, Parvez sprang across the hall and set his ear to
35 Ali's door. A muttering sound came from within. Parvez was puzzled but relieved.

Once this clue had been established, Parvez watched him at other times. The boy was praying. Without fail, when he was at home, he prayed five times a day.
40 Parvez had grown up in Lahore, where all young boys had been taught the Koran. To stop Parvez from falling asleep while he studied, the *maulvi* had attached a piece of string to the ceiling and tied it to Parvez's hair, so if his head fell forward, he would instantly jerk awake. After this indigni-
45 ty, Parvez had avoided all religions. Not that the other taxi-drivers had any more respect than he. In fact, they made jokes about the local mullahs walking around with their caps and beards, thinking they could tell people how to live

---

drawer *Schublade*
to probe to examine sth closely
syringe [sɪˈrɪndʒ] *Spritze*
rock (sl) crystallized form of cocaine

to flinch to draw back as with fear or pain
gaze long, steady look
sullen silent and bad-tempered
hint sign

reluctantly unwillingly
to abandon to give up
to resemble to look like

to donate sth to give sth to a charity

to mutter to mumble

without fail without exception

maulvi teacher of the Muslim religion
indignity humiliation

to rove over to keep looking at sth intensely and in every detail

inquisitive curious
odd strange

to yearn to do sth to want to do sth very much, esp when it is very difficult to do

mac short form of mackintosh, a raincoat

unimpeded with nothing blocking or stopping sb/sth

imminent coming up soon
to crunch to crush sth noisily between your teeth when you are eating
poppadum thin, crispy Indian bread
to castigate *geißeln*
insolent extremely rude and showing a lack of respect

while their eyes roved over the boys and girls in their care. Parvez described to Bettina what he had discovered. He informed the men in the taxi office. His friends, who had been so inquisitive before, now became oddly silent. They could hardly condemn the boy for his devotions.   5

Parvez decided to take a night off and go out with the boy. They could talk things over. He wanted to hear how things were going at college; he wanted to tell him stories about their family in Pakistan. More than anything, he yearned to understand how Ali had discovered the "spiritual dimen- 10 sion", as Bettina called it.

To Parvez's surprise, the boy refused to accompany him. He claimed he had an appointment. Parvez had to insist that no appointment could be more important than that of a son with his father.   15

The next day, Parvez went immediately to the street corner where Bettina stood in the rain wearing high heels, a short skirt, and a long mac, which she would open hopefully at passing cars.

"Get in, get in!" he said.   20

They drove out across the moors and parked at the spot where, on better days, their view unimpeded for miles except by wild deer and horses, they'd lie back, with their eyes half-closed, saying, "This is the life." This time Parvez was trembling. Bettina put her arms around him.   25

"What's happened?"

"I've just had the worst experience of my life."

As Bettina rubbed his head Parvez told her that the previous evening, as he and his son had studied the menu, the waiter, whom Parvez knew, brought him his usual whisky- 30 and-water. Parvez was so nervous he had even prepared a question. He was going to ask Ali if he was worried about his imminent exams. But first he loosened his tie, crunched a poppadum, and took a long drink.

Before Parvez could speak, Ali made a face.   35

"Don't you know it's wrong to drink alcohol?" he had said.

"He spoke to me very harshly," Parvez said to Bettina.

"I was about to castigate the boy for being insolent, but I managed to control myself."

Parvez had explained patiently that for years he had worked 40 more than ten hours a day, had few enjoyments or hobbies, and never gone on holiday. Surely it wasn't a crime to have a drink when he wanted one?

"But it is forbidden," the boy said.

Parvez shrugged. "I know."   45

"And so is gambling, isn't it?"

"Yes. But surely we are only human?"

Each time Parvez took a drink, the boy winced, or made some kind of fastidious face. This made Parvez drink more quickly. The waiter, wanting to please his friend, brought another glass of whisky. Parvez knew he was getting
5 drunk, but he couldn't stop himself. Ali had a horrible look, full of disgust and censure. It was as if he hated his father.
Halfway through the meal, Parvez suddenly lost his temper and threw a plate on the floor. He felt like ripping the cloth
10 from the table, but the waiters and other customers were staring at him. Yet he wouldn't stand for his own son's telling him the difference between right and wrong. He knew he wasn't a bad man. He had a conscience. There were a few things of which he was ashamed, but on the whole he
15 had lived a decent life.
"When have I had time to be wicked?" he asked Ali.
In a low, monotonous voice, the boy explained that Parvez had not, in fact, lived a good life. He had broken countless rules of the Koran.
20 "For instance?" Parvez demanded.
Ali didn't need to think. As if he had been waiting for this moment, he asked his father if he didn't relish pork pies?
"Well." Parvez couldn't deny that he loved crispy bacon smothered with mushrooms and mustard and sandwiched
25 between slices of fried bread. In fact, he ate this for breakfast every morning.
Ali then reminded Parvez that he had ordered his wife to cook pork sausages, saying to her, "You're not in the village now. This is England. We have to fit in."
30 Parvez was so annoyed and perplexed by this attack that he called for more drink.
"The problem is this," the boy said. He leaned across the table. For the first time that night, his eyes were alive. "You are too implicated in Western civilisation."
35 Parvez burped; he thought he was going to choke. "Implicated!" he said. "But we live here!"
"The Western materialists hate us." Ali said. "Papa, how can you love something which hates you?"
"What is the answer, then," Parvez said miserably, "accord-
40 ing to you?"
Ali didn't need to think. He addressed his father fluently, as if Parvez were a rowdy crowd which had to be quelled or convinced. The law of Islam would rule the world; the skin of the infidel would burn off again and again; the Jews and
45 Christers would be routed. The West was a sink of hypocrites, adulterers, homosexuals, drug users and prostitutes. While Ali talked, Parvez looked out the window as if to check that they were still in London.

---

to wince [wɪns] to suddenly make an expression with your face that shows that you are feeling pain or embarrassment
fastidious here: disapproving

censure strong criticism

wicked morally bad, evil

to relish to enjoy
pork pie Schweinepastete

to smother with to cover sth thickly with sth

implicated involved
to burp to belch
to choke to suffocate

rowdy [ˈraʊdi] noisy
to quell to stop violent behaviour
infidel a person who does not belief in religion, etc
Christer Christian
to rout [raʊt] to defect
hypocrite a person who pretends to have moral standards or opinions that they do not actually have
adulterer Ehebrecher

persecution to treat sb in a cruel and unfair way, esp because of their race, religion or political beliefs
jihad holy war of the Muslims

to urge to advise or to try very hard to persuade sb to do sth
to mend to improve

to usher to take or show sb where they should go

rear view mirror *Rückspiegel*

wing mirror *Seitenspiegel*

to scrape to rub sth accidentally so that it gets damaged or hurt
to haul oneself up to pull up with a strong effort
to dislodge to force or knock sth out of its position

usury [juːʒərɪ] the practice of lending money to people at unfairly high rates of interest

"My people have taken enough. If the persecution doesn't stop, there will be *jihad*. I, and millions of others, will gladly give our lives for the cause."
"But why, why?" Parvez said.
"For us, the reward will be in Paradise." 5
"Paradise!"
Finally, as Parvez's eyes filled with tears, the boy urged him to mend his ways.
"But how would that be possible?" Parvez asked.
"Pray," urged Ali. "Pray beside me." 10
Parvez paid the bill and ushered his boy out of there as soon as he was able. He couldn't take any more.
Ali sounded as if he'd swallowed someone else's voice.
On the way home, the boy sat in the back of the taxi, as if he were a customer. "What has made you like this?" Parvez 15
asked him, afraid that somehow he was to blame for all this. "Is there a particular event which has influenced you?"
"Living in this country."
"But I love England," Parvez said, watching his boy in the 20
rear view mirror. "They let you do almost anything here."
"That is the problem," Ali replied.
For the first time in years, Parvez couldn't see straight.
He knocked the side of the car against a lorry, ripping off the wing mirror. They were lucky not to have been stopped 25
by the police: Parvez would have lost his licence and his job.
Back at the house, as he got out of the car, Parvez stumbled and fell in the road, scraping his hands and ripping his trousers. He managed to haul himself up. The boy didn't 30
even offer him his hand.
Parvez told Bettina he was willing to pray, if that was what the boy wanted – if it would dislodge the pitiless look from his eyes. "But what I object to," he said, "is being told by my own son that I am going to Hell!" 35
What had finished Parvez off was the boy's saying he was giving up his studies in accounting. When Parvez had asked why, Ali said sarcastically that it was obvious. "Western education cultivates an anti-religious attitude."
And in the world of accountants it was usual to meet wom- 40
en, drink alcohol, and practise usury.
"But it's well-paid work," Parvez argued. "For years you've been preparing!"
Ali said he was going to begin to work in prisons, with poor Muslims who were struggling to maintain their purity 45
in the face of corruption. Finally, at the end of the evening, as Ali went up to bed, he had asked his father why he didn't have a beard, or at least a moustache.

"I feel as if I've lost my son," Parvez told Bettina. "I can't bear to be looked at as if I'm a criminal. I've decided what to do."
"What is it?"
"I'm going to tell him to pick up his prayer mat and get out
5 of my house. It will be the hardest thing I've ever done, but tonight I'm going to do it."
"But you mustn't give up on him," said Bettina. "Many young people fall into cults and superstitious groups. It doesn't mean they'll always feel the same way." She said
10 Parvez had to stick by his boy.
Parvez was persuaded that she was right, even though he didn't feel like giving his son more love when he had hardly been thanked for all he had already given.

For the next two weeks, Parvez tried to endure his son's looks
15 and reproaches. He attempted to make conversation about Ali's beliefs. But if Parvez ventured any criticism, Ali always had a brusque reply. On one occasion, Ali accused Parvez of "grovelling" to the whites: in contrast, he explained, he himself was not "inferior"; there was more to the world than the
20 West, though the West always thought it was best.
"How is it you know that?" Parvez said. "Seeing as you've never left England?"
Ali replied with a look of contempt.
One night, having ensured there was no alcohol on his
25 breath, Parvez sat down at the kitchen table with Ali. He hoped Ali would compliment him on the beard he was growing, but Ali didn't appear to notice it.
The previous day, Parvez had been telling Bettina that he thought people in the West sometimes felt inwardly empty
30 and that people needed a philosophy to live by.
"Yes," Bettina had said. "That's the answer. You must tell him what your philosophy of life is. Then he will understand that there are other beliefs."
After some fatiguing consideration, Parvez was ready to
35 begin. The boy watched him as if he expected nothing. Haltingly, Parvez said that people had to treat one another with respect, particularly children their parents. This did seem, for a moment, to affect the boy. Heartened, Parvez continued. In his view, this life was all there was, and when
40 you died, you rotted in the earth. "Grass and flowers will grow out of my grave, but something of me will live on."
"How then?"
"In other people. For instance, I will continue – in you."
At this the boy appeared a little distressed.
45 "And in your grandchildren," Parvez added for good measure. "But while I am here on earth I want to make the best of it. And I want you to, as well!"

superstitious believing in magic, ghosts, etc

to venture to dare to express

to grovel to crawl

contempt scornful disregard

fatiguing tiring
haltingly hesitantly

to affect to have an effect on

a bottomless pit *ein Fass ohne Boden*

to oppress to treat sb in a cruel and unfair way, esp by not giving them the same freedom, rights, etc as other people

"What d'you mean by 'make the best of it'?" asked the boy.
"Well," said Parvez. "For a start … you should enjoy yourself. Yes. Enjoy yourself without hurting others."
Ali said enjoyment was "a bottomless pit".
"But I don't mean enjoyment like that," said Parvez. "I 5
mean the beauty of living."
"All over the world our people are oppressed," was the boy's reply.
"I know," Parvez answered, not entirely sure who "our people" were. "But still – life is for living!" 10
Ali said, "Real morality has existed for hundreds of years. Around the world millions and millions of people share my beliefs. Are you saying you are right and they are all wrong?" And Ali looked at his father with such aggressive confidence that Parvez would say no more. 15
A few evenings later, Bettina was riding in Parvez's car after visiting a client when they passed a boy on the street.
"That's my son," Parvez said, his face set hard. They were on the other side of town, in a poor district, where there were two mosques. 20
Bettina turned to see. "Slow down, then, slow down!"
She said, "He's good-looking. Reminds me of you. But with a more determined face. Please, can't we stop?"
"What for?"
"I'd like to talk to him." 25
Parvez turned the cab round and pulled up beside the boy.
"Coming home?" Parvez asked. "It's quite a way."
The boy shrugged and got into the back seat. Bettina sat in the front. Parvez became aware of Bettina's short skirt, her

gaudy too brightly coloured in a way that lacks taste

gaudy rings and ice-blue eyeshadow. He became conscious 30
that the smell of her perfume, which he loved, filled the cab. He opened the window.
While Parvez drove as fast as he could, Bettina said gently to Ali, "Where have you been?"
"The mosque," he said. 35
"And how are you getting on at college? Are you working hard?"
"Who are you to ask me these questions?" Ali said, looking out of the window. Then they hit bad traffic, and the car came to a standstill. 40

inadvertently by accident, without intending to

By now, Bettina had inadvertently laid her hand on Parvez's shoulder. She said, "Your father, who is a good man, is very worried about you. You know he loves you more than his own life."
"You say he loves me," the boy said. 45
"Yes!" said Bettina.
"Then why is he letting a woman like you touch him like that?"

If Bettina looked at the boy in anger, he looked back at her with cold fury.

She said, "What kind of woman am I that I should deserve to be spoken to like that?"

5 "You know what kind," he said. Then he turned to his father. "Now let me out."

"Never," Parvez replied.

"Don't worry, I'm getting out," Bettina said.

"No, don't!" said Parvez. But even as the car moved forward, 10 she opened the door and threw herself out – she had done this before – and ran away across the road. Parvez stopped and shouted after her several times, but she had gone.

Parvez took Ali back to the house, saying nothing more to him. Ali went straight to his room. Parvez was unable to 15 read the paper, watch television, or even sit down. He kept pouring himself drinks.

At last, he went upstairs and paced up and down outside Ali's room. When, finally, he opened the door, Ali was praying. The boy didn't even glance his way.

20 Parvez kicked him over. Then he dragged the boy up by the front of his shirt and hit him. The boy fell back. Parvez hit him again. The boy's face was bloody. Parvez was panting; he knew the boy was unreachable, but he struck him none the less. The boy neither covered himself nor retaliated; 25 there was no fear in his eyes. He only said, through his split lip, "So who's the fanatic now?"

to pant to breathe heavily

to retaliate [rɪˈtælɪeɪt] to do sth harmful to sb because they have harmed you first

Salman Rushdie
Good Advice Is Rarer than Rubies

On the last Tuesday of the month, the dawn bus, its headlamps still shining, brought Miss Rehana to the gates of the British Consulate. It arrived pushing a cloud of dust, veil-30 ing her beauty from the eyes of strangers until she descended. The bus was brightly painted in multicoloured arabesques, and on the front it said "MOVE OVER DARLING" in green and gold letters; on the back it added "TATA-BATA" and also "O.K. GOOD-LIFE". Miss Reha-35 na told the driver it was a beautiful bus, and he jumped down and held the door open for her, bowing theatrically as she descended.

Miss Rehana's eyes were large and black and bright enough not to need the help of antimony and when the advice ex-

to veil verschleiern

TATA Indian company producing vehicles

to bow [baʊ] to move your head or body forwards and downwards as a sign of respect or greeting

antimony cosmetic substance that makes the eyes shine

lala guard (Persian)

cockade royal sign

courtesy polite behaviour
gruffly unfriendly and impatient
sahib Arabian word for sir

compound area, esp surrounded by a fence or wall

vulnerable weak and easily hurt physically or emotionally
supplicant a person who asks for sth in a humble way, esp from a God or a powerful person

to munch to eat sth steadily and often noisily, esp sth crisp
chilli-pakoras fried chilli-pies
digestive tract *Verdauungssystem*

alas unfortunately
orphan a child whose parents are dead

to be well tempered here: has matured, developed in a good way

volition free will

shanty-town an area in or near a town where poor people live in small huts

pert Muhammad Ali saw them he felt himself becoming young again. He watched her approaching the Consulate gates as the light strengthened, and asking the bearded lala who guarded them in a gold-buttoned khaki uniform with a cockaded turban when they would open. The lala, usually ₅ so rude to the Consulate's Tuesday women, answered Miss Rehana with something like courtesy.
"Half an hour," he said gruffly. "Maybe two hours. Who knows? The sahibs are eating their breakfast."

The dusty compound between the bus stop and the Consu- ₁₀ late was already full of Tuesday women, some veiled, a few barefaced like Miss Rehana. They all looked frightened, and leaned heavily on the arms of uncles or brothers, who were trying to look confident. But Miss Rehana had come on her own, and did not seem at all alarmed. ₁₅ Muhammad Ali, who specialised in advising the most vulnerable-looking of these weekly supplicants, found his feet leading him towards the strange, big-eyed, independent girl.

"Miss," he began. "You have come for permit to London, I think so?" ₂₀
She was standing at a hot-snack stall in the little shanty-town by the edge of the compound, munching chilli-pako-ras contentedly. She turned to look at him, and at close range those eyes did bad things to his digestive tract.
"Yes, I have." ₂₅
"Then, please, you allow me to give some advice? Small cost only."
Miss Rehana smiled. "Good advice is rarer than rubies," she said. "But alas, I cannot pay. I am an orphan, not one of your wealthy ladies." ₃₀
"Trust my grey hairs," Muhammad Ali urged her. "My advice is well tempered by experience. You will certainly find it good."
She shook her head. "I tell you I am a poor potato. There are women here with male family members, all earning good ₃₅ wages. Go to them. Good advice should find good money."
I am going crazy, Muhammad Ali thought, because he heard his voice telling her of its own volition. "Miss, I have been drawn to you by Fate. What to do? Our meeting was written. I also am a poor man only, but for you my advice ₄₀ comes free."
She smiled again. "Then I must surely listen. When Fate sends a gift, one receives good fortune."

He led her to the low wooden desk in his own special corner of the shanty-town. She followed, continuing to eat ₄₅ pakoras from a little newspaper packet. She did not offer him any.

Muhammad Ali put a cushion on the dusty ground. "Please to sit." She did as he asked. He sat cross-legged across the desk from her, conscious that two or three dozen pairs of male eyes were watching him enviously, that all the other shanty-town men were ogling the latest young lovely to be charmed by the old grey-hair fraud. He took a deep breath to settle himself.

"Name, please."

"Miss Rehana," she told him. "Fiancée of Mustafa Dar of Bradford, London."

"Bradford, England," he corrected her gently. "London is a town only, like Multan or Bahawalpur. England is a great nation full of the coldest fish in the world."

"I see. Thank you," she responded gravely, so that he was unsure if she was making fun of him.

"You have filled application form? Then let me see, please."

She passed him a neatly folded document in a brown envelope.

"Is it OK?" For the first time there was a note of anxiety in her voice.

He patted the desk quite near the place where her hand rested. "I am certain," he said. "Wait on and I will check." She finished the pakoras while he scanned her papers.

"Tip-top," he pronounced at length. "All in order."

"Thank you for your advice," she said, making as if to rise. "I'll go now and wait by the gate."

"What are you thinking?" he cried loudly, smiting his forehead. "You consider this is easy business? Just give the form and poof, with a big smile they hand over the permit? Miss Rehana, I tell you, you are entering a worse place than any police station."

"Is it so, truly?" His oratory had done the trick. She was a captive audience now, and he would be able to look at her for a few moments longer.

Drawing another calming breath, he launched into his set speech. He told her that the sahibs thought that all the women who came on Tuesdays, claiming to be dependents of bus drivers in Luton or chartered accountants in Manchester, were crooks and liars and cheats.

She protested, "But then I will simply tell them that I, for one, am no such thing!"

Her innocence made him shiver with fear for her. She was a sparrow, he told her, and they were men with hooded eyes, like hawks. He explained that they would ask her questions,

---

envious wanting sth that sb else has
to ogle to look hard at sb in an offensive way, usually showing sexual interest
fraud swindler

fiancée the woman that a man is engaged to (= has officially agreed to marry)
fiancé (male form)

to pat to touch sb/sth gently several times with your hand flat, esp as a sign of affection
to scan to look quickly but not very carefully at a document, etc

to smite to hit

oratory the skill of making powerful and effective speeches in public
captive impressed and attentive

to launch into to start with great energy and force
set planned and prepared before-hand
chartered accountant *Bilanzbuchhalter*
crook criminal

hood *Kapuze*

personal questions, questions such as a lady's own brother would be too shy to ask. They would ask if she was virgin, and, if not, what her fiancé's love-making habits were, and what secret nicknames they had invented for one another. Muhammad Ali spoke brutally, on purpose, to lessen the ₅ shock she would feel when it, or something like it, actually happened. Her eyes remained steady, but her hands began to flutter at the edges of the desk.
He went on:
"They will ask you how many rooms are in your family ₁₀ home, and what colour are the walls, and what days do you empty the rubbish. They will ask your man's mother's third cousin's aunt's step-daughter's middle name. And all these things they have already asked your Mustafa Dar in his Bradford. And if you make one mistake, you are finished." ₁₅
"Yes," she said, and he could hear her disciplining her voice. "And what is your advice, old man?"

It was at this point that Muhammad Ali usually began to whisper urgently, to mention that he knew a man, a very good type, who worked in the Consulate, and through him, ₂₀ for a fee, the necessary papers could be delivered, with all the proper authenticating seals. Business was good, because the women would often pay him five hundred rupees or give him a gold bracelet for his pains, and go away happy. ₂₅
They came from hundreds of miles away – he normally made sure of this before beginning to trick them – so even when they discovered they had been swindled they were unlikely to return. They went away to Sargodha or Lalukhet and began to pack, and who knows at what point they ₃₀ found out they had been gulled, but it was at a too-late point, anyway.
Life is hard, and an old man must live by his wits. It was not up to Muhammad Ali to have compassion for these Tuesday women. ₃₅

But once again his voice betrayed him, and instead of starting his customary speech it began to reveal to her his greatest secret.
"Miss Rehana," his voice said, and he listened to it in amazement, "you are a rare person, a jewel, and for you I ₄₀ will do what I would not do for my own daughter, perhaps. One document has come into my possession that can solve all your worries at one stroke."
"And what is this sorcerer's paper?" she asked, her eyes unquestionably laughing at him now. ₄₅
His voice fell low-as-low.

authenticating seal
Echtheitssiegel

bracelet a piece of jewellery worn around the wrist or arm

to gull sb to trick sb

compassion sympathy

to betray to give secret information to an enemy
customary typical of a person

sorcerer magician, wizard

"Miss Rehana, it is a British passport. Completely genuine and pukka goods. I have a good friend who will put your name and photo, and then, hey-presto, England there you come!"

pukka goods really good (Hindi)

5 He had said it!
Anything was possible now, on this day of his insanity. Probably he would give her the thing free-gratis, and then kick himself for a year afterwards.
Old fool, he berated himself. *The oldest fools are bewitched*
10 *by the youngest girls.*

insanity madness

to berate to scold
bewitched under a magic spell

"Let me understand you," she was saying. "You are propos-ing I should commit a crime …"
"Not crime," he interposed. "Facilitation."
"… and go to Bradford, London, illegally, and therefore
15 justify the low opinion the Consulate sahibs have of us all. Old babuji, this is not good advice."
"Bradford, *England*," he corrected her mournfully. "You should not take my gift in such a spirit."
"Then how?"
20 "Bibi, I am a poor fellow, and I have offered this prize because you are so beautiful. Do not spit on my genero-sity. Take the thing. Or else don't take, go home, forget England, only do not go into that building and lose your dignity."
25 But she was on her feet, turning away from him, walking towards the gates, where the women had begun to cluster and the lala was swearing at them to be patient or none of them would be admitted at all.
"So be a fool," Muhammad Ali shouted after her. "What
30 goes of my father's if you are?" (Meaning, what was it to him.)
She did not turn.
"It is the curse of our people," he yelled. "We are poor, we are ignorant, and we completely refuse to learn."
35 "Hey, Muhammad Ali," the woman at the betel-nut stall called across to him. "Too bad, she likes them young."

to propose to suggest

to interpose to interrupt
facilitation act to make sth easier

babuji (Hindi) respectful for dear Sir
mournful very sad

bibi (Urdu) lady, madam
generosity the act of being generous (= willing to give sb money, gifts, time or kindness freely)
dignity the fact of being treated with honour and respect by people
to cluster to come together in small groups

That day Muhammad Ali did nothing but stand around near the Consulate gates. Many times he scolded himself, *Go from here, old goof, lady does not desire to speak with you*
40 *any further.* But when she came out, she found him waiting.
"Salaam, advice wallah," she greeted him.
She seemed calm, and at peace with him again, and he thought, *My God, ya Allah, she has pulled it off. The Brit-ish sahibs also have been drowning in her eyes and she has*
45 *got her passage to England.*

goof (infml) idiot

wallah (Hindi) a person who renders a service to sb

to pull sth off (infml) to succeed in doing sth

He smiled at her hopefully. She smiled back with no trouble at all.
"Miss Rehana Begum," he said, "felicitations, daughter, on what is obviously your hour of triumph."
Impulsively, she took his forearm in her hand.   5
"Come," she said. "Let me buy you a pakora to thank you for your advice and to apologise for my rudeness, too."

They stood in the dust of the afternoon compound near the bus, which was getting ready to leave. Coolies were tying bedding rolls to the roof. A hawker shouted at the passen-   10
gers, trying to sell them love stories and green medicines, both of which cured unhappiness.
Miss Rehana and a happy Muhammad Ali ate their pakoras sitting on the bus's "front mud-guard", that is, the bumper. The old advice expert began softly to hum a tune from a   15
movie soundtrack. The day's heat was gone.

"It was an arranged engagement," Miss Rehana said all at once. "I was nine years old when my parents fixed it. Mustafa Dar was already thirty at that time, but my father wanted someone who could look after me as he had   20
done himself and Mustafa was a man known to Daddyji as a solid type. Then my parents died and Mustafa Dar went to England and said he would send for me. That was many years ago. I have his photo, but he is like a stranger to me. Even his voice, I do not recognise it on the   25
phone."

The confession took Muhammad Ali by surprise, but he nodded with what he hoped looked like wisdom.
"Still and after all," he said, "one's parents act in one's best interests. They found you a good and honest man who has   30
kept his word and sent for you. And now you have a life-time to get to know him, and to love."

He was puzzled, now, by the bitterness that had infected her smile.
"But, old man," she asked him, "why have you already   35
packed me and posted me off to England?"
He stood up, shocked.

"You looked happy – so I just assumed ... excuse me, but they turned you down or what?"
"I got all their questions wrong," she replied. "Distinguish-   40
ing marks I put on the wrong cheeks, bathroom decor I

completely redecorated, all absolutely topsy-turvy, you see."
"But what to do? How will you go?"

"Now I will go back to Lahore and my job. I work in a great house, as ayah to three good boys. They would have been sad to see me leave."

ayah (Hindi) nanny

"But this is tragedy!" Muhammad Ali lamented. "Oh, how
5 I pray that you had taken up my offer! Now, but, it is not possible, I regret to inform. Now they have your form on file, cross-check can be made, even the passport will not suffice.
It is spoilt, all spoilt, and it could have been so easy if ad-
10 vice had been accepted in good time."
"I do not think," she told him, "I truly do not think you should be sad."

Her last smile, which he watched from the compound until the bus concealed it in a dust-cloud, was the happiest thing
15 he had ever seen in his long, hot, hard, unloving life.

to conceal to hide

Biographies

Joseph Conrad (1857–1924)

Józef Teodor Konrad Korzeni-owski (Conrad's original name) did not speak English before he was 21 years old. He was born in Berdichev, in the Ukraine, in ₅ a region that had once been a part of Poland but was then un-der Russian rule. His father Apollo Korzeniowski was an aristocrat without lands, as well ₁₀ as a poet and translator of the works of Shakespeare and Victor Hugo in the Polish lan-guage. Conrad's parents both died early of tuberculosis. From then on, he led an adventurous life. An uncle took care of him and sent him to the best schools in Kraków ₁₅ but Conrad soon lost interest in learning. He first joined the French Marines, later in 1878, the British Merchant Navy. There, he became captain in 1886 and was grant-ed British citizenship in the same year. He sailed his ship, the "Otago", across the oceans to many ports and ₂₀ thus travelled to many parts of the world (Africa, Aus-tralia, the Malay states, Borneo and several South Pa-cific islands), which later on provided the exotic settings for his fiction. In one of his most famous novels *Heart of Darkness* (1899; filmed with Marlon Brando as *Apoca-* ₂₅ *lypse Now*), Conrad draws richly from his most impres-sive steamboat journey up the Congo river. He had al-ready begun writing as a seaman, but in 1894 he became seriously ill and could no longer go to sea, so he then devoted himself entirely to literature. In 1895, his first ₃₀ novel, *Allmayer's Folly,* was published, quickly followed by *An Outcast of the Island* (1896). Both texts are written

exuberant rich and lively
en vogue fashionable

in the exuberant style of tropical exoticism that was very much *en vogue* in the 19th century. *The Nigger of the "Narcissus"* (1897), though, shows the beginning of his ₃₅ literary skills and his typical technique of giving insights

and theoretical reflections in a preface to his works. With *Lord Jim* (1900), he presents his attitude towards art and literature. This attitude shows the features of realism and
40 symbolism in combination with a philosophical and natural scientific approach. He describes the purpose of this as follows: "by the power of the written word to make you hear, to make you feel, – it is before all to make you *see*". Conrad became one of the few major
45 authors of the 20th century English novel.

feature mark, sign

William Somerset Maugham
(1874–1965)

William Somerset Maugham started his literary career as a playwright. He was the highest-paid author in the world in the
5 1930s, however, he is not acknowledged as one of the major authors in English. His worldwide fame is mainly based on the novels *Of Human Bond-*
10 *age* (1915) and *The Razor's Edge* (1944). It was especially in these two works that he used autobiographical material.

Maugham was born in the British Embassy in Paris. His
15 father was a famous attorney; later, his brother even became England's Lord Chancellor. So a career as a lawyer was set up for him by way of family tradition. Unfortunately, Maugham suffered from a bad stammer, so that he shied away from speaking in public and became
20 rather introverted. A cruel stroke of fate further aggravated his situation. At the age of ten he became an orphan and his further education was laid in the hands of an uncle, a clergyman. Maugham attended King's school in Canterbury, Kent. He studied philosophy and
25 literature at Heidelberg University, but then turned to medicine and became a surgeon in London. There, he performed his practical year in the slums of the East End. This period left deep impressions and he drew

to shy away from to try to avoid
to aggravate to make worse
orphan a child whose parents are dead

richly from these experiences for his literary work. After his first successes as a writer, he gave up his medical ₃₀ career and went into more adventurous activities. Disguised as a reporter, Maugham worked for the British Intelligence in Russia during the Russian Revolution in 1917. As his health and his stuttering grew worse, he had to give up this exciting job. After a series of travels ₃₅ to eastern Asia, the Pacific Islands, and Mexico, he dedicated himself to writing entertaining stories against the background of his international experiences. He was a cosmopolitan with an observer's eye and thus his style is marked by sceptical criticism. He presents life and ₄₀ people in a detached, sober and rather cool way, detecting psychological deficits and social evils without ever being biased or advocating a fixed ideology or political principles.

detached objective, neutral

biased prejudiced

George Orwell (1903–1950)

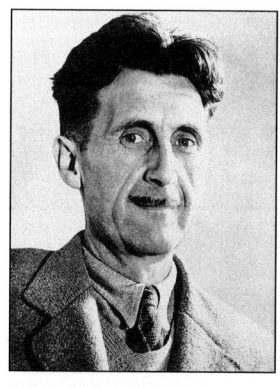

Orwell was born in Motihari, India as Eric Arthur Blair, son of parents who were members of the Indian Civil Service. He spent the years from 1917 to 1922 at ₅ Eton College, in London where he received a classical intellectual education. At the early age of six, he had already made up his mind and determined for himself ₁₀ to become a famous writer.

After his studies in England, he returned to India to join the Indian Imperial Police in Burma, an experience that later found expression in the novel *Burmese Days* (1934). He quit that job, however, because he devel- ₁₅ oped a strong affinity for the destitute, the poor Burmese suffering under the imperial regime, whose rigid and sometimes inhumane laws he had to enforce. His distaste for "every form of man's dominion over man", i.e. autocratic and totalitarian forms of government grew ₂₀ at that time. He returned to England, and living in deliberately self-imposed poverty, explored the lives of the poor, be it the living conditions of the impoverished

destitute without hope

autocratic ruled by a tyrant

deliberately intentional

miners in Lancashire or his self-experiment as a dish-
25 washer in Paris or as a tramp in London. For a short
time, he was enthusiastic about communist ideals. So,
when the Spanish Civil War broke out, he fought as a
member of the Marxist party for a classless society. The
war itself and his observations of various communist
30 practices turned him into a strong critic of communism.
His war participation ended dramatically. He was se-
verely wounded and had to flee for his life. His reflections on these events and experiences can be found in
his most famous anti-fascist and anti-totalitarian works,
35 *Animal Farm* (1945), a modern beast-fable attacking
Stalinism, and *Nineteen Eighty-Four* (1949), an anti-uto-
pian novel setting out his fears of an intrusively bureau-
cratized state of the future with absolute governmental
control and observation manifested in the installation of
40 "big brother". Orwell's reputation rests not only on his
political shrewdness and his cutting satires but also on
his marvellously clear style and superb essays, which
rank among the best ever written.

intrusive entering sth in an unpleasantly direct and intensive way

Doris Lessing (1919–2013)

The novels of Doris Lessing reflect the political conflicts of
South Africa; the social, especially sex-related problems, of
5 women in a permissive society
and the fears caused by nucle-
ar armament that are shared by
people all over the world. Her
works show autobiographical
10 traces and use the rich experiences Lessing has had
during her unconventional life as an emancipated woman to give greater impetus to the feminist movement of
the 20th century.
15 Doris Lessing was born Doris May Tayler in Persia (now
Iran). Her parents moved to the British colony in Southern Rhodesia (now Zimbabwe). They had emigrated because of an official call in 1925 offering landed property
to farmers and the prospect of becoming rich by grow-

permissive esp in sexual matters, liberal and free

arable cultivable

charge person one has
responsibility for

preconception prejudice

ing maize there. However, reality was harsh, especially ₂₀
on her father, who did not succeed in turning the thou-
sand-odd acres of bush he had bought into an arable
area. Only her mother adapted to the situation and tried
vigorously to establish a civilized life in Edwardian fashion in the rough settlement. Since she was obsessed ₂₅
with raising a proper daughter, she enforced a rigid system of rules and hygiene at home, and finally placed
Doris in a convent school, where nuns terrified their
charges with stories of hell and damnation. Lessing was
later sent to an all-girls high school in the capital of ₃₀
Salisbury, but soon dropped out. At this time she was
thirteen; it was to be the end of her formal education.
Lessing's first marriage with a colonial civil servant did
not last long. Meanwhile the effects of World War II influenced her political interests. After her divorce she ₃₅
married Gottfried Anton Lessing, a German communist
emigrant but soon after this marriage also ended in
divorce. In 1949, she settled down in England, joining
the Communist Party, but was soon disillusioned with it
and left it altogether in 1956. It was in England that she ₄₀
started her professional literary career with the publishing of *The Grass is Singing* (1950). The book explores
the complacency and shallowness of white colonial
society in southern Africa. Her fictional scope comprises books from her communist-feminist phase such as ₄₅
the series *Children of Violence* (1952–1958) about her
semi-autobiographical protagonist Martha Quest and
the highly-acclaimed *The Golden Notebook (1962)* as
well as non-fictional essays and science-fiction novels
that she wrote in the 1970s–1980s. Lessing's more re- ₅₀
cent novels have continued to confront taboos and
challenge preconceptions, thus generating many different and conflicting critical opinions (*The Good Terrorist
1985; The Fifth Child 1988*).
She is now widely regarded as one of the most impor- ₅₅
tant post-war writers in English and has received numerous outstanding literary awards and honours all over
the world. Her latest book, *The Grandmothers*, a collection of four short novels centred around an unconventional extended family, was published in 2003. ₆₀

Rasipuram Krishnaswami Narayan (1906–2001)

Narayan was born and educated in Madras, India. Apart from his various travels, he has lived in India ever since. Most of his work, starting from his first novel *Swami and Friends* (1935) is set in the fictional town of Malgudi. He was voted third most popular writer in an Indian poll of the best writers of the 20th century. However, his literary career, which he began as a short story writer and correspondent for a Madras-based newspaper, was full of obstacles, since he could not find a publisher for his early novels for quite a long time. His story-telling is marked by traditional Indian features: an ironic outlook on the human condition, accepting the social system as it is, making no attempt to criticize social evils or deal with the plight of the underdog. He mainly uses male protagonists belonging to the middle class and makes no attempt to present India in an exotic light for the sake of foreign audiences. His language is plain and simple English, which makes his narration transparently clear. In his novel *The Dark Room* (1938), he treats the topic of Hindu marriage sombrely, while *The English Teacher* (1945) is a tragic-comedy depicting human aberration and attainments. Narayan has also published various short stories (13 collections among which his ninth collection *Under the Banyan Tree*, which included "A Horse and Two Goats", was a bestseller), an excellent autobiography *My Days,* (1975) and has brought out a collection of Indian legends drawn from the Mahabharata and the Puranas entitled *Gods, Demons and Others* (1964). He has been awarded great literary honours in America and India.

plight difficulties

aberration behaviour outside the norm
attainments (pl) abilities, accomplishments

Chinua Achebe (1930–2013)

Albert Chinualumogu Achebe was born at Ogidi in eastern Nigeria. He studied English, theology and history. After graduation, he travelled in Africa and [5] America, worked for a short time as a teacher and then returned home to start a job with the Nigerian Broadcasting Company in Lagos in 1954. [10] During the Nigerian Civil War (1967–1970) he served in the Biafran government, and then taught at American and Nigerian universities. His first novel about the rise and fall of a man called Okonkwo, a native "big man" (*Things Fall Apart*) was released [15] in 1958 and translated into 50 languages. The clash of traditional Igbo life with the colonial powers in the form of missionaries and governmental influences was Achebe's concern in the following novels (*No Longer at Ease,* 1960; *Arrow of God,* 1964). Achebe was one of [20] the founders of Nigeria's new literature that draws substance from "both traditional oral literature and from the present and rapidly changing society". He is not only one of the finest Nigerian writer but has acquired a worldwide readership and has become one of the best [25] novelists now writing in the English language. Achebe's work reflects the idea at the heart of the African oral tradition: that "art is, and always was, at the service of man. Our ancestors created their myths and told their stories for a human purpose." He is the first writer to [30] succeed in combining European and African art forms in a most appealing way. His stories do not focus on the psychological depths and aberrations of the individual and his or her character development in an isolated or detached way. It is the individual integrated in commu- [35] nal life and thus his or her development under and attempts to cope with the influences, customs and rites of the community that concern him. His style is therefore more abundant and aesthetic following the rhythm of traditional tribal life and oral tradition. Achebe's literary [40] language is standard English blended with pidgin, Igbo vocabulary, proverbs, images and speech patterns. He

---

Igbo (or Ibo) name of the Negroid people and the main literary and cultural language of South Nigeria

abundant *üppig*

Pidgin a hybrid language made up of elements of two or more languages

has defended the use of the English language in the production of African fiction, insisting that the African
45 novelist has an obligation to educate, and has attacked European critics who have failed to understand African literature on its own terms.

As an essayist, Achebe has gained fame with the collections *Morning yet on Creation Day* (1975), *Hopes*
50 *and Impediments* (1988) and his long essay *The Trouble with Nigeria* (1983). In 1990, Achebe was paralyzed from the waist down in a serious car accident, but despite this he is still a prolific author.

Ngugi wa Thiong'o (born 1938)

Ngugi wa Thiong'o was born in Kamiriithu, near Limuru, Kenya, in 1938, when the country was still under British rule (it re-
5 mained so until 1963). Ngugi's family belonged to Kenya's largest ethnic group, the Gikuyu. His father, Thiong'o wa Nducu, was a peasant farmer,
10 who was forced to become a squatter after the British Impe-   **squatter** illegal land-user
rial Act of 1915. Ngugi attended the mission-run school at Kamaandura in Limuru, Karinga school in Maanguu, and Alliance High School in Kikuyu. During these years,
15 Ngugi became a devout Christian. Later he rejected Christianity, and changed his original name in 1976 from James Ngugi, which he saw as a sign of colonialism, to Ngugi wa Thiong'o. He studied at Makerere University College in Kampala (Uganda) and the University of
20 Leeds (UK). After his graduation from Makerere University in 1963, Ngugi worked briefly as a journalist in Nairobi. When he was at school in England, he had started his first novel in the form of the European *Bildungsroman*. *Weep not, Child* (1964) was the first novel in Eng-
25 lish to be published by an African author. The most prominent theme in Ngugi's early work was the conflict between the individual and the community.

harassment intimidation, attack

indigenous native

In 1977, Daniel arap Moi, then vice-president, ordered Ngugi to be detained under the Public Security Act for a year without trial for his involvement with a communist 30 theatre. His novel, *Petals of Blood* (1978), with its dangerous change of perspective from depicting the problems of the colonial era to the current corruption and exploitation in present-day Kenyan politics worsened his situation even more. 35

After his imprisonment, Ngugi was not reinstated to his university post, and his family was subjected to frequent harassment. Since 1982, he has lived in exile. It is due to this experience of violence and humiliation that he turned to writing solely in his mother tongue, Gikuyu. He 40 became a fervent fighter for the use of indigenous languages, arguing that literature written by Africans in a colonial language was not African literature, but "Afro-European literature". Writers should use their native languages to give African literature its own genealogy and 45 grammar. In his 1986 *Decolonising the Mind*, his "farewell to English", Ngugi describes language as a way people have not only of describing the world, but of understanding themselves. For him, English in Africa is a "cultural bomb" that continues the process of erasing 50 memories of pre-colonial cultures and history and acts as a way of installing the dominance of new, more insidious forms of colonialism. Writing in Gikuyu, then, is Ngugi's way not only of harkening back to Gikuyu traditions, but also of acknowledging and communicating 55 their present. In a general statement, Ngugi points out that language and culture are inseparable, and that therefore the loss of the former results in the loss of the latter. The transition from colonialism to postcoloniality and the crisis of modernity has been a central feature in 60 Ngugi's writings. His works function as an important link between the pioneers of African writing and the younger generation of postcolonial writers. In 1992, Ngugi became professor for Comparative Literature and Performance Studies at New York University. He has also 65 taught at the University of Bayreuth in Germany, at the University of Auckland, in New Zealand; and at several renowned American universities.

Muriel (Sarah) Spark
(1918–2006)

Muriel Spark was born and educated in Edinburgh. She is of Italian-Jewish descent. In 1954, Spark converted to the Roman Catholic faith, which greatly influenced her life and literary work. Spark travelled to South Africa and spent several years in Rhodesia (now Zimbabwe). She returned to England in 1944 to work in the Foreign Office on anti-Nazi propaganda. During World War II, she started writing non-fictional texts while working on documents for the British Political Intelligence Office. Her literary career, however, was triggered off after winning a fiction writing contest in 1951. Her first novel *The Comforters* (1957) was well-received by the readers. She has written 17 novels so far. She became most famous for *The Prime of Miss Jean Brodie* (1961), which was performed on stage and turned into a very successful film. In the 80s, she dealt with religious themes such as the concepts of good, evil and the writer's mind in *Loitering with Intent* (1981), and in *The Only Problem* (1984), a witty meditation on the Old Testament Book of Job. Her most recent books are *Aiding and Abetting* (2000) and *The Complete Short Stories* (2001). She is also a highly-acclaimed poet and writer of short stories and literary criticism. Her stylistic trademarks are "a taut, nervy, controlled style; precise characterization; and a deadly accurate wit which entertains and appals at the same time. The Sparkian world is peopled by ordinary, familiar characters and frequently features powerful and iron-willed women; it has an edge of bleakness and frequently sinister undertones." David Lodge, a contemporary critic and a famous writer himself, praises "I should say that I consider Mrs. Spark to be the most gifted and innovative British novelist of her generation, one of the very few who can claim to have extended and altered the possibilities of the form for other practitioners." As one of the most prolific English writers, Muriel Spark

taut tight, well-written

to appal to shock

bleakness hopelessness, coldness

was awarded the Order of the British Empire in 1971 and created Dame of the British Empire by Queen Elizabeth in 1993.

Qaisra Sharaz (born 1958)

Qaisra Sharaz was born in Pakistan but came to England at the age of eight. She has been living in Manchester ever since. As well as being a strong, ac- ⁵ tive member of the Pakistani Community in the UK, she has excellent links with Pakistan in various capacities. All three of her novels and drama serials ₁₀ are set in Pakistan, exploring themes and issues which are universal. She is committed to raising awareness of many issues, particularly in education and health. She is mother to three sons and manages two thriving careers in literature and in educa- ₁₅ tion. Sharaz has gained three degrees: a BA Honours in English Literature and Classical Civilisations from the University of Manchester as well as two Masters Degrees from the University of Salford, the first in European Literature and the second in Scriptwriting for Televi- ₂₀ sion. **To enhance** her cultural, religious and historical knowledge of the Muslim world, she also undertook a Higher Certificate in Islamic Studies at the Metropolitan University of Manchester. Her career in education ranges from teaching, teacher training and lectures, as well ₂₅ as college inspections. Over a number of years, she has given seminars and lectures on educational issues and literature at universities and colleges in England and throughout Pakistan. **Under the auspices** of the British Council, she has more than once delivered training and ₃₀ workshops on the subjects of Quality of Education, Inspections and Literature at Agha Khan University (Karachi), Allama Iqbal University (Islamabad), The University of Punjab (Lahore) and numerous colleges. She feels passionately about women-related issues and through- ₃₅ out her work, whether in writing or in education, her aim

to enhance to improve

under the auspices with the support of

is to empower women, to enhance their quality of life and allow them to have access to opportunities that she herself enjoys through living in a developed country. Her
40 first novel *The Holy Woman* (2001) (winner of the Golden Jubilee Award) and its sequel *Typhoon* (2003) have been part of many prestigious literary festivals in the United Kingdom. Her 14 episode drama serial *Dil Hee to Hai* recently won two TV awards in Pakistan. Her award-
45 winning short stories are studied throughout Europe-in schools and colleges. She was short-listed for the Asian Woman's Achievement Awards and Awards for Excellence by the *Muslim News*. She has also been included in the *Asians in the Millennium Book* for her achieve-
50 ments, and in 2002, she was appointed Fellow of the Royal Society of Arts.

Hanif Kureishi (born 1954)

Hanif Kureishi was born in Bromley, London. As son of a Pakistani father and an English mother, he experienced the fre-
5 quent clashes of race and culture at an early age. His own struggle to develop a cultural identity was the impetus for his decision to become a writer from his teenage years on-
10 wards. He published his first plays and filmscripts during his studies in philosophy at the University of London. His first play, *Soaking Up the Heat*, was produced in 1976 at London's Theatre Up-
15 stairs. One of his later plays was even performed by the Shakespeare company. He gained international recognition, especially in America, with his screenplay for the film *My Beautiful Laundrette* (1985). It tells the story of a young Pakistani immigrant who opens a laundrette with
20 his gay, white lover. Critics from both sides of the Atlantic praised Kureishi for his humorous, modern portrayal of the immigrants neither as victims nor as tradition-bound aliens. In answer to some Pakistani organizations that felt offended by his representation of

the Pakistani families he declared that he is not acting 25
as a presenter or ambassador for his minority but for
the depiction of the realities of racism and class divisions affecting his generation and their parents. *My
Beautiful Laundrette* won the New York Film Critics Best
Screenplay Award and an Oscar nomination for Best 30
Screenplay. In 1988, the film *Sammy and Rosie Get Laid*
based on Kureishi's screenplay was released. It explores the world of a racially-mixed couple living in London during the race riots. Both films have reached cult
status with audiences. 35

His first novel was published in 1990. *The Buddha of
Suburbia* is the semi-autobiographical story about the
life of a young bisexual man, who is half-Indian and
half-English, growing up in London. It won the Whitbread Book of the Year Award for the first novel catego- 40
ry of the Booksellers Association of Great Britain and
Ireland. It has recently been filmed.

Salman (Ahmed) Rushdie
(born 1947)

Salman Rushdie was born in
Bombay, India, in June 1947,
almost exactly two months before India gained her independence from Britain. As the child 5
of wealthy, Indian middle-class
parents, he was isolated from
India's slums and poor people.
His world was that of Aladdin,
Sinbad the Sailor, and the flying 10
carpets of his favourite book
Arabian Nights. His family was very eager to give him a
British education, so at the age of 14, with rather idealistic ideas about Britain, he was sent to England to attend Rugby School. There, he experienced a shock, 15
which caused him to reflect upon his whole upbringing
and thinking, and which only found an outlet in writing.
Used to being "the little prince" at home, in England he
was treated as an inferior "wog", an outsider who was
discriminated against not only by fellow students but 20

wog offensive name for dark-skinned persons

also by the teachers. After his graduation, he went to
Pakistan, where his parents had moved to in the meantime. But, even at home, he was now an outsider. At
school he had become more independent, more force-
25 ful in his opinions, and his English pronunciation had
changed from its original Bombay accent to the more
superiorsounding English that older Indians associated
with former British colonial officials. In 1965, he returned
to England, making good use of a scholarship at Cam-
30 bridge. Rushdie graduated in 1968 with a Master of Arts
in History with honours, and then returned to his family's home in Karachi. He spent two unsuccessful years
working at a television station, whose constant censor-
ship frustrated him. Following that, he emigrated to
35 England and returned to London in 1970. There, he was
fostered by such renowned authors as James Joyce
and Günter Grass in Germany. His first novel *Grimus*,
was published in 1975. In 1981, he was awarded Britain's prestigious Booker Prize for *Midnight's Children*,
40 which later received the "Booker of Bookers" Prize as
the best of the award's recipients in its 25-year history
(1993). In 1983, he was selected as one of Granta's
Best Young British Novelists. He has also received Germany's author of the Year Award, the French Prix Meil-
45 leur Livre Etranger, and many more international awards.

His novels are important examples of mystic realism.
They show a deep concern for the individual living in an
age in which identities are fractured by imperialism, and
in which demystification intrudes the realms of man's
50 emotional and religious needs as well as his imagination, leaving only blank spaces there instead. Until 1988,
his works had been well-received by the public, but
neither he nor his publishers were prepared for the extremely negative reception of *The Satanic Verses*. The
55 novel starts *in media res* with the "angelic devilish fall"
of the two main protagonists to the earth in Britain as
their hijacked aircraft explodes. Religion, particularly Islam, seems to be mocked in the course of the story and
the novel was declared as blasphemy by many Muslims
60 right from the first days of its release. It was banned
almost immediately in India, while disturbances in
Pakistan, Saudi Arabia, Egypt and South Africa made
publishing there almost impossible. In England, demon-
strations and book burnings took place.

realm (fig) kingdom; sphere

The most severe reaction, however, came from the Ira- 65
nian Ayatollah Khomeini. On Valentine's Day, 1989, a
"fatwa," or decree was announced, sentencing not only
Salman Rushdie, but also all of the publishers and
translators of *The Satanic Verses*, to death. Hence,
Rushdie was forced into hiding. Khomeini himself died 70
that year, but for many years to come Rushdie, nevertheless, had to live under constant police protection,
and all his public appearances took place only with the
highest security. Salman Rushdie has continued to write
and publish books. He now lives in America and is an 75
Honorary Professor in the Humanities Faculty at the
Massachusetts Institute of Technology (MIT), and a
Fellow of the Royal Society of Literature.

Historical Background: From Empire to Commonwealth – From Imperialism to Multiculturalism

The Commonwealth Today

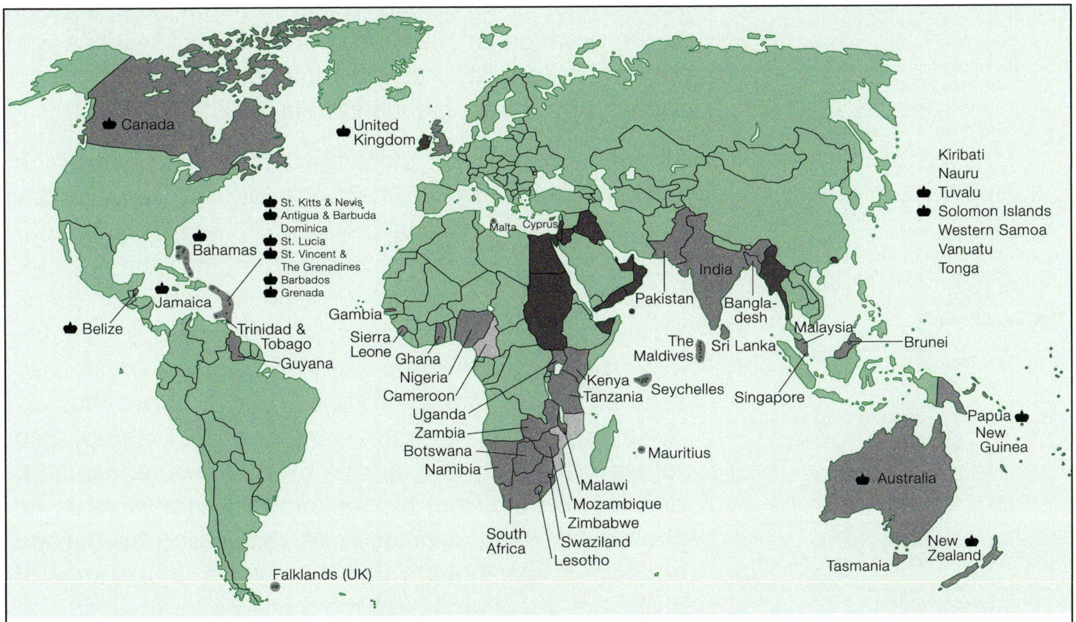

Canada
United Kingdom

Kiribati
Nauru
Tuvalu
Solomon Islands
Western Samoa
Vanuatu
Tonga

St. Kitts & Nevis
Antigua & Barbuda
Dominica
St. Lucia
Bahamas
St. Vincent &
The Grenadines
Barbados
Grenada

Malta Cyprus

India

Jamaica

Belize

Gambia

Pakistan

Bangla-desh

Malaysia

Brunei

Trinidad & Tobago
Guyana

Sierra Leone
Ghana
Nigeria
Cameroon
Uganda
Zambia
Botswana
Namibia

The Maldives

Sri Lanka

Kenya
Tanzania Seychelles Singapore

Papua New Guinea

Mauritius

Australia

Malawi
Mozambique
Zimbabwe
South Swaziland
Africa Lesotho

Tasmania

New Zealand

Falklands (UK)

on a scale of 1:200 mio

■ Former dependencies; not members of the Commonwealth
■ Former dependencies; members of the Commonwealth
■ Not part of the Empire; now members of the Commonwealth
♣ Here the Queen is still Head of State

A Historical Comparison: 1909

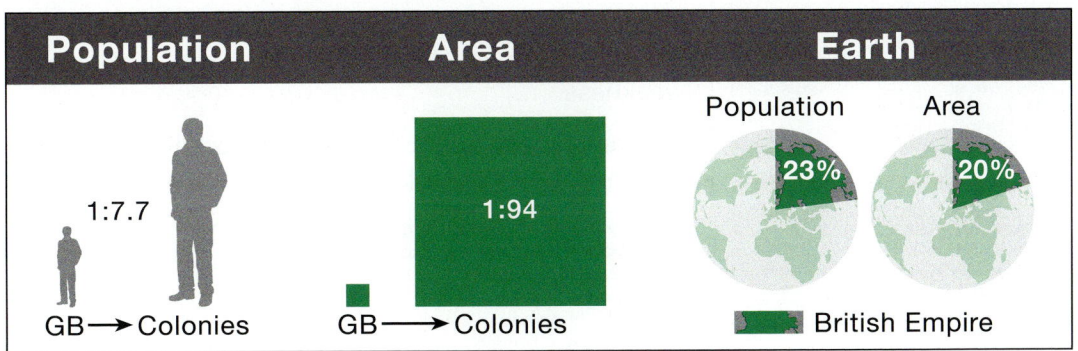

Population	Area	Earth
1:7.7	1:94	Population 23% Area 20%
GB → Colonies	GB → Colonies	■ British Empire

Some important data up to World War I

Date	The Empire	Britain
1497	John Cabot's first transatlantic voyage for England (Newfoundland, North America)	1558–1603 Queen Elizabeth I
1578–1580	Francis Drake's circumnavigation (West Indies)	1616 Shakespeare's death (*1564)
INDIA		
1600	First Charter of the East India Company: establishment of trading posts	1603–1625 James I
1661	Bombay is added to the bases at Madras and Calcutta	1625–1649 Charles I (beheaded)
1757	British victory over the French: beginning of the British Empire in India	1653–1658 Cromwell, Oliver ("Lord Protector of the Commonwealth")
THE CARIBBEAN		
1605	Barbados settlement	1660–1685 Charles II
1609	Bermuda settlement	1685–1688 James II
1655	Jamaica captured from Spain	1688 Glorious Revolution
NORTH AMERICA		1689–1702 William III
1607	Jamestown first permanent settlement in North America	1689 Bill of Rights
Up to 1750	Establishment of the thirteen American colonies	1702–1714 Anne
1756–1763	The Seven Year's War: Fighting between the French and the British colonies in North America; 1763 The Peace of Paris leaves Britain supreme in America; French Canadian possessions given to Britain.	1707 Act of Union ("United Kingdom of Great Britain") 1714–1727 George I 1727–1760 George II
1776–1783	War of Independence: Britain loses her thirteen American colonies, which become the United States of America	
BRITAIN OVERSEAS: AFTER THE LOSS OF THE AMERICAN COLONIES		1760–1820 George III
1788	Convict colonies in Australia	

The British Empire

"The sun never sets on Britannia's Empire" is a famous cliché used to describe the heyday[1] of Great Britain's imperial past, especially the era under Queen Victoria's rule (1837–1901). Lord Joseph Chamberlain (1836–1914), the "Empire Builder" and Colonial Secretary from 1895–1903, described Britain's imperial past that led to the creation of the Commonwealth of Nations and paved the way for today's multicultural society in his speech at the Imperial Institute in 1895:

"It seems to me that there are three distinct stages in our Imperial history. We began to be, and we ultimately became, a great Imperial power in the eighteenth century, but, during the greater part of that time, the colonies were regarded, not only by us, but by every European power that possessed them, as possessions valuable in proportion to the pecuniary[2] advantage which they brought to the mother country, which, under that order of ideas, was not truly a mother at all, but appeared rather in the light of a grasping and absentee landlord desiring to take from his tenants[3] the utmost rents he could exact. The colonies were valued and maintained because it was thought that they would be a source of profit – of direct profit – to the mother country. That was the first stage, and when we were rudely awakened by the War of Independence in America from the dream that the colonies could be held for our profit alone, the second chapter was entered upon, and public opinion seems then to have drifted to the opposite extreme; and because the colonies were no longer a source of revenue[4], it seems to have been believed and argued by many people that their separation from us was only a matter of time, and that that separation should be desired and encouraged lest haply[5] they might prove an encumbrance[6] and a source of weakness. [...]"

The first stage towards the global association of nations was the age of colonialism. In fact, Britain's imperial

---

[1] **heyday** the most powerful time of sth
[2] **pecuniary** connected with money
[3] **tenant** *Pächter, Mieter*
[4] **revenue** income
[5] **haply** (arch) perhaps
[6] **encumbrance** burden

drive goes back to the early age of discoveries and can be traced down to the first transatlantic voyage of John Cabot, who in 1497 discovered Newfoundland and North America for the British crown. From the 16th
5 century on, Britain expanded continually. The economic heart of the up and coming British Empire was the establishment of the East India Company in 1600. The beginning of the British Empire can be dated back to the Victory of Clive in the "Seven Year's War" between
10 the English and French colonies in North America and India. The subsequent Peace of Paris (1763) left Britain reigning supreme in America and Canada.

After the loss of the American colonies in 1783, British colonialism expanded around the whole globe, with
15 India being the most cherished[1] colony. The second stage of imperialism, the aggressive extension of British authority on a global scale for capitalist benefits, took place. While Canada, Australia, New Zealand and the Cape Colony were settlement colonies, most of the other
20 ones were used for trading (e.g. India: spices, cotton, tea) or were regarded as important strategic locations (Gibraltar, Malta, Cyprus and the Suez Canal acted as a chain of communication through the Mediterranean to India). All the colonies were under the direct rule of
25 Britain.

The present Commonwealth gradually evolved out of this imperial past, mainly through decolonization, the effects of two world wars and changing patterns of international relations.

30 Today, from Africa to Asia, from the Pacific shores to the Caribbean, the Commonwealth's 1.7 billion people in 54 countries make up 30% of the world's population. Officially, its purpose is to advance democracy, human rights and enduring economic and social development
35 within its member countries. It is loosely bound together by a common working language and similar systems of law, public administration and education.

Modern Commonwealth

The modern Commonwealth has its roots in the 19th century. In 1867, Canada became the first colony to be

---

[1] **to cherish** to love

Year	Event	Monarch
1788	First settlement at Botany Bay (New South Wales-Australia)	
1795	Ceylon (today Sri-Lanka) occupied	
1800	Malta occupied	
1807	Abolition of British slave trade	
1819–1824	Occupation of the western coast of the Malay peninsula (Malacca)	
1819	Singapore purchased	
1826	Parts of Upper Burma ceded to the East India Company	
1829–1835	Colonization of the west and south of Australia	
1829	Suttee ['s] the practice of widow burning forbidden in India	1820–1830 George IV
1839	Abolition of slavery in the British colonies	1830–1837 William IV
1840	New Zealand annexed Hong Kong annexed Natal annexed	
1846–1849	Kashmir conquered	1837–1901 Victoria
1850	Danish settlements on the Gold Coast purchased	
1851–1853	Gold rush in Australia, Australia completely under British rule	
1857	End of East India Company	
1867	Formation of Dominion of Canada	
1891–1895	Rhodesia (today Zimbabwe) and Nyasaland conquered, 1893 Uganda British	1876 Queen Victoria proclaimed "Empress of India"
1899–1902	Boer War (South Africa)	
1901	Commonwealth of Australia – Dominion Status	1901–1910 Edward VII
1907	Dominion Status for New Zealand	
1911	First Imperial Conference (formerly Colonial Conference)	1910–1936 George V
WORLD WAR I 1914–1918		

transformed into a self-governing Dominion; a status which came to imply[1] equality with the United Kingdom. In Australia in 1884, the British politician Lord Rosebery described this changing empire as a Commonwealth of Nations. Australia became a Dominion in 1900, New 5 Zealand in 1907, South Africa in 1910 and the Irish Free State in 1921. At the Imperial Conference of 1926, the various prime ministers adopted the Balfour Report, which defined the Dominions as "autonomous communities within the British Empire, equal in status, in no 10 way subordinate one to another in any aspect of their domestic or external affairs, though united by common allegiance[2] to the Crown, and freely associated as members of the British Commonwealth".

This definition was adopted into British law in 1931 as 15 the Statute of Westminster. In 1930, the first Empire (later Commonwealth) Games were held as a means to strengthen the ties between the member countries.

The Second World War changed the face of the modern world forever. It also changed the nature of the British 20 Commonwealth, marking its transition to a multiracial association of sovereign and equal states. That process began with India's and Pakistan's independence in 1947. With India's desire to become a republic, yet remain in the Commonwealth, the principle of Common- 25 wealth membership had to be rethought. A conference of Commonwealth prime ministers in 1949 revised this criterion and decided to welcome India as the Commonwealth's first republican member. They all agreed, however, to recognize King George VI as the "symbol 30 of their free association and thus Head of the Commonwealth." At the same time, the word *British* was dropped from the association's title to reflect the Commonwealth's new reality. Committed to racial equality and national sovereignty, the Commonwealth became 35 a natural association of choice for many new nations emerging out of decolonization in the 1950s and 1960s. Ghana achieved independence in 1957 and became the first majority-ruled African member. From 1960 onwards, the Commonwealth expanded rapidly with new 40 members from Africa, the Caribbean, the Mediterranean and the Pacific. Today, 33 members are republics

---

[1] **to imply** to mean
[2] **allegiance** loyalty

and five have national monarchies, of their own (Brunei Darussalam, Lesotho, Malaysia, Swaziland and Tonga). Sixteen are constitutional monarchies, which recognize Queen Elizabeth II as their Head of State. All, howev-
5 er, accept the Queen as Head of the Commonwealth. The Commonwealth's opposition to all forms of racism, and especially apartheid, led to the withdrawal of South Africa in 1961. In 1994, following
10 the end of apartheid and the establishment of a non-racist government, South Africa rejoined the association. In 1965, another milestone was reached
15 when Commonwealth leaders established the Commonwealth Secretariat in London to be the association's own independent civil service, headed by the
20 Commonwealth Secretary General. In 1991, the Harare Commonwealth Declaration set the association firmly on a new course for a new century: that of
25 promoting democracy and good government, human rights and the rule of law, as well as the equality of women, universal access to education, and sustain-
30 able economic and social development. At their 1997 summit in Edinburgh, Commonwealth leaders agreed on a similar set of economic principles and
35 practical activities. In the same year, the last important British Crown Colony, Hong Kong, was handed back to China. The British Prime Minister Blair has
40 recently formulated new goals for the Commonwealth, including fighting AIDS, avoiding economic downturns and ending terrorism.

THE 🛡 TIMES

Britain in decline

British industry is crumbling. Our factories are now mere warehouses for imported goods. Who is to blame? Tomorrow, in the first of a three-part series, *The Times* investigates

THE TIMES 30p

Multiculturalism in Britain today

As British subjects[1], people from the Empire were expected to fight in all Britain's wars, and the part they played in both world wars made a decisive difference to Britain's future prospects. Faced with the massive task of reconstruction after the Second World War and acute 5 labour shortages, the British government encouraged immigration, first from among European refugees displaced by the war, and then from Ireland and the Commonwealth. Before long, the great majority of workers in some factories were Asian or Black: Afro-Caribbeans 10 from the West Indies as well as from the mainland territories of Guyana and Belize, and immigrants from Hong Kong and the Indian subcontinent. Until 1962, Commonwealth citizens had always been free to enter Britain. Since many British people complained that their 15 "homogenous" Anglo-Saxon society had been seriously undermined by the massive immigration, the government decided that it was necessary to limit the influx of immigrants to a number the country could absorb, both economically and socially. Further Immigration Acts fol- 20 lowed. The majority of those who are now allowed to settle in Britain are spouses[2] or dependants of people who are British citizens. People from the New Commonwealth countries make up more than 55% of the total number accepted. Nationwide, non-whites make up 25 about 6% of the population. The highest concentration of ethnic minorities is in Greater London, where nearly 50% of all minorities live, making up approximately 20% of the capital's population. It is home to over 30 ethnic communities of more than 10,000 residents each. In this 30 city, over 300 languages are spoken. Nevertheless, the settlement patterns within the ethnic minorities are quite diverse: whereas nearly 60% of Afro-Caribbeans live in London, only about 35% of South Asians do. Many South Asians live in the West Midlands, Leicestershire 35 and West Yorkshire. The ethnic minorities, as elsewhere in Europe, are mainly represented in the large cities and towns and are rarely found in small towns or rural areas. In Scotland and Wales, ethnic minorities make up just over 1% of the population. 40

---

[1] **subject** *Untertan*
[2] **spouse** wife or husband

This great pluralism contributes to the cultural and economic vitality of the British nation. For example, hundreds of thousands of visitors are attracted by London's Caribbean Notting Hill carnival every year.

5 Britain continues to be the preferred location for multinational companies setting up in Europe because of the linguistic variety of the staff that they can recruit there. Today, curries and Chinese takeaways are as popular as fish and chips. Members of the ethnic minorities as 10 a whole, though, experience a greater number of social disadvantages than other groups. Their children are more likely to need special help in education; unemployment is higher among the ethnic minorities than among the population at large, particularly among the younger 15 age group, and racial discrimination is often experienced on a daily basis. In the 1980s, there were riots and urban disorder in Brixton, Birmingham and Liverpool, which highlighted the breakdown in trust between the police and certain members of the community, both 20 black and white. Recent racial clashes[1] have occurred in the industrial towns of Oldham (May 2001) and Bradford (July 2001). As among the whites, forces of conservatism also exist in the non-white population of Britain. Many Black and Asian Britons feel that they will lose 25 their roots if they become too British. Above all, they argue for special schools and spaces.

However, despite some negative aspects of life in Britain for ethnic minorities, they are probably better integrated into society than ethnic minorities in many other 30 European countries. The percentage of mixed-race relationships is among the highest in the world. The Indian food industry produces a turnover that is higher than that of the coal, steel and shipbuilding industries combined. Virtually[2] everyone has British citizenship, and 35 even citizens of Commonwealth countries who are not British citizens may vote in elections if they reside in Britain. However, only five of the 659 members of Parliament are Black or Asian.

---

[1] **clash** violent confrontation
[2] **virtually** practically

Elements of Short Stories

General Definition

The first attempt at describing the characteristics of the literary form that was to be known later on as the 'short story' was made by E. A. Poe in his review of Nathaniel Hawthorn's 'Twice-told tales' (1842).

According to this essay 'the short prose narrative' should

- take between half an hour and two hours to read
- be read 'at one sitting'
- present a 'totality' of effects
- follow one general idea which determines the course of the narrative
- carry out all the author's intentions
- control the reader's emotions while he/she is reading it

Poe's definition laid the foundation for the writing of short stories and their literary criticism in the one and a half centuries that followed. Points of emphasis have varied in the course of time but one can safely deduce a number of characteristics that will help students of short stories to understand their structure.

The short story generally

- has an open beginning and an open ending
- comprises one plot
- describes a single, decisive incident in the life of its protagonist and his or her reaction to it
- shows the development of its protagonist's character through his or her actions
- proceeds directly to its climax
- has a small number of characters
- creates the impression of unity through place, time, action, theme, character, tone, etc

Short Story and Novella

novella *Novelle*

At first sight, the difference between an English short story and a German novella might seem to be confusing. If one takes a closer look, one can find elements that both literary forms have in common but can also distinguish features that clearly set them apart.

short story	novella
open beginning – open ending	exposition – conclusion
single plot	single plot
rising action – climax – falling action	rising action – climax – falling action
	central symbol
	turning point
small number of characters	small number of characters

Developing Skills

Useful Words and Phrases

- sequence of events in a narrative
  rising action: events that lead to the climax
  falling action: events that follow the climax

  action

- tone or mood of a text created by the setting and the characters

  atmosphere

- the writer of a story

  author

- a person in a story

  character

climax	• the highest point of tension or suspense
hero/heroine	• main character
narrator	• the person who tells the story (not identical with the author)
	first person narrator: the story is told by one of its characters (point of view: 1st person singular)
	third-person narrator: the story is told from the point of view of one of its characters (point of view: 3rd person singular)
	omniscient narrator: the story is told by a narrator who has insight into the complete action and into all the characters
open beginning	• the action sets in immediately, there is no introduction
open ending	• the action simply ends, the reader is left with the task of finding answers to questions which have been raised in the course of the action
plot	• causal sequence of events
protagonist	• major character
setting	• time and place of action
story	• chronological sequence of events
story and plot	• (def. see above): 'Peter played football in the rain and then he got a cold.' This is a story because it gives us just the chronological sequence of events. 'Peter got a cold because he had played football in the rain.' This is a plot because it explains one event as the cause of another.
symbol	• sth that represents sth else, usually by convention

Acknowledgements

Texts

Joseph Conrad: "An Outpost of Progress" from *The Penguin Book of English Short Stories* ed. by Christopher Dolley, London, Penguin 1981, pp. 56–80

W. Somerset Maugham: "The Force of Circumstance" from *Collected Short Stories* by W. Somerset Maugham, London, Penguin 1992, pp. 42–64

George Orwell: "Shooting an Elephant" from *Shooting an Elephant and Other Essays* by George Orwell, San Diego, Harcourt Trade Publishers 1950

Doris Lessing: "The Second Hut" from *Winter in July* by Doris Lessing, London, Grafton 1966, pp. 7–28

R. K. Narayan: "A Horse and Two Goats" from *A Horse and Two Goats and Other Stories* by R. K. Narayan, London, Bodley Head 1970, pp. 7–24

Chinua Achebe: "Dead Men's Path" from *Girls at War and Other Stories* by Chinua Achebe, London, Heinemann 1972, pp. 70–74

Ngugi wa Thiong'o: "A Meeting in the Dark" from *Secret Lives* by Ngugi wa Thiong'o, London, Heinemann 1992

Muriel Spark: "The Black Madonna" from *The Complete Short Stories* by Muriel Spark, New York, Viking 2001, pp. 417–437

Qaisra Shahraz: "A Pair of Jeans", © Qaisra Shahraz, Manchester

Hanif Kureishi: "My Son the Fanatic" from *Love in a Blue Time* by Hanif Kureishi, London, Faber and Faber 1998, pp. 72–97

Salman Rushdie: "Good Advice Is Rarer than Rubies" from *East, West* by Salman Rushdie, London, Vintage 1995, pp. 63–81

"Some important data up to World War II" from LEU, Materialien Englisch, E 21; Michael Lutz: From Empire to

Commonwealth, pp. 2–3 and LEU, Materialien Englisch, E 40; Lutz/Preissler: Das heutige Großbritannien vor dem Hintergrund seiner Geschichte als Weltmacht – Eine Verbindung von Landeskunde und Literatur

Joseph Chamberlain: "Speech at the Imperial Institute, 1895", taken from LEU, Materialien Englisch, E 21; Michael Lutz: From Empire to Commonwealth, p. 2, 7

Illustrations |Alamy Stock Photo (RMB), Abingdon/Oxfordshire: Destefanis, Marco 149.1; jeremy sutton-hibbert 151.1. |archivberlin Fotoagentur, Berlin: Adams, B.J. 5.2. |Arco Images GmbH, Iserlohn: Dieterich, W. 5.1; Moellers, F. 4.1. |argus Fotoagentur GbR, Hamburg: Schwarzbach, Hartmut 4.4. |Art Explosion, Calabasas, CA: 3.1, 3.2, 3.3, 3.4, 3.5, 26.1, 48.1, 75.1, 80.1, 135.1. |Avenue Images GmbH, Hamburg: Index Stock/Galloway, Ewing 142.1; Index Stock/Pat Canova 5.6. |Bundesministerium für wirtschaftliche Zusammenarbeit und Entwicklung (BMZ), Berlin: 4.3. |Focus Photo- u. Presseagentur GmbH, Hamburg: © Leonardo Cendamo 153.1. |Getty Images, München: Stock Montage 161.1. |INNOVA-Agentur - Graphik & Design, Borchen: 157.1, 157.2. |iStockphoto.com, Calgary: Lipowski, Milan 5.5. |juniors@wildlife Bildagentur GmbH, Hamburg: Mallwitz, J. 4.5. |Klett-Cotta Verlag, Stuttgart: 145.1. |Lorenz, Thomas, Hamburg: 5.4. |Picture-Alliance GmbH, Frankfurt/M.: dpa-Bildarchiv 143.1; dpa/Settnik, Bernd 154.1; Herve Champollion / akg-images 5.3. |Qaisra Shahraz: 152.1. |Reinhard-Tierfoto, Heiligkreuzsteinach: 4.2. |Suhrkamp Verlag AG, Berlin: Foto: Bauer, Jerry 148.1. |The Times a. The Sunday Times, London, SE1 9GF: 4th February 1990 161.2. |ullstein bild, Berlin: 144.1. |Unionsverlag, Zürich: 147.1.

Wir arbeiten sehr sorgfältig daran, für alle verwendeten Abbildungen die Rechteinhaberinnen und Rechteinhaber zu ermitteln. Sollte uns dies im Einzelfall nicht vollständig gelungen sein, werden berechtigte Ansprüche selbstverständlich im Rahmen der üblichen Vereinbarungen abgegolten.